WHAT PEOPLE ARE SAYING ABOUT
RIC EDELMAN:

"Ric has the uncanny ability to present crafty financial advice in terms the average man and woman can understand and enjoy."

—DEREK McGINTY
CBS-TV's *Public Eye with Bryant Gumbel*

"He understands how real people think and feel about money, where they make their biggest mistakes, and what they need to know to achieve financial success."

—ROBERT CLARK
Editor-in-Chief, *Dow Jones Investment Advisor*

"Ric speaks in plain English, with an easy-to-digest style."

—PAT LAWSON MUSE
WRC-TV

"[He] offers intelligent and practical insights that can help readers achieve their financial goals."

—U.S. SENATOR CHRISTOPHER J. DODD
Member, Senate Budget Committee

"He makes a difficult concept, like money, a lot simpler and easier to understand."

—MIKE POMP
WTSN Radio

"Ric Edelman gives the best financial advice in the country. This is one financial advisor who has no personal ax to grind but simply wants the ordinary person to succeed."

—PAUL WEYRICH
President, NET Cable Network

the
new
rules
of
Money

the
new
rules
of
Money

---

88 STRATEGIES FOR FINANCIAL SUCCESS TODAY

RIC EDELMAN

 **HarperPerennial**
A Division of HarperCollinsPublishers

This book is dedicated to the staff of
The Edelman Financial Center.
It is my privilege to be associated
with this outstanding group of people.
There are none finer in the
financial services community.

The Library of Congress has catalogued the hardcover edition as follows:

Edelman, Ric.
 The new rules of money : 88 strategies for financial success today / Ric Edelman.
  p. cm.
 Includes index.
 ISBN 0–06–270219–X
 1. Finance, Personal. 2. Investments. I. Title.
HG179.E346 1998
332.029—dc21   97–42402

ISBN 0–06–272074–0 (pbk.)

99 00 01 02 03 ❖/RRD 10 9 8 7 6 5 4 3 2 1

How to Use This Book

Married

Retired

Female

**The Child
of Aging
Parents**

Contents

Acknowledgments

Credit for this book belongs primarily to my wife, Jean, who joined me at the beach for three weeks in rotten weather so I could type away, far from the office and in quiet solitude. Jean took care of the dogs, Dojar and Liza (and me!), so I could be free to fuss over the book. She stopped me when I got tired, and kick-started me when I got lazy. This book would not have been written without her support, assistance, and, as always, endless patience.

Many thanks go to Graham Casserly, CFP, for his extensive research assistance. I also am indebted to the many members of my staff who reviewed the manuscript: James Baker, CPA, CVA; Cindee Berar, MBA, RFC; Jack Bubon, CFP; Marty Corso, CHFC, CLU, CFP; John Davis, Mary Davis, CFP; Pat Day, CFP; Jeff Douglas, Joe Gilmore, RFC; Colin Grote, Mark Katzenberger, Lisa Korhnak, Jan Kowal, MBA, CPA, CFP; Yale Lewis, Andrew Massaro, CFP, CFS; Edward Moore, CFP; Betty O'Lear, MBA, RFC; Doug Rabil, RFC; Kathy Renzetti, Carol Roberts, Catherine Smith, Kelsey Williams, RFC; and Rosa Zediker. Thanks also to Mary Lawrence, ESQ; Carol Terwilliger, ESQ; and title settlement expert Jerry Boutcher.

Thanks also to Gail Ross; Robert Wilson and the rest of the team at HarperCollins Publishers; Adrian Reilly for his artwork; and to Georgetown University Press's John Samples, for if he didn't take a chance by publishing my first book, this one never would have happened.

Foreword

I've been called unconventional, and I'm afraid this book will perpetuate that accusation. Indeed, inside you'll read things that few other financial advisors tell you. Things like never buy a condo (Rule #14), never accept a new job just for a higher salary (Rule #3), always carry a big, long mortgage (Rule #21), don't bother sending your kids to college (Rule #13), stay away from S&P 500 Index Funds (Rule #36), learn the problem with diversification (Rule #42 and #44), and forget about retirement as you know it (Rule #88).

I say things like this for two reasons. First of all, it's solid advice—as the facts and supporting data will prove. Second, and more importantly, these strategies force you to consider a perspective on each subject that you probably have never considered. And you never thought about these things because most advisors don't talk about them. It's highly unlikely, for example, that your accountant would tell you to stop investing in tax-free bonds (Rule #75), or for your lawyer to brag about TOD (Transfer On Death) registration (Rule #60). Insurance agents are unlikely to tell you to stop buying policies on children (Rule #79), and stockbrokers are not likely to consider themselves dinosaurs (Rule #52).

There are two reasons most advisors don't talk about these things with their clients. A few suffer from conflicts of interest. They fret that telling you to do what's in your best interest won't help them earn a living. But these days, few advisors are guilty of this. Most of those crooks have long since been blown out of the business. No, based on my experience, the reason most advisors tend to present you with "conventional" advice is because most merely repeat what they've been told. Few have done the research on their own. They merely accept the teachings and writings of others. It's taken for granted, for example, that your kids are supposed to get your money as an inheritance, after you've died. Thus, most planners help their clients design elaborate estate plans to accomplish this goal. I, on the other hand, argue that you should start giving away your money now, while you're still alive (Rule #55), and I offer some pretty compelling arguments to support this position. Ditto for Dividend Reinvestment Plans. Everyone from your grandfather to today's personal finance columnists tout DRPs as a great way to invest, so people repeat the refrain without investigating whether it's still true (it isn't, and Rule #50 explains why).

It is said that myths repeated often enough become facts, and so it is with much of the misinformation passed along as "advice." People who know little about personal finance often repeat what they've heard, not knowing if what they heard is correct, or even if they are repeating it accurately. And, too often, those listening fail to challenge what they hear, and they fail to evaluate whether the claims are applicable to their own situation.

In this book, I take these truisms head on. By presenting you with a different perspective, you will find yourself forced to defend strategies that you always assumed were correct, strategies that you thought needed no defending. And in the end, while you may disagree with some of what you read inside, you often will be persuaded that I am right, and you'll conclude that you need to change the way you think about personal finance.

So get ready to read some unconventional advice. Get ready to be shocked. And above all, get ready to think. For whether you conclude that I am right or wrong, you'll be better off. Because you'll know that you'll have reached a decision based on careful consideration, not mere assumption or myth, and that decision therefore will be the best one for you.

And helping you reach those right decisions is what this book is all about.

Ric Edelman
October 1998

Preface

This book contains performance data. Presentation of this data is not meant to imply that similar results will be achieved in the future. Rather, past performance is no indication of future success and any assertion to the contrary is a federal offense. The data are provided merely for illustrative and comparative purposes. Performance data using a wide variety of time periods are provided. Rather than focusing on the specific time periods used, the reader should focus on the underlying principles instead.

None of the material presented here is intended to serve as the basis for any financial decision, nor does any of the information contained within constitute an offer to buy or sell any security. Such an offer is made only by prospectus, which you should read carefully before investing or sending money.

The material presented in this book is accurate to the best of the author's knowledge. However, laws frequently change,* and the author's advice could change with them. Therefore the reader is encouraged to verify the status of such information before acting.

While all the stories and anecdotes recited here are true, all of the names have been changed to protect each individual's privacy. It is impossible to ascertain the identity of any person based solely on the information in this book, so if you're a client, friend, or relative of the author, you can relax.

---

*See Rule #69.

your income, expenses— and debt

RULE #1

DO NOT USE A HOME EQUITY LINE OF CREDIT AS A SUBSTITUTE FOR CASH RESERVES.

I am a firm believer in cash reserves. Except for participating in a company retirement plan, you should not begin to invest in stocks, bonds, mutual funds, real estate, or any other asset class until you first set aside some money as cash reserves.[1]

The amount you need in reserves is based on how much money you *spend* (not on what you earn) and on the *stability* of your income (not the income itself). For example, because my clients Richard and Catherine are married[2] and each have secure jobs, two months' worth of spending is probably sufficient. However, another client, June, a single mom who earns sales commissions, ought to keep 12 months' worth of spending in cash reserves. The point is that every person or family should maintain in cash reserves enough to get through those unexpected but inevitable rough times.

As important as that is, it's equally important that you maintain *only* enough in reserves, because the interest rate your reserves will earn is terribly low—lower, in fact, than what you'll earn on virtually any other investment.

Once you determine how much you need for reserves, you must keep your reserves *safe* (meaning you cannot lose this money) and *liquid* (meaning you can get to it at any time without penalty). Only six places qualify: Your mattress, savings accounts, checking accounts, money market funds, U.S. Treasury bills, and short-term bank CDs.

---

[1]And you shouldn't even maintain the reserves until you're out of debt. But that's a different Rule.
[2]To each other, wise guy.

Although most folks who are attentive to their finances agree with this concept, over the past several years, many have become unhappy with the idea of stashing $15,000 or $20,000 into low-interest bank accounts, where the money just sits for a rainy day that might never come, while their investments in stocks and mutual funds have been earning 15% a year or more.

Increasingly, I have come across people who are not maintaining any money in cash reserves. Instead, they're taking out home equity lines of credit at the bank.

It's a great idea, they say. Because they bought their houses many years ago, they now have substantial equity in their homes, enabling them to obtain a $20,000 or sometimes even a $50,000 line of credit. This way, they tell me, they can fully invest all their cash and, if the roof suddenly needs repairs, they can simply draw against the credit line to pay the bill. Besides, they argue, I want them to carry a big, long mortgage anyway, right?[3]

Yes, I do want them to get a big, long mortgage,[4] but their attempt to use that point in this conversation is obfuscation.[5]

Although their plan sounds good, it is predicated on two things: Good performance from their investments and a short-lived, although not necessarily inexpensive, crisis. I'm not sure I'd categorize a new roof as an economic crisis (at least, it shouldn't be one). No, in my opinion, a real crisis would be you losing your job because your company went broke—rendering worthless all of your company stock and tying up in litigation your 401(k) plan because the company owner was stealing from it in a vain attempt to keep the company afloat.[6]

That's what happened to a client of mine. He lost his job when his company went broke, and fearing that he might be out of work for months, he went to the bank to seek an

---

[3]See Rule #21.
[4]See Rule #21.
[5]Cool word.
[6]See Rule #87.

increase in his credit line. When asked why he wanted the increase, he replied to the loan officer, "Well, I've just lost my job, so I want this to help tide me over."

Bad move. Not only did they deny his request, the bank canceled his existing credit line![7]

Remember, it's called *cash* reserves for a reason. So, while you can be as clever as you want when it comes to selecting your investments, don't get too creative when it comes to building and maintaining your cash reserves. Because when that crisis hits, you'll agree: There is no substitute for cash.

RULE #2 NEVER PICK THE MONEY FUND OFFERING HIGHER RATES THAN EVERYONE ELSE.

Since lines of credit are not acceptable for cash reserves (see previous Rule), you have no choice but to stash some cash away for that rainy day. A natural tendency is to put the cash into the highest-yielding account you can find.

Money market funds are a good choice, because they don't charge fees, they offer free check-writing privileges, and they pay interest rates that usually are a little higher than what banks offer. But you must no longer choose the money fund that is offering the *highest* rate, and if that's where your money already is, get it out *now*.

Money market funds, like all mutual funds, give you shares when you make a deposit. But unlike mutual funds, where share prices change daily, money market share prices are always $1, and they do not fluctuate. At least, they're not supposed to. They maintain consistency by

---

[7]Remember, as Rule #22 explains, mortgage loans and home equity lines of credit are based on your income, not on the equity in your house. With no current income, he no longer qualified for the credit line!

investing in short-term (30-day) U.S. Treasury bills or "commercial paper," which are like T-bills except that they're issued by corporations instead of the federal government.

Say you saw ads in the newspaper for two money market funds. One offers a rate of 4.3%, while the other offers 4.7%. Which would you buy?

In a world where the greater the return, the greater the risk, you might anticipate that the fund offering the higher yield must be doing something to get that higher return. And you'd be right: Funds that offer higher returns invest in higher-risk securities.

Just ask the people at Strong Capital Management, one of the largest mutual fund companies in America. They offer the Strong Institutional Money Market Fund. To attract investors, they offered a higher interest rate than other money funds. To get that rate, though, they invested in riskier investments. And when one of those investments lost 85% of its value, Strong's money market fund ran the risk of falling below $1 per share.

This would have been a momentous occurrence, something that technically has never happened. Many say it never will.[8] But Wall Street has a name for it anyway. It's called "breaking the buck." The fear is that if someone breaks the buck in the money market fund business, the ensuing panic would have incredible repercussions throughout the investment community. After all, most people think money market funds are as safe as bank accounts, and if that perception were broken, millions of investors would withdraw their money, creating a "run" on the funds like we once saw in banks.

So in the face of this huge loss, why didn't Strong "break the buck"? Well, actually it did. But to avoid any problems, Strong paid for the loss out of its own pocket, thus preserving the $1 share price. This is not the first time a mutual fund company had to cover losses to avoid breaking the buck, but it raises some questions: What if next time the

---

[8]Probably children of the same people who said the Titanic was unsinkable.

fund company does not step up to protect its shareholders? What if next time the drop is more calamitous? What if the declines are more widespread, deeper, longer lasting? How far would Strong go—how far *could* Strong go—to absorb the losses?

No buck has ever been broken, yet several times in the past 10 years various mutual fund companies have "eaten losses" to avoid breaking the buck. We've been lucky so far, but the day may come.

So if you invest in a money market fund, be careful about which fund you choose. Investing in the fund that brags it has the highest yield could be a big mistake. You'd be more prudent to choose a money fund that has a slightly lower return, such as one that invests only in U.S. Treasuries. If you handle your money fund that way, buck-breaking will never break your back.

Besides, for your limited cash reserves, is earning 4.7% really all that much better than 4.3%? Say your family spends $3,000 per month and you and your spouse have stable incomes. Rule #1 suggests you might maintain as little as $10,000 in reserves. Based on that, the four-tenths-of-one-percent difference between the two funds translates to a whopping $40 per year—and that's before taxes! Is the forty bucks worth the risk of subjecting yourself to a buck-breaker? I don't think so.

RULE #3 NEVER ACCEPT A NEW JOB JUST TO GET A HIGHER SALARY.

The days of womb-to-tomb employment are over. Today the average worker changes jobs every five years or less— meaning that 20% of the workforce changes jobs *every year*. The most common reason cited is career growth. But does career success always translate to financial success? Not necessarily.

To see why, compare Brenda and Monica. Both graduated from college at age 22, and both got jobs with the same employer, earning $20,000 a year. Both receive 4% annual pay increases, and both began to contribute 5% to the company 401(k) plan when they became eligible after their first year of employment. The company also supported the 401(k), contributing 2% of their pay to the plan as a basic contribution, another 1.5% in the form of a matching contribution, and another 3% as a profit-sharing contribution. All told, for every dollar Brenda and Monica deposited into the 401(k), their employer contributed $1.30.

After five years, Brenda left for a new job, where she enjoyed a 10% pay increase and all the same 401(k) benefits she enjoyed previously. She continued to change jobs every five years until she retired at age 65, and each time she moved to a new job, she got another 10% boost in her salary. While with each employer, she received a 4% annual pay increase, so by the time she retired, Brenda's salary was $175,000.

Monica, meanwhile, never left her first employer, and she too retired at age 65. She never enjoyed a 10% salary increase in any one year (while Brenda got nine such increases), so her income at retirement was only $112,000—significantly less than Brenda's.

But look at the value of their respective 401(k) accounts. By the time she retired, Brenda the job-changer had amassed $1,497,000 in her retirement plan. But Monica, who never changed jobs and who was earning only 64% as much as Brenda by the time she retired, had somehow managed to accumulate $1,546,000 in her 401(k) plan—*nearly $50,000 more than Brenda!* How is this possible?

There are several reasons, and understanding them is key to helping you learn how wealth is created. First, you need to understand how retirement plans operate. In order to participate in a company retirement plan, you must meet certain eligibility requirements. Although they vary from company to company, they typically prohibit employees from joining the plan until each has been with the employer for a minimum period of time—usually one year, which is the time frame used in my example of Brenda and Monica.

It is exactly this requirement that reduced Brenda's ability to save as much money as you would have expected her to save. Indeed, every time she changed jobs, she made herself ineligible to participate in her new employer's 401(k) plan for one year. That means she was not able to contribute to the plan, and her employer did not contribute for her, either. By changing jobs every five years throughout her career, she kicked herself out of 401(k) eligibility an astonishing 20% of the time! So even though Monica was earning only 64% as much as Brenda by the time they retired, Monica actually was able to accumulate more money because she was able to participate in the 401(k) more consistently!

Still, you might be challenging this notion, arguing that Brenda's substantially higher income would have allowed her to save outside the company retirement plan much more easily than could Monica. While this is true, it does not necessarily mean that a real-life Brenda would indeed have saved more money than Monica. Everybody knows that Americans fail to save.

There is no question, though, that Brenda would have enjoyed a better lifestyle than Monica. She'd likely live in a bigger, more expensive home, and drive newer, nicer cars. But do not confuse *income wealth* with *asset wealth*. Having worked with thousands of clients from around the country, I can assure you that there is a big difference between the two.

In that sense, Monica quite possibly may prove to be the wealthier of the two. Why? Let's assume that, like many Americans, neither Brenda nor Monica saved outside of their company retirement plan. By the time they retired, Brenda had enjoyed her $175,000 income, and the lifestyle that went along with it, while Monica was earning only $112,000. But now, as they both enter retirement, each must live on the income that can be generated by assets held in their 401(k) plans.

Let's assume they can generate an 8% annual income from their accounts. Based on their account values, Brenda is able to earn $119,760 from her 401(k), while Monica receives $123,680. Thus, compared to their final year's pay, Brenda must face a 32% cut in income, while Monica's income actually increases by 10%!

So, you tell me: Which of the two is likely to have the more enjoyable retirement? Which would you say has therefore achieved greater financial success? Oh, sure, Brenda might have achieved greater career success, and more material wealth, but does that necessarily translate into greater overall personal financial success?[9]

You'll have to make that decision for yourself. But please do—*before* you spend a career jumping from job to job, relocating from city to city. There's more to life than making money, and as Brenda and Monica demonstrate, *making less money* doesn't have to mean you will *accumulate less money*.

RULE #4   YOU MUST PREVENT YOUR CREDIT RECORD FROM BECOMING *TOO* GOOD.

When evaluating your application for a mortgage or other loan, lenders ask themselves one basic question: Are you likely to default? To help them answer that question, the Fair, Isaac Company (FICO) has devised a method of "scoring" individuals based on their credit histories. This practice, which compares your credit report with data compiled from millions of other borrowers, enables FICO to predict your likelihood of default.

---

[9]This analysis doesn't even take into consideration the seniority benefits that Monica accrues but which Brenda does not. For example, with 25 years of service, Monica is probably enjoying four weeks of vacation per year, and possibly even an occasional six-month sabbatical, while Brenda never stays with any company long enough to earn more than a week or two off. I'm sure you can think of other examples, too.

FICO's point system, developed over the past four decades, gives a variety of values for the types of accounts you hold, as well as your history, such as delinquencies. The higher your FICO score, the better. For example: You get 15 points if you have no credit cards, 22 points for one card, and 30 points for two to four cards. So, is approval from several lenders better than approval from one or none? Yes, but only to a point: You get only 20 points if you carry five credit cards. Thus, the message is clear: Carrying too many cards is held against you.

In fact, merely *asking* for a new credit card can be as bad as being *denied* one. You lose 10 points for each credit inquiry (an inquiry is made whenever you apply for credit), because FICO has learned that those in (or expecting) financial trouble try to increase their lines of credit. Thus, completing a dozen applications in a brief period makes you a suspect credit risk.

If you have no public record (meaning no one has ever taken you to court for unpaid bills), you get 75 points; if five months have passed since a public record has been filed, you get 10 points; and 25 points if the most recent public record is a year old or more. So the longer you've been out of trouble, the better.

If you're among the "smart consumers" who have a credit card "just in case" you need it, you're actually hurting yourself: You lose points if you have a credit card but never use it. Of course, delinquencies count against you, too. How much depends on their severity, and how recent and frequent they are. And some delinquencies outweigh others— missing a mortgage payment is considered worse than missing a credit card bill.

Because so much data is used to calculate your score, FICO does not disclose how your score is determined, although the company is quick to state that age, race, religion, color, national origin, marital status, and sex are not considered. It also should be noted that correcting erroneous information in your credit report does not necessarily mean your score will be increased.

To get a high FICO score—which is important if you one day want to buy a home or apply for a car loan—you should:

- Have and use few bank cards;
- Close any unused credit card accounts;
- Keep your credit limits and outstanding balances down;
- Satisfy any public records (such as tax liens or judgments);
- Avoid late payments; and
- Limit the number of accounts you open.

This last item can be difficult to avoid. Many department stores give you discounts for opening an account, and credit card offers flood your mailbox. Keep in mind, though, that opening these new accounts—even if doing so lowers your payments—also lowers your FICO score. So, if you are planning to buy a home in the next 12 months, think twice about accepting these new offers, and order a copy of your credit report to make sure it's accurate.

RULE #5
IF YOU WANT TO AVOID FINANCIAL FAILURE, WATCH THE PENNIES YOU SPEND— NOT THE DOLLARS.

In the old days, your ability to save was predicated largely upon how much money you spent on a house, car, and other big-ticket items. Today you have far less discretion over your spending.

Consider taxes. Under the current tax law, you have few deductions, and therefore little opportunity to lower your tax bill. And because your total tax burden has never been higher, you are devoting more and more of your income to tax payments. I'm not just talking about federal income taxes (28% for most people)—I'm also talking about state income taxes (6% is the national average), Social Security and other payroll taxes (15.3% of earned income),[10] sales taxes, property taxes, gasoline taxes, and many more. All told, close to 50% of your income is lost to taxes.

Then there's housing. As explained more fully in Rule #22, most people spend 28% of their income on rent or mortgage payments. Add another 7% for home-related expenses, including insurance, repairs, and maintenance, and you've just spent another 35% of your income.

So before you eat dinner, before you buy a pair of pants, and before you hail a cab or buy a car, 85% of your total income is already gone. And since a college degree is a virtual requirement in today's workforce, you also can regard the money you're saving for college to be a tax of sorts. Clearly, your remaining 15% must go a looooooooong way.

With those precious few remaining pennies, you decide to buy soda with lunch. No big deal, you say. After all, it's only a dollar. Considering the huge amounts you're spending on taxes, homes, cars, clothes, insurance, food, and day care, what possible difference could one little dollar make?

A $190,000 difference, that's what.

It's true. Spending one dollar a day (instead of investing it) for 40 years—a normal working career—on sodas, candy bars, even the daily newspaper—translates to $190,000 that you won't have when you retire. Can you afford to throw away nearly two hundred grand? Because that's what you're doing by buying that soda or ice cream.

Under **The New Rules of Money**, you simply are not in daily control over most of the money you spend. That is why it is crucial that you carefully allocate the money that *is* in your control. So the next time you reach for that soda on the supermarket shelf, or head to the fast-food joint, or subscribe to all the premium channels on cable, ask yourself one simple question: Is this expense going to help you achieve your financial goals?

---

[10]Although your paycheck is reduced by only 7.65% for payroll taxes, keep in mind that your employer pays an equal amount on your behalf.

RULE #6

STOP SPENDING MONEY ON THINGS THAT FALL IN VALUE.

Without question, "the good life" is within the grasp of more people than ever before. However, many people are trying nonetheless to live a life they cannot yet afford. Too often they act like they have wealth even though they are not, in fact, wealthy.

For example, you probably can't afford to buy a $15,000 Rolex; it's likely you won't even try. But you might be willing to spend $400 on a Raymond Weil or Gucci watch. Not that you should, mind you. Because to spend $400, you first must earn $667 (or so—see Rule #5), while that money, if invested for 40 years at 8%, would grow to nearly $10,000.

But you won't have that ten grand, because you'll have spent the $400 instead. The biggest irony is that the watch won't be worth anywhere near $400 in 40 years. In fact, it'll be a surprise if you still have it. On the other hand, you'll not only still have the Rolex, it will have held its value, and probably have even appreciated—not just because expensive watches become collector's items, but because such watches are laden with gold, a valuable commodity in any form.

So if you really want to boost your ability to build a large net worth, stop buying assets that you really can't afford to buy, like $400 watches. Either buy a $15,000 watch (which is likely to hold its value or appreciate) or buy a $25 Timex. Better yet, ask a rich friend what time it is.

RULE #7

YOU MUST CUT YOUR DEBT LOAD BY 33%— *TO BREAK EVEN.*

Does it seem harder than ever to pay off your debts? Well, you're not crazy—it *is* harder than ever. In fact, it's 33% harder.

Here's why: Under the old tax rules, the interest you paid for credit cards and auto loans was tax-deductible. That means if you owed $5,000 on a credit card that charged 18%, you spent $900 in interest—and got a $900 tax deduction. And if your taxable income was as little as $18,300, you would have been in the 33% tax bracket, meaning that a $900 interest payment saved you $300 in taxes.

But under **The New Rules of Money**, interest payments are no longer tax-deductible.[11] That means you are not getting the tax break you once got. Although the government might have hoped that eliminating the tax deduction for debt payments would encourage consumers to eliminate their personal debt,[12] it hasn't happened. Instead, personal bankruptcies are now at record highs, partly because the loss of tax savings has increased the cost of debt.

Therefore, mortgages aside, if you must carry debt, you should carry only two-thirds as much as you might have carried back in the 1980s.

RULE #8

OBSERVE THE NEW RULES FOR SURVIVING THE HOLIDAYS.

The numbers are astounding. Retailers sell 35% of their entire year's products between Thanksgiving and New Year's—and toy stores rack up 60% of annual sales during the holiday season. That's why the day after Thanksgiving is known as "Black Friday"—it puts retailers, who have been losing money all year, into the black.

Indeed, the holidays put people into a shopping frenzy, with budgets ignored in favor of the latest gifts and gadgets. When the bills arrive, people often realize they spent more than they could afford—way, way, way more!

---

[11]Except for new student loans (see Rule #69), investment interest, and mortgage interest (see Rule #21).
[12]Yeah, right. Congress merely was trying to raise revenue.

You must no longer allow the holidays to bust your budget. Instead, despite your best intentions, recognize that you *will* spend money. Every year, we tell ourselves we won't spend too much. But who[13] are we kidding?

You're going to spend a ton of money. You always do. If you don't believe me, just look at last year's checkbook and credit card bills (and the year before that, and the year before that). Go back to last December, January, and February. I'm willing to bet that you will spend as much or more next time, too.

What's startling is that people are shocked when they discover how much money they have spent. But the holiday season comes every year, so stop acting like it's a surprise. Instead, plan on it. If you spent $1,200 last year on holiday expenses (gifts, parties, food) you need to save $100 a month all year long. For just this purpose, banks used to offer special savings accounts called the "Christmas Club." Regrettably, few still do.

To help you survive the next holiday season, follow these steps:

1. Make a list—not of *what* you're going to buy—but *for whom* you are going to buy: Family, friends, business associates, and so on.
2. Next to each name write—not what you're going to give—but *the amount you're going to spend* on that person's gift.

   Too often people focus on the gift they plan to buy rather than the gift's cost. If you decide to give a sweater to Cousin Sara, you're forcing yourself to spend whatever sweaters cost, even if they cost more than you should spend. ("It wasn't my fault I spent so much," you'll rationalize later. "That's what the sweater cost.") Therefore, you need to decide the amount you'll spend on Sara, and if you can't buy a sweater for that amount, then buy something else.

---

[13] I mean "whom."

3. Once your list is complete, total it up.[14] If you're happy with that number, great. If you're not happy, start cutting. Remove people from your list,[15] reduce the amount you're intending to spend on each person, or both.

4. Now your list is ready—but don't head off to the mall yet. First, you have to go to the bank to get some cash (or travelers checks if carrying lots of cash makes you nervous). Why bother with cash when you have credit cards? Because *you're going to leave all your credit cards at home!* You overspend because your credit card is a virtual bottomless pit, but your wallet isn't. So if your list adds up to $800, go to the bank and withdraw $800. Then head to the mall, and spend freely. And when you run out of cash, *you're done!*

Following this strategy will keep you from overspending, and it will reduce or eliminate impulse buying. You will force yourself to spend your cash wisely, or the last person on your list will get a five-cent lollipop!

And let me add this point: Don't buy gifts just because you feel obligated. Spending more than you can afford is *not* mandatory. You can make a charitable donation for the entire family, giving each person a card saying, "I made a donation in your name to so-and-so charity." Or make your own gifts—bake cookies, even. Everybody loves chocolate chip cookies.

January should start off with Baby New Year knocking at your door, not creditors.

---

[14]And check it twice.
[15]Especially those who were naughty, not nice!

the new rules regarding college planning

RULE #9

DO NOT SAVE MONEY IN A CHILD'S NAME.

Many parents are doing a wonderful job saving for their kids' college education. But too many parents continue to operate under a set of tax laws that haven't existed for more than 10 years.[16]

In the old days, putting money in your kids' names made great sense, because parents lost to the IRS as much as 70% of what they earned, while children were able to earn money tax-free. This created a huge incentive to save in children's names, using something called the Uniform Gift to Minors Act.

But the Tax Reform Act of 1986[17] closed this loophole by creating the so-called Kiddie Tax. Today, you are much more likely to be in the 28% or 31% tax bracket—a far cry from the 70% top marginal bracket of the old tax code. Your kids, meanwhile, are no longer earning money tax-free like they used to. Today, only the first $650 earned by a child under 14 is tax-free; money earned between $650 and $1,300 is taxed at the 15% rate, and everything they earn over $1,300 is taxed at their parent's rate. After age 14, they pay taxes at their own rate.

Thus, there is now very little tax incentive to save money in the name of children. And I'll give you two good disincentives, the first of which is this: When children have money, their ability to qualify for college financial aid is reduced. It's easier to get student loans when the child's *parents* have the money instead. If that isn't enough to dissuade you from putting money in a child's name, then consider this letter I once received from a listener to my radio show:

---

[16]For an example, see Rule #73.
[17]That's right—1986! Where've you been?

Dear Ric,

My husband's mother passed away some years ago, and when she died, she left some money to my daughter. The money was supposed to be used to help pay for college. I have been very fortunate, and through some good investments, I have been able to increase the size of her account to about $72,000. I am concerned because my daughter has spent some time in an institution due to a drug habit. Joanne recently got out (this was her third time), and although she's been able to stay off drugs so far, we've been through this before, and we are worried that she will once again return to drugs. Joanne knows about the money that her grandmother left her, and she told me to keep the money away from her, because she knows that if she gets ahold of it, she will spend it on drugs. Can you tell me, is there anything I can do to keep this money from her? She turns 18 in just a few months, and my broker has already told me that he will have to remove me as custodian of her account. Can you help me?
—Betty

Are you *sure* you want to save money in your child's name?

RULE #10 NEVER PARTICIPATE IN COLLEGE TUITION PREPAYMENT PLANS.

More than half of the nation's 50 states now offer programs that allow parents to prepay college tuition. I've always hated them, and now Congress and President Clinton have provided two more reasons for you to stay away from these gimmicky programs.

With college costs skyrocketing, most every parent is concerned about paying for their child's college education. Thus, to the rescue comes tuition prepayment programs, which claim they "guarantee" to pay for college tuition. All you need to do, the state bureaucrats say, is pay a certain amount of money to the state—either in a single lump sum, or as a series of monthly payments from now until your child reaches age 18. If you participate, the state assures you that your child's tuition will be paid. Just rely on us, says the government, and you'll have no more worries.

As I've said for years, these programs are too good to be true. First, despite their claims, these prepayment programs *do not* pay for college. They pay for *tuition only*—NOT room and board. This is a critical distinction, because room and board account for 50% to 60% of the total cost of college. Since the plans don't cover these expenses, guess who does when Junior heads off to school?

Furthermore, pay attention to the word *guaranteed*. That word applies to *tuition,* not *acceptance.* That's right: Participating in these programs does not mean that your child's admission to a state college is guaranteed. It merely means that tuition costs are covered if he or she is accepted. What happens if your 18-year-old doesn't qualify? You're out of luck: In many programs, the state will merely refund your contributions, without interest. In other states, you'll get your money back with a meager 4% interest. A few will cover a portion of the tuition costs of colleges outside their program.

Here's the worst part of the fine print: If you cancel your participation in the program for any reason between birth and age 18, the government will return your investment to you—but with little or no interest!

If all these reasons weren't enough for you to avoid these state-sponsored college tuition prepayment plans, Congress and President Clinton have now given you two new reasons: First, thanks to a 1996 law, participants of college prepayment plans now face a huge tax liability. Here's how it works: Say you prepay tuition by making a lump sum payment of $10,000. This means your child can attend college in the future without paying tuition when he or she enrolls. But say the true cost of tuition at that time is $50,000.

According to the law, you have a $40,000 profit, and it's now considered taxable income. So when you send your son or daughter off to college, plan on sending thousands of dollars to the IRS.

Indeed, you stand to lose to taxes as much as a third of the "savings" you expected to enjoy by participating in a tuition prepayment plan. Since these plans covered only half of the true cost of college anyway, parents who thought they were solving the college cost problem by participating in these programs could discover that they are still short of their goal by as much as 75%! This is a far cry from having college fully paid for, which is no doubt what parents who participate in these programs are expecting.

Also, those who enroll in tuition prepayment plans are prohibited from contributing to the new Education IRA, which was passed into law in 1997. Parents who participate in both face big tax problems. (For more on this, see Rule #69.)

For all of these reasons, you need to reject these programs. Instead, take any money you plan to save and invest it on your own or with the help of a financial advisor. It is far more likely that you will end up with much more money. Not only that, but you will enjoy complete control and flexibility over your assets. If the child doesn't go to college, all the money is yours; if he or she wants to go to another college, you can spend the money as you wish; or if he or she wins a scholarship, you get to keep it all!

The bottom line:[18] Stay away from college prepayment plans!

---

[18]And I can't say it enough!

RULE
#11 APPLY THE ECONOMIC PRINCIPLE OF ROI TO CHOOSE A COLLEGE.

If your 16-year-old asked you to buy him a car for $25,000, would you? Would you take out another mortgage, liquidate your investments, get a second job, or go into debt to give your kid the money? You're probably saying, "No way!"

But what will you say when the money is needed to pay for college? In that case, parents often will do most anything to enable their child to attend the college of his or her choice. After all, your child's future is at stake.

So is yours.

It's time for parents and their children to treat college like any other investment. You need to look at it from the economic principle of "Return on Investment." What will your child receive from this investment? Surely you wouldn't spend a quarter of a million dollars on a house you'll never live in. Or $30,000 on a new car you never drive. But you'd be amazed how many college graduates are not in the workforce at all (being stay-at-home parents), or have jobs in fields unrelated to their degrees. (Just ask around at your office.)

Thus, I ask this question: If your child's major does not point to a specialized career path, such as medicine, engineering, or law, why spend $100,000 when you can buy the degree for a quarter of that cost? At $50 per share, IBM is a great buy; at $500, it's a lousy deal. The same concept applies to a college degree: You must calculate the expected "Return on Investment" *before* you invest. If you haven't thought of a college degree as an investment, you need to— because at today's costs, that's exactly what it is.

The investment comes in two parts: *Actual cost* (tuition, room, board, travel, books, and other expenses) and *Opportunity cost* (income and retirement benefits not earned because the student isn't working during college years). Parents and their kids regard this investment to be worthwhile (and I don't disagree) on the presumption that the degree will lead to a career that offers a higher income and better benefits than would be available without the degree. In the long run, it is held, the investment more than pays for itself in ways both tangible and intangible.

But will spending $100,000 on that degree produce benefits four times greater than spending $25,000? This is where high school seniors and I part company.

Take the example of my friend, Jasmine. Her daughter wants to be a teacher and has decided on a college that costs $18,000 a year. That's $72,000 for the degree. Teaching is a fine profession, but first-year teachers often earn less than $30,000 and the profession is not exactly known for offering rapid salary growth. Since the economic rewards will be limited, Jasmine's daughter should limit the cost of the investment accordingly. If she doesn't, she'll graduate with debt that could take her 20 years to pay off—and in the interim, she'll be sorely challenged in her efforts to buy a home and live the lifestyle she wants. That, in turn, will not produce the personal fulfillment she's supposed to enjoy as a result of going to college.

Thus, Jasmine's daughter will enjoy life much more if she pays $25,000 for her degree instead of $72,000. The question then becomes this: Can she find a college offering a suitable degree in that price range?

The answer is "yes." Oh, sure, she might not get to Harvard that way. She might have to accept her third or fourth choice instead of her first. Maybe she (shivers!) even has to attend an in-state school, or live at home instead of on campus. But life is full of choices, and while we'd all rather be driving a Rolls Royce, few can claim they're suffering just because they're in a Chevy.

And none of this deals with the increasing likelihood that your child will be interested in obtaining a graduate or doctoral degree. Depending on your child's chosen field of study, an advanced degree might be essential. That could double or triple the cost of a college education. A bachelor's degree in philosophy, for example, is of questionable economic value.[19, 20]

And don't assume that a PhD is a guaranteed road to success.[21] According to the National Research Council, the number of PhDs finding positions in academia[22] is falling rapidly. While 80% of social and behavioral sciences PhDs obtained teaching jobs in 1970, of those who graduated in 1993, only 53% found jobs. Life sciences and education graduates experienced 30% drops in academic employment as well. Boston University's Thomas Parker told *American Demographics* magazine in January 1997 that "Many graduate students are like ghetto kids hoping to make the NBA. From a financial standpoint, it's not necessarily a rational decision." Laura Green-Knapp, an education consultant, agreed: "More so than 10 years ago, people with graduate degrees can't find work, especially with general degrees like MBAs. If you have a PhD in philosophy and you decide you don't want to teach, your degree is worthless."

Every situation is different, of course, and some can argue that the expensive schools and advanced degrees are worth the price. But in all cases, parents need to explain to their children the economic implications of their decision. If your child wants to attend an undergraduate school costing $25,000 a year, or plans to get a master's degree or doctorate, make him or her examine the economic results experienced by people who chose the same career path.

One method is to have your kids talk with 10 people who have degrees in their intended field of study; half who graduated five years ago, and half 10 years ago. Key question: "Regarding your current job, would you have been hired even if you had graduated from a different (cheaper, lower

---

[19]A friend of mine's son, who recently received a philosophy degree, asked me for some job-hunting tips. I told him to look for a job with a philosophy company.
[20]Hey, I was just being sarcastic.
[21]Any more than college is at all. See Rule #13.
[22]After all, with a doctorate in Irish Ethnomusicology, where else are you going to get a job—at General Motors?

quality, other state, etc.) school?" Your kids will discover a common theme: While an *alma mater* might help in landing that first job, it is rarely a factor in obtaining subsequent jobs. Employers are much more concerned about a person's work history and ability to do the job—and less interested in your pedigree. This homework assignment will be an eye-opening experience for your kids. And maybe for you, too.

One way or the other, your children are going to learn about the economic realities of earning a college degree. The only question is whether they learn this lesson before they go to college, or after they've had you take out a second mortgage, liquidate your investments, and get a second job, and after they've saddled themselves with huge debt from student loans that will haunt them for decades.

If you're not careful, college will give you a *real* education.

RULE #12   NEGOTIATE COLLEGE COSTS AND FINANCIAL AID PACKAGES LIKE YOU WOULD THE PRICE OF A NEW CAR.

A generation ago, when it came to selecting a college, there used to be two kinds—the Ivy League, and everyone else. Show me a kid who's accepted to Harvard, and I'll show you a parent who will do anything—anything—to pay for it. All the kids who were rejected by Harvard, meanwhile, would turn to a good private school, and those who didn't even *bother* to apply to Harvard headed off to a public college or university.

Today it's much different. Now there are three groups of colleges, not two. The first consists of the top 50 schools in the country.[23] The second group consists of public colleges and universities, which have solid reputations not only for

---

[23]You know who they are.

being able to provide a very good education, but also for costing much less than private schools. And that is indeed the third group—small, private schools whose names you've never heard.

The common misconception is that you might as well send your child to the local state college because the nearby private school is both far too expensive and, considering the quality of the public school, not worth the extra money— especially after reading Rule #11.

But don't be too quick to dismiss that private school. Public schools have gotten very crowded, while private school enrollments are now down. For example, state budget cutbacks in California have made it so hard to get key courses that some advisors reportedly are warning parents that students there will need to attend for five years in order to get a degree. Meanwhile, Pine Manor College of Massachusetts, Ohio's Muskingum College, and Waldorf College in Iowa, like other private colleges, actually have cut tuition costs for new students. Still others, like Vermont's Bennington College, North Carolina's Guilford College, and West Coast University in California have frozen tuition levels.

This is a dramatic shift from the past. You're used to skyrocketing tuition costs—since 1980, college tuition costs have risen an astonishing 256%, compared to just 79% for the Consumer Price Index—but we are now witnessing an important change in the cost of college, and you can turn this to your advantage. Also, many private schools offer financial aid packages that make them as affordable as state schools.

When those letters of acceptance start to arrive, don't assume you must either accept or reject the school's offer of financial aid. In many cases, you can negotiate a better loan or grant package. Just treat the transaction like you would when dealing with a new car—the first offer you get is rarely their last.

And who knows, you just might be able to send your kid to that fancy school after all—without violating Rule #11.

RULE #13 RECOGNIZE THAT COLLEGE IS NO LONGER NECESSARILY THE ROAD TO FINANCIAL SUCCESS.

You've heard the statistics: College graduates earn substantially more money than those who have only a high school diploma. And since most Americans choose spouses with similar levels of education, this difference is usually amplified by marriage.

Indeed, according to Census Bureau data, the average household income of married couples is more than $77,000—for families, that is, where both spouses have a college degree. But when both spouses merely graduated from high school, the average household income drops to $41,000, and for families where both spouses are high school dropouts, the average household earnings are just $25,000.

A college degree clearly is a good investment.[24] According to research at the University of Chicago, a college graduate earns 73% more money per hour than a high school graduate. The U.S. Department of Education says that women who graduate college earn nearly twice as much as women who don't have a degree.

Clearly, going to college is an important element to achieving financial success. But is it a *prerequisite*? Are those who go to college *guaranteed* to achieve a greater degree of financial success than those who do not go to college? Considering that Bill Gates is a college dropout,[25] I doubt anyone would make the claim that college is the only way to achieve financial success. Still, the statistics do provide pretty convincing evidence.

So allow me to present a different view.

All the data regarding the benefits of college, including those I've mentioned here, demonstrate that a college education is key to earning a higher income. But when it comes

---

[24]Provided you don't overpay for that investment. See Rule #11.
[25]Okay, so he's a *Harvard* dropout.

to personal finance, there are two kinds of wealth, as discussed in Rule #3: *Income* wealth and *asset* wealth. College can help you provide the former, but does a college degree boost your chances of creating the latter?

To answer that question, consider this financial analysis, a comparison of two high school seniors. Upon graduation, Doug is headed off to college, while Kelsey is going directly into the workforce. Here are the assumptions I used in the analysis:

Doug starts out with $50,000, which he invests for a 10% annual return until needed to pay for college.[26] College costs $12,500 in his first year, and this cost will increase 4% per year. He'll get his degree in four years, then enter the workforce. When he does, he'll earn $45,040 (equivalent to the $38,000 a year that the Census Bureau data mentioned above says is the average salary for a college graduate, adjusted by a 4% annual increase during each of the four years it'll take Doug to get there). His salary will then continue to increase 4% per year until retirement. Beginning at age 22, during his first year in the workforce, Doug will contribute $2,000 to an IRA, and he'll continue to do that every year until he retires at age 65. He'll also save 10% of his salary every year, and all of his savings will grow at the rate of 10% annually.

Kelsey, meanwhile, will enter the workforce at age 18. With only a high school diploma, he'll earn just $20,500, matching the Census Bureau data. Because he is deemed to have more limited career growth than Doug, Kelsey's salary will grow by only 2% per year until age 65, or half as much as Doug's will grow. Like Doug, however, Kelsey will contribute $2,000 every year to an IRA, which he'll start to do when he enters the workforce at age 18. He'll also save some of his salary each year, but because he's not earning

---

[26]To keep the analysis even, Kelsey also will leave high school with $50,000. I could have started them both out with nothing (which is more typical of high school graduates), but that would have required Doug to take out student loans, which would have created unnecessary complications in this spreadsheet analysis. By starting them both with $50,000, the calculation is more straightforward, and the results are unaffected.

as much as Doug, he'll only be able to save 5% of his pay, whereas Doug is able to save 10%, or twice as much. Like Doug, all of Kelsey's savings and investments will grow at the rate of 10% annually.

By the time they reach retirement, the numbers are what you'd expect them to be. Well, the income numbers are, anyway. Because Doug started out earning more than twice as much as Kelsey, and because his salary grew twice as fast as Kelsey's, Doug was earning at age 65 (his final year of work prior to retirement) $243,238. Kelsey, by contrast, was earning by then only $51,995. There is no question that Doug's college investment paid off in terms of income wealth.

But in terms of asset wealth, the numbers reveal a very different story. By the time he retired, Doug had accumulated total savings of $6.8 million. But Kelsey, who didn't incur the cost of college, and who was able to start saving four years sooner than Doug, entered retirement with $8.3 million—a full million and a half dollars more than Doug, even though he was saving substantially less than Doug, and even though he earned only a fraction of what Doug was earning. Clearly those handicaps didn't matter.

Or, rather, they *did* matter: When it comes to your ability to accumulate wealth, it just might be true that college does more harm than good.

No, I'm not about to say that college is a waste of money, or that today's high school graduates shouldn't attend. I highly recommend that you obtain a college degree, for college offers an outstanding experience, and a degree opens doors for you that otherwise would be closed. But if your only reason for endorsing college is because it improves one's ability to achieve wealth, you might want to rethink that position.

Just ask Bill Gates.

mortgages, home ownership, and real estate

RULE #14 FORGET ABOUT BUYING A CONDO.

Thinking about buying a new home or investing in real estate? Forget about buying a condominium, and if you already own one, you have my condolences.

Most condos are small, and their tiny size leads to very low prices, which makes them attractive to college graduates, newlyweds, and others just starting out in life.[27]

It's a very attractive sales pitch—builders require very small down payments, and after factoring in the tax deduction, the mortgage is often as low as a rent payment. So (as you can read in every newspaper's weekend real estate section), why rent when you can own your own home? This is a tremendous tug on your desire to live the American Dream.

But that dream can turn into a nightmare.

First, consider the condo association fee. As the owner of one of the building's units, you're required to pay this fee, which covers the building's common areas and grounds. But unlike a mortgage, you never pay it off! (So much for the dream of owning your home with no payments.)

Second, the association fee is *guaranteed* to rise over time—simply due to inflation. Worse, many of those "common areas" are expensive to maintain, such as elevators, swimming pools, and heating systems. As any longtime condo owner can attest, condo fees can rise dramatically. Thus, your condo fee actually can be more than your mortgage payment—and guess what: It's not tax-deductible!

Third, many condo buyers are first-time buyers, and they fully expect to "move up," perhaps after marrying and having kids. If that describes you, you're in for a big surprise: When you're ready to move, you probably won't be able to

---

[27]I'm not talking here about high-end luxury buildings, where condos routinely cost several hundred thousand dollars or even millions, or condos in high-density urban areas, such as Manhattan.

sell the condo for what you paid (and you almost certainly can forget about selling for *more* than you paid, despite promises from the builder or real estate agent). Why will the condo fall in price? Because condo builders are continuing to build—so why should a prospective buyer choose your (old) condo in an even older building instead of a brand-new condo in a brand-new building? To find a buyer, you'll have to lower your price—and when you do, you'll get no tax deduction for the loss!

Even if new condos do not pose much of a competitive threat, two other problems do. For one, only Generation X-ers, divorcees, and retirees are potential buyers (because of their often limited income). Therefore, unless there's dramatic salary growth among these demographic groups, your property cannot grow in value, or it'll exceed their ability to buy. After all, those who can afford to buy a town house or single-family home almost certainly will (just like you would if you could afford to).

The second threat to your condo's value is, simply, all the other condo owners. Check out any building, and look at all the condos for sale or rent. With so many from which to choose, why would a buyer select yours? Since the floor plans are all identical, the only way to attract a buyer is to lower the price. This makes it hard for condos to maintain their value.

And it gets worse. For a buyer to qualify for a mortgage, your condo must be appraised. Since all the units are the same, the appraiser will simply compare your unit to other recent sales in the building. Say another tenant needs to sell in a hurry and therefore sells his condo for $15,000 less than what he paid. Guess what? This "comparable" will serve as the basis for the appraisal—and it could serve as the new pricing standard for the building, to the consternation of the other owners in the building.

Have you ever noticed that a lot of condo units in a given building are available for rent? Ask around, and you'll discover that many (even most) of the owners used to live there themselves—until they wanted to "move up" as you'll want to do. Why are they renting? Because they couldn't find a buyer, yet they needed to move and couldn't afford to let the condo sit vacant. Thus, they've become landlords, which leads us to the next problem.

If you plan to rent your condo, beware of several things. For one, you'll be competing with the builder. To beat him, you must give the renter a better deal (after taxes) than the builder is offering. This means you probably will find your-self receiving less in rental income than what you spend on the mortgage and association fee. I'm assuming that you do indeed find a tenant—I won't even talk about the costs you'll incur by renting to the Tenant from Hell. You know him. He's the guy who fails to pay the rent or trashes the place—or both. When your tenant moves out, you'll spend several months finding a replacement—with you paying the mortgage and condo fee in the meantime.

Having many investors and former owners trying to rent their condo units leads to another problem: You might not be able to sell your condo—even if you *have* a buyer! This is because most mortgage lenders will reject your buyer's application unless two-thirds of the building is owner-occupied. You see, lenders realize that renter-filled buildings usually are not maintained as well as buildings whose own-ers live in them. When a building isn't maintained well, it falls into disrepair. Tenants begin to move out faster than new tenants move in, and property values fall—placing the lender's loan at risk. (In the worst cases, the buildings become slums, and many well-intentioned investors and owners find that they've become slumlords. If you think this can't happen to your building, think about it: Nobody ever builds a slum.)

Therefore, if you were planning to buy a condo, STOP. DON'T DO IT.

If you're looking for a real estate investment, look else-where. If you're looking for a place to live, rent the condo instead (because, as a renter, you can walk away anytime). And never buy a home that you aren't willing to live in for a long, long time.

RULE #15 FORGET ABOUT A "STARTER" HOME.

When did the idea of buying a "starter" home start, anyway? And what's the point of it?

The idea is that you buy a small, inexpensive home—usually when you're single or newly married—with the intent to sell in a few years. Ostensibly, your income will have grown by then, allowing you to afford a larger, more expensive home, or by then you'll have started having kids and the needs of your growing family will simply *demand* a bigger house.

You see this concept frequently put into action by young couples. They buy a condo[28] or a town house, and then they sell it in a few short years and move into a single-family house.

From a financial perspective this makes absolutely no sense. Consider:

Newlyweds Bill and Susan were renting an apartment for $650 per month. He was earning $20,000; she, $25,000. They had no children, but figured that would change someday. Based on their combined income, they were able to qualify for a $120,000 mortgage, so they took their $3,000 in savings, borrowed $15,000 more from Bill's parents, and started looking to buy a house.

It didn't take long to find one (about two weekends, actually[29])—a new end-unit town house, in a new community not far from the center of town (well, not too far, anyway). They put down 10% ($13,000), leaving them with a $117,000 mortgage at 8%. The monthly cost: $858 plus taxes and insurance. Not bad, considering the rent on Susan's apartment was $650. Besides, they figured, the mortgage payment would give them a hefty tax deduction they didn't get from renting.

---

[28]Ugh! See Rule #14.
[29]Funny how easy it is to buy a house.

Like all first-time home buyers, they were excited but nervous, yet confident that they could afford the house. After all, they considered everything, hadn't they?

Not really.

They discovered their first miscalculation on settlement day. The settlement agent showed them the total costs involved, and it turned out that they needed cash for a lot more than just the $13,000 down payment. When they got approved for their loan, they were worried that interest rates might rise, and therefore Bill and Susan had agreed to pay 2½ points to lock in that 8% rate—but they forgot that doing so meant they had to pay an additional $2,925 *right now*, at settlement. It created a bit of a cash-flow crisis, but they told each other that it'd be worth it in the long run, because paying the points enabled them to obtain a lower interest rate, which in turn lowered their monthly mortgage payment.[30] There were other charges, too, so the total settlement costs—including the points—came to about $19,000, or $6,000 more than they had anticipated. Susan wrote a check.

Next came the move. The first expense was renting a truck ($500). Then, after a long day aided by friends paid in the form of pizza and beer, they finally finished. Susan decided to take her first shower in their new home, and Bill, with his last bit of energy, collapsed onto the bed. Suddenly, Susan screamed, and Bill bolted upright and darted into the bathroom.

"I can't use this bathroom!" Susan shrieked.

"What's the matter?" Bill asked, quickly scanning the master bath for signs of a problem.

"Look!" Susan yelled, waving her arm at the far wall. Bill looked. He turned to Susan, then looked at the wall again. "What?" he asked, unable to see the problem. He knew his next sentence would land him in trouble. "I don't see anything."

---

[30]Points, after all, merely are a prepayment of mortgage interest. See Rule #24.

"There are no curtains in here!" Susan yelled, pointing to the unadorned windows. "Our neighbors can see us from across the yard!"

She was right. By purchasing a new home, it had no curtains on the windows, and no blinds. Bill tacked a couple of bath towels onto the wall, covering the windows for the night. The next morning, he headed to Home Depot. He came home with blinds for every window in the house, plus contact paper to line the shelves in the kitchen cabinets, along with doormats, a hose, and sundry other items. Cost: $350. "Well," Bill said to himself as he reached for his Visa at the register, "this certainly wasn't expected."

Nor did he expect the sight that he beheld outside his house that Saturday. Every family on the street was busy gardening. Susan, acting like she had just come from a Monty Python movie, was already talking shrubbery. Bill knew he'd soon be returning to the Depot.

Several months and nearly $1,000 later, Bill and Susan had become expert landscape designers. It's money well spent, they figured, for the new bushes and flagstone would certainly add to the property's value.

So will all the paint we're buying, they said as they began covering their home's rental-white walls with more pleasing colors—the kind that an *owner* would have. They spent $175 on paint and materials.

During their first summer, they bought a lawn mower ($300); that winter, a snowblower ($400).

Over the next four years, they added a deck ($3,000), track lighting in the living room ($1,200), and a chair rail in the dining room ($350). They bought a grill for the deck, and continued to upgrade the flowered planters alongside their sidewalk. They stopped counting how much they were spending, but it was a far cry more than the $650 a month Susan had paid in rent for her old apartment.

By now they had one child and were preparing to have another. Increasing the number of people in the house by 50% when Cindee was born was challenging enough, but Susan was adamant that a second child would stretch their needs further than the home could handle.

"We need to move, Bill," she said one evening. Bill said nothing. His mental math was giving him a headache. He calculated that over the past four years they had spent about $25,000 in cash to buy, move into, decorate, maintain, and improve their home. They also spent about $3,000 a year in property taxes (something renters don't have to pay). So, Bill figured, their total outlay had been $37,000, and to recoup that money, they'd have to list their town house for about $167,000.

When he added it up, Bill was upset with himself for having spent so much money to maintain a house that he knew from the beginning they wouldn't live in forever. At least they'd get most of it back when they sell, he figured, and they'd be able to use that money as a down payment on their next home.

Then their real estate agent, Carol, gave them some bad news. The real estate market has been soft for the past couple of years, she told them. There had been substantial overbuilding in the area, and there were many builders still constructing new town houses. There were about a dozen units for sale on Bill and Susan's own street—including three of their same floor plan—and the two most recent sales were for $120,000, or $10,000 *less* than what Bill and Susan had paid just four years ago. And that was before counting all the extra money they spent. Nor did this include the real estate commission, which would lop off another 6%—$7,200—from the total.

Their mortgage balance was now about $112,000 and, Carol told them, that's about what they could expect to net from the sale of the house. So if they still wanted to sell, she said, they would probably walk away with nothing. And they should consider themselves lucky that they won't actually have to bring money to the settlement table. "That's happened to some of my other clients," Carol said.

Perhaps buying a starter home once made sense. Perhaps in the heyday of the 1980s, when real estate values were quickly escalating in pockets around the country, buying a home with the intention of flipping it in just a few years might have worked. After all, if Bill and Susan's town house had grown in value by 8.2% per year, the property would now be worth $178,000—exactly enough to let them pay the real estate commission and still walk away with the money they had spent on the place.

But assuming your home will grow in value at an annual rate of 8.2% is pure speculation. It's a poor basis for deciding to buy a home, and such a stance certainly does not work under **The New Rules of Money**.

Of course, Bill and Susan are now left with a dilemma. They need to move to a bigger home—and they can forget about getting money out of their current house to help them afford it. So what should they do? Should they sell the town house and take the loss, or rent it and wait for property values to recover? To find the answer, read the next Rule.

RULE #16   NEVER RENT REAL ESTATE YOU'D RATHER SELL.

When you're ready to sell your current house, go right ahead. If you are unable to sell it for the price you want, either lower your price as needed (see Rule #18), or keep living in it. But do not attempt to rent it instead, on the theory that you'll simply let your tenant cover the costs until property values rise enough to allow you to sell for the price you want. If you try this, you're almost certain to lose money.

Mark serves as a good example. He bought a town house for $160,000, and a few years later, decided to move to a bigger home. Although he had finished the basement, added a deck, and made other improvements for a total of about $25,000, he found that a soft real estate market had reduced the value of his property to only about $150,000. Rather than sell for a loss, he decided to rent the town house instead.

Because he had put down 20% when he bought the town

house, Mark's monthly mortgage payment was $940; add taxes, insurance, maintenance, and repairs, and Mark figured that he'd need to charge $1,200 in rent to break even. No problem, he figured. Finding a tenant would be as easy as placing an ad in the classifieds.

He was wrong. It took him six weeks to sign a tenant—and he could get only $850 a month. He discovered that those who rent private homes rarely are able to collect enough rent to cover their property's carrying costs. In real estate circles, this is known as "negative cash flow," meaning that Mark would not be earning enough on a monthly basis to cover his costs.

But that's okay if real estate prices are increasing. For example, if Mark's town house was to grow in value by just 3% in a year—the equivalent of an extra $375 every month—that plus the $850 he gets from his tenant would give him the $1,200 or so he's looking for. Thus, by assuming he'll get that appreciation, Mark technically could afford to accept less rent from his tenant. To make this work, Mark simply would need to be able to live without that extra $375 every month (at least for now, since it would come back to him later—supposedly).

Mark also was making one other key assumption: That he would indeed be collecting rent every month. He quickly learned that this does not always happen. Mortgage bankers know that rental units are routinely vacant 25% of the time, and Mark must cover the entire carrying cost of the property during these periods.

Even getting a tenant doesn't guarantee success. Unhappily, Mark discovered that he had rented his house to the aforementioned Tenant from Hell, Andrew. First, Andrew failed to pay rent one month, and then the next month's check bounced—which caused Mark's own mortgage check to bounce. Mark got rid of Andrew, but Mark remained liable for the rental's mortgage payments as well as those on his own home.

Mark found new tenants—after another two months of looking—and although the couple, Mary Jane and Jim, seemed stable and mature, Mark's problems weren't over.

He got a call one night from Jim, shortly after a bad storm had hit the area. There was severe flooding in the basement, Jim said, and part of the roof suffered wind damage. Although his insurance company eventually paid for most of the repairs, Mark nonetheless suffered both out-of-pocket expenses and the Hassle Factor.

Let's face it: Being a landlord can offer a unique investment experience; Mark would never get a phone call in the middle of the night because something went wrong with his mutual fund.

And for all his trouble, the biggest irony is that Mark didn't improve his finances by renting the house he originally wanted to sell. By the time he'd had enough, he sold the town house for $150,000—exactly what he could have sold it for in the first place. He'd have been a lot better off if he had simply sold the property instead of renting it. Keep that in mind when you're faced with the same decision.

RULE #17 TRYING TO SELL YOUR HOUSE? USE RANGE PRICING.

Kathy's house is on the market, listed at $299,990. Will her house sell for that price?

Of course not. Everyone knows that houses rarely sell for the listing price. Yet, the listing price is important, even critical, to the home buying/selling process. Why? It has to do with the Multiple Listing Service. Real estate agents around the country use it or a similar system to list homes for their client-sellers and to find homes for their client-buyers.

Consider Wendy and Adrian. They want to buy a house. They've been prequalified by their lender, and they know how much they can afford to pay for their new home. They also know how much they'd *prefer* to pay. So when they hire their real estate agent, Rosa, they do what all buyers do: They give their real estate agents an upper limit.

"We'll consider anything up to $200,000," they tell Rosa, even though they'd really rather spend—and they hope they find something for—just $175,000.

"No problem," Rosa says, who then goes about the process of finding every house in the area that is being offered for sale for $200,000 or less. It takes her about five minutes.

Rosa sits at her computer screen and accesses the MLS. At her desk, Rosa tells the computer the criteria to use in producing its list of candidates. Of all the criteria Rosa uses, one piece of data is more important than all the others: The sales price. She enters $200,000.

Minutes later, Rosa has a detailed printout of every house for sale in the area with a list price of $200,000 or less. She picks a dozen homes from this list that seem to match Wendy and Adrian's other criteria and the house-hunting begins. If Wendy and Adrian don't find what they want in this group, Rosa will produce a second list for another day of house-hunting.

Eventually they find something they like. It's the house Kathy has listed. Wendy and Adrian make her an offer, which Rosa will present for them to Kathy's real estate agent.

You can be sure of one thing: Wendy and Adrian will not offer to pay Kathy's asking price of $199,990. Therefore the negotiations begin. They'll offer less, Kathy will counter-offer, and eventually everybody will reach an agreement. Or not, in which case Wendy and Adrian will bid Kathy good-bye and continue their search.

The only person truly unhappy in this entire process is Will. He lives down the street from Kathy, in a house similar to hers, but with a finished basement. Will figures his house is worth *at least* $200,000, though he might be willing to accept a bit less. Kathy's house is worth only $185,000, he figures, but if she's listing hers for $199,990, then he'd better list his for more. So he prices his for $210,000.

But he'll never get an offer from Wendy and Adrian. Even though he's willing to accept less than $200,000, and even though Wendy and Adrian are willing to pay up to $200,000, the two parties will never meet. That's because Rosa worked from a list of all the homes listed for $200,000 or less. That's just too bad.

It's also too absurd. Everybody knows that the listing price is bogus. It's merely a starting point, and not necessarily an accurate or realistic one at that. So even though Wendy, Adrian, and Will are all willing to be flexible in their pricing, the MLS and similar systems aren't. You tell the computer $200,000, you get $200,000.

This is why real estate agents tell sellers to list their homes for amounts just below certain thresholds, and it explains why you see houses listed for seemingly silly prices, such as $199,999 or $149,499. You might ask yourself, "Who is that seller trying to fool?" It's not you they're trying to fool—it's the *computer* they're trying to fool! But many sellers, like Will, do not price their houses this way. It's either because their real estate agent isn't sharp enough to recommend that strategy[31] or because Will has rejected the idea.[32] After all, Will figures, if he lists the house for $210,000, he might get $205,000—but if he lists it for $199,999, he's certain *not* to get $205,000. So he lists it for $210,000—and gets nothing.

This also is why real estate agents tell buyers to increase the maximum amount they're willing to pay, at least for purposes of accessing the computer. Rosa wanted to produce a list of all the homes selling for up to $250,000—not just $200,000—because that would have enabled her to include houses like Will's. But many buyers, like Wendy and Adrian, often do not accept that idea. It's either because their real estate agent isn't sharp enough to recommend that strategy[33] or because Wendy and Adrian have rejected the idea[34] as a mere tactic to get them to buy a more expensive house, which would increase Rosa's commission. So they stick to their $200,000 limit—and they never see their "Dream House" that Will is selling.

---

[31]Not likely.
[32]More likely.
[33]Not likely.
[34]More likely.

If you think about it, this entire process is dumb. It places incredible importance on the listing price, even though everybody involved in the process—the buyers, the sellers, and their agents—know that the list price is not going to be the house's ultimate selling price.

There's a new, better idea. It's called range pricing.

The next time you list your house for sale, don't list a price. Instead, assign a range of prices that you're willing to consider. For example, Will should list his house for $175,000–$215,000. Worried that buyers will simply offer you the low end of the range? Don't be: In San Diego, where this idea was first test-marketed, houses using range pricing tended to sell *above* the range's midpoint. As long as the range is reasonably based, buyers have proven to be fair.

And the best news is that houses listed with range pricing have sold in a fraction of the time it normally takes to sell a house. Why? Because by listing the entire range, more potential buyers are exposed to the house, and the more people you get to see your house, the quicker it will sell.

The only problem with range pricing is that, so far, the MLS system cannot handle it. The system demands that you enter only one price for the listing. But you can get around this problem easily. First, list in this space the lowest price in your range (so that the house will be included in the type of search Rosa did), and then add a footnote to the listing that describes the range pricing. Then make sure all your other marketing—newspaper ads, flyers, and for-sale signs—prominently displays your range pricing.

This is a fabulous new idea, and it's quite possible that your real estate agent hasn't yet heard of it. If your agent is not willing to try this idea, find one who will. People who do this never go back to the old way of selling real estate, and it will be only a matter of time before the MLS and competing systems catch up with this new, improved way to sell homes.

RULE #18 IF YOU'RE THE SELLER, ACCEPT A LOWER PRICE.

In many parts of the country, the real estate market has been in the doldrums for several years. Much of this is due to unrealistic attitudes about the local real estate marketplace. So allow me to offer two kind and gentle words of advice to those selling real estate, and to the real estate agents assisting them.

Get real!

The price you have set is too high. There has been a recession in the real estate market for years now, and your home is not worth as much as you think. It might not even be worth as much as it was 10 years ago. If you want to sell your house, *you need to lower your price.*

Just because *you* think your home is worth a certain amount of money doesn't mean it *is* worth that amount. Put yourself in the buyer's shoes: Would you buy your house for the price you are demanding? I don't think so. *You need to lower your price.* Maybe not by the 40% that the buyer wants, but by something. So exactly how do you determine how much your house is worth?

- Many people who are preparing to sell their houses begin by looking at what they paid for their house. Wrong. The price you paid is *irrelevant.*
- Adding up what you paid in improvements and decorating? *Irrelevant.*
- Looking at your current mortgage balance? *Irrelevant.*
- Basing the sales price on what you need in order to buy your next home? *Irrelevant.*
- Calculating what the sales price needs to be so that the house will have proved a profitable investment? *Irrelevant.*
- Comparing the value of your house with other sales that have occurred in the neighborhood over the years you've lived there? *Irrelevant.*

When selling a house, there is only one relevant number that matters, and that is *the price a buyer is willing to pay.* I know your heart and soul are built into your house, that feelings of family and self-worth are painted on every wall. But the simple truth is that none of that matters. The people purchasing your home are merely *buying* it, after all. They are not *adopting* it. Stop emotionalizing[35] the transaction. The house's price is what the buyer will pay. Nothing more, and nothing less. Since you are too close to the situation, you need to defer to your real estate agent and appraiser, both of whom will give you a much more realistic view of the current market value of the house. Listen to them, and act accordingly.

You can resist this advice all you want. It won't change anything, because you'll eventually do what I'm telling you to do. It's just that doing it now will save you a lot of money, as one client of mine can tell you.

Jan called me one day, quite discouraged. He'd been trying to sell his house for six months without success. He originally listed his property for $410,000 (which he knew was too high), and later dropped the price to $389,000 (more in line with recent sales in his neighborhood). Still, no offers.

"My real estate agent wants me to cut the price to $379,000," he told me. "But I want to see if anyone will accept $389,000 first."

I asked, "How long do you think it will take you to get an offer at $389,000?"

"Four or five months," he replied.

"And how quickly do you think the house will sell if you price it at $374,000?" I asked.

"Right away!" he exclaimed. "It's already on the low side compared to recent sales on my street, and I've got a finished basement. At $374,000 it's a steal."

"One last question," I said to him. "How much is the house costing you to maintain?"

"Well," he pondered. "If you factor in everything—the

---

[35]Emotionalizing?

mortgage, utilities, maintenance, and so forth—I guess about $4,000 a month."

"Then the answer is obvious," I said. "You need to price your house at $374,000 right away." That was $5,000 lower than even his real estate agent, Marty, had suggested.

"What?" he demanded. "I'll take a bath!"

"You're taking a bath now," I said. "You just don't know it."

I quickly went through the numbers with him. If it takes four months to sell the house at $389,000 as he said it would, Jan will spend $16,000 carrying the property in the meantime—cutting his profit to $373,000. Therefore, by listing the house at $374,000 right now, he'll sell the house immediately—and net $1,000 more than if he holds on for the next four months—which will only happen, by the way, if some poor clod agrees to pay $21,000 too much, which is highly unlikely. Therefore, if Jan tries that gamble, it's more likely that he'll just end up selling the place for $374,000 anyway—after he's wasted four months and $16,000.

If you have a house to sell, drop your price. And get on with your life.

RULE #19 IF YOU'RE THE BUYER, RAISE YOUR OFFER.

In many parts of the country[36] the real estate market has been in the doldrums for several years. Much of this is due to unrealistic attitudes about the local real estate marketplace. So allow me to offer two kind and gentle words of advice to those who are thinking of buying real estate:

Get real!

The price you are offering for the house of your dreams is too low. The real estate recession that the nation has

---

[36]Gee, this paragraph looks familiar. See Rule #18.

experienced for the past several years has not decimated the market. Therefore, you need to be much more realistic about the value of the property that you want to purchase. *You need to raise your offer.*

As a buyer, you are supposed to buy a home because you want to live there: You like the house, you like the neighborhood, you like its proximity to schools and work and shopping, you like the nice flowering trees and playgrounds for the kids, and you like it because your friends and family live nearby.[37]

You should not buy a home because you think it's going to double in value in five years, let alone six months, for a home is not an investment, nor is it your biggest asset. *Stop pretending it is.*

Your home is a place to live. *Period.* If it grows in value, consider yourself lucky, not smart.

RULE #20 STOP THINKING THAT YOUR HOME IS THE BEST INVESTMENT YOU'LL EVER MAKE.

In fact, as I just said in Rule #19, your home is not an investment at all. It's merely a place to live.

And yet, many people continue to say, "My house is the best investment I ever made!" Whenever I hear this, I inevitably discover that their home is the *only* investment they ever made.

To demonstrate, say you bought your home in 1980 for $150,000 and sold it 10 years later for $500,000.[38] That $350,000 profit represents a gain of 233%. That seems like an awesome return by anybody's standard.

But is it really? During the same 10-year period, the Dow Jones Industrial Average grew from 800 to 3,000—a gain of

---

[37]Or maybe because they don't live nearby!
[38]You wish.

275%. Thus, the stock market performed even better than this fictional house.

But if you're a real estate investor, you might argue that the house could have been the better deal. Why? Because when you bought that $150,000 house, you didn't need $150,000 in cash! You merely needed a down payment of 10%, or $15,000. Then that $15,000 cash outlay grew to $350,000—and *that's* a total return of 2,333%—far outpacing the measly 275% earned by the stock market.

This is cheating, of course, because in that scenario, it's not the *house* that produced such profits, it was the *leverage*, i.e., the fact that *you borrowed money to buy the house.* If you wanted to, you could have borrowed money to invest in stocks.[39] And if you had put that same loan into stocks instead of the house, you would have accumulated a lot more than $350,000!

Of course, doing so would have been highly speculative,[40] because you must repay the loan even if the investment goes down in value, as many investors—in both stocks and real estate—can attest.

I am not suggesting that you go out and borrow a huge amount of money for the purpose of investing. In fact, I refuse to allow my clients to borrow money for such a purpose—and that includes investing in real estate. But why, then, do I say it's okay to borrow money to buy a home?[41] Because your home is not a real estate investment. It's merely a place to live. You buy a home because you love it and because you want to live there—not because you think it will grow in value. If it does, consider yourself lucky, not smart.

---

[39]It's called a margin account. With it, you can borrow money, using your stocks as collateral, to buy even more stocks.

[40]And illegal, too, because when borrowing against a stock portfolio, your loan is limited to 50% of the value of the stocks. There is no such limit when borrowing against real estate.

[41]See Rule #21.

RULE #21

NEVER OWN YOUR HOME OUTRIGHT. INSTEAD, GET A BIG 30-YEAR MORTGAGE, AND NEVER PAY IT OFF—*REGARDLESS OF YOUR AGE AND INCOME.*

Last year, Wal-Mart sold several hundred thousand drills to people who didn't want them.

What these people wanted was a hole in the wall, but to get one, they first had to buy a drill.

The same is true for your mortgage: You didn't want that, either. What you did want was a house—but to get a house, you first had to obtain a mortgage. If you're like most folks, you hate your mortgage, and you'd love to get rid of it as soon as possible. You consider every monthly payment you make to be a waste of money, and you know that over 30 years, you'll spend more on interest on the loan than you paid to buy the house in the first place. That's why you put down as much money as possible—to keep the mortgage as small as possible. You also chose a 15-year loan—to get the loan paid off in half the time, compared to a conventional 30-year mortgage—and you make extra payments whenever possible to further accelerate the payoff. In fact, you might even have signed up for one of those new biweekly loan programs, which have you make half the payment every two weeks instead of a single, full payment once a month. You do all these things because your parents taught you that mortgages were expensive and dangerous, and the key to achieving financial success was to own your home outright.

Although their advice was once correct, it is now completely wrong. All wrong.

The New Rules of Money are clear: A big, 30-year mortgage is the best thing you can have. You should get as big a loan as possible, and never pay it off. Forget about 15-year loans, never make extra payments, and forget about those biweekly mortgage payment plans.

Before you dismiss all this as craziness, read on—

because I'm about to save you (and make you) incredible amounts of money.

First, understand that everything you know about mortgages—and particularly what you fear about them—was told to you by your parents and grandparents. They told you that mortgages are dangerous, that having one means you can lose your home. They told you this because they remember the Depression, when millions of Americans lost their homes. But by learning why your elders were correct to pay off *their* mortgage, you'll come to understand why you'll be *right* to keep *yours*.

The story begins with federal law. In the 1920s and 1930s, banks were permitted to cancel mortgage loans at any time. During the Depression—when banks ran out of cash and needed more—that's exactly what they did: Bicycling messengers throughout the nation delivered telegrams informing home owners that they had 120 days to pay off their mortgage—or face foreclosure. The result: Millions of Americans lost their homes, and the lesson—that you must own your home without a mortgage to make sure you'll never lose it—was burned into the American psyche.

What you and your parents have failed to realize, though, is that Congress has changed the rules. Now **The New Rules of Money** are in place. This means banks no longer are permitted to cancel mortgage loans prematurely. If you have a mortgage, you have no risk that the bank will make you pay off the loan any quicker than is demanded by your regular payment schedule. Therefore, carrying a mortgage is not the risky tactic it once was.

Fine, you say. *So the bank can't call the loan. That doesn't mean carrying a big, long mortgage is a good idea.*

No, but what it does mean is that mortgages are not as scary as you thought they were.

Is your apprehension over mortgages weakening? Well, hey, I'm just getting started.

You say you don't want a mortgage because it costs you so much money. That's why you send in extra cash every month—to get the loan paid off more quickly. You know that paying off the mortgage early will save you a ton of money in interest charges.

Although that is correct, you need to turn that coin over, because there's another side you have completely overlooked. It's a critical point, too: Every time you send an extra $100 to your mortgage company, you deny yourself the opportunity to invest that $100 elsewhere.

In business school, this is called *opportunity cost*. It means, essentially, that every time you turn left, you deny yourself the opportunity to turn right.[42] So while paying off the mortgage saves you interest, you deny yourself the chance to *earn* interest with that money. And with mortgage rates so low, it is relatively easy today to earn more from an investment than what the loan is costing you.

Think about it. Your mortgage is probably costing you 8% or less. Over the next 30 years, can you earn (on average) at least that much from investments? Absolutely: Even long-term government bonds pay nearly that amount, and stocks have been averaging more than 10% since 1926. Although "past performance is no indication of future success," these long-term performance records do provide some comfort that at least it's been done before. I don't know about you, but I'm happy to pay 8% out of my left pocket if I can earn 10% in my right pocket.

In fact, keeping that mortgage allows you to earn money two ways: First, you get to invest the money that you otherwise would have spent on extra mortgage payments. Second, your home will grow in value *even if you have a mortgage*. Think about it. Your home's value will rise or fall whether there's a mortgage or not. Therefore, owning your home outright is like having money buried under the mattress: None of that cash, in effect, is earning any interest. You wouldn't stuff ten grand under your mattress, so why stash two hundred thousand into the walls of the house?

Carrying a mortgage gets to be more fun, too. Yes, *fun*. My father used to love to talk about his mortgage—all $98

---

[42]For an example of opportunity cost, see Rule #13.

per month of it. You see, he and my mom bought their home in 1959 for the whopping price of $19,500! Yet, my Dad tells how *his* father—my Grandpop Max—thought Dad was crazy. How in the world was my father going to be able to handle such a huge mortgage payment, Max wondered. After all, my dad was earning less than $3,000 a year back then. To spend $1,200 a year on mortgage payments—well, Grandpop Max thought my Dad was nuts![43]

Of course, by the 1970s, Dad was laughing about it. Why? It's simple: Because in 1974 his monthly payment was the very same amount that he paid back in 1959. Yet during that time, of course, Dad's income steadily rose. Thus, by the 1970s, Dad's mortgage payment had become insignificant compared to his income—not to mention that his house had grown in value substantially.

That's lesson number two in carrying a big, long mortgage: The payments get cheaper over time, even though they never actually change. This is possible because the payments are fixed, though your income grows.

Your defense of mortgage apprehension just took a big body blow, but you're still not convinced. Okay, try this: It's a given that you are going to borrow money during the course of your life, right? So doesn't it make sense to borrow money as inexpensively as possible?

That translates to a mortgage. Why carry 18% credit card debts—which are not tax-deductible—when you can instead carry an 8% mortgage that *is* tax-deductible? Ditto for auto loans and personal loans. Your mortgage is the cheapest money you'll ever buy, so it makes sense to use it as much as you can. The next time you buy a car, finance it with a home mortgage instead of a car loan.

There I go again, talking about carrying debt. That's what scares you. You know that if you owe $5,000 to credit cards and then lose your job, Visa can't reclaim that sweater you bought. But if you have a home equity line of credit which you fail to repay because you're out of work, the bank can

---

[43]As all parents think of their kids!

take your house. That's why you don't want to borrow against your house—in case you're out of work and money gets tight; it sure would be a relief knowing that you don't have a big mortgage payment to make.

That's wrong again, I'm afraid. First, you're unlikely to find yourself in such dire straits. But then, that's what financial planning is all about, so let me do some effective planning for you.

Let's look at Pat and Ed. They both earn $50,000 a year. Both have $20,000 in savings. Both buy a $120,000 house. Pat wants to minimize his mortgage, so he uses his $20,000 in savings as a down payment, and he opts for a 15-year loan at 7.5%. His monthly payment is $927, but only 67% of that payment is tax-deductible interest; the rest is principal.[44] Therefore, Pat's net after-tax cost for his mortgage is $742. And to pay off his mortgage even quicker, Pat sends in an extra $100 with every payment. Of course, these payments are devoted entirely to principal, and therefore provide no tax deduction.

Ed listens to me, and therefore obtains a 30-year mortgage at 8%,[45] putting down just 5% and financing the rest. Even though his mortgage balance is bigger than Pat's ($114,000 compared to $100,000), his monthly payment is just $837. That's not all: A full 90% of the payment is interest, meaning that Ed's after-tax cost is just $586 a month— $156 less than what Pat has to pay! Ed invests this savings of $156 each month for five years, earning 8% after taxes per year. And instead of sending an extra $100 a month to his mortgage company, as Pat does, Ed adds it to his savings. Result: Over five years, Ed accumulates nearly $19,000. Because he kept $14,000 from his original $20,000, he's able to keep that money invested, too. Now, that money has grown to $21,000. All told, Ed has accumulated $40,000 in savings and investments.

---

[44]With 30-year loans, much less of each payment goes toward principal. That's why it takes 30 years to repay it.

[45]30-year loans typically charge higher rates than 15-year loans. This seems to bolster the defenders of 15-year loans, but keep reading.

Suddenly, both men find themselves out of work. Because Pat used all of his money as a down payment, he has no savings to tide him over. True, he's got $48,000 worth of equity in his house, but he can't access it. He tried, but the bank turned him down for the loan. "But I've got all this equity in my house!" Pat exclaimed. It didn't matter, the loan officer said, because banks only lend money to people who can repay the loans. With no job, Pat has no income and therefore he cannot qualify for a loan.

Indeed, Pat has fallen victim to the biggest misconception in real estate: That a mortgage is a loan against the house. It isn't. A mortgage is a loan against *your income*. Without an income, you cannot obtain a loan.[46] If Pat doesn't fix his income problem in a hurry, he'll lose his house. How ironic: Pat, who never wanted a mortgage in the first place, is now in financial jeopardy because he was trying to get rid of one too quickly, and now can't get another!

Ed, though, is in much better shape. With $40,000 in savings, he's easily able to make his payments each month. In fact, even if he doesn't find work for a long time, his home is not in jeopardy. At the rate of $586 a month, Ed won't run out of money for nearly eight years!

And that's really my point: When you have a mortgage, you are required to make only that month's payment. As I explained at the beginning, you are never required to pay off your loan immediately. You might *want* to do so, but that doesn't mean you *must* do so.

Face it. You're beaten. You're just lying in the sand, begging me not to pummel you with any more great reasons to carry a big, long mortgage. Okay, but let's make sure you learned your lesson.

1. You must no longer send extra payments to your mortgage lender.

Invest that money instead, just as Ed did.

---

[46]You are able to borrow at such low rates because the loan is secured by your home. Credit cards, which have no collateral to seize if you default, therefore charge much higher rates. "Ah," I hear you saying, "now this whole thing is becoming clear."

2. Never prepay your mortgage payments like Pat did.

Once you give money to a lender, the only way you'll ever get it back is to reborrow the money or sell the house. Selling your home is the last thing you want to do,[47] and you probably will be unable to get a loan when you need it most. Besides, if you're simply going to borrow it back later, why bother giving the money to the lender in the first place?

3. Stop participating in biweekly loan programs.

This is nothing more than a marketing gimmick by firms that capitalize on your hatred—and fear—of mortgages. Somebody figured out that if you make half the payment every two weeks, you can pay off a 30-year loan in about 21 years. It sounds harmless—after all, what's the difference between making a full payment on the 30th and paying half on the 15th and the other half on the 30th?

There would be no difference—if that were how biweekly mortgages worked. But they don't work that way: You don't make *two payments a month*, you make *half a payment every two weeks*. There's a big difference between those two statements. With a biweekly mortgage, you make 26 half-payments a year. And 26 half-payments is the same as 13 full payments. In other words, biweekly mortgages require you to make one extra payment per year—13 instead of 12. Therefore you're merely making extra principal payments, which, as you've learned by now, is the wrong thing to do.

4. Recognize that agreeing *not* to prepay your mortgage actually can earn you a *lower* interest rate, which will save you a lot of money.

Given the choice, most people would prefer a loan that does not have a "prepayment penalty" over one that does. In fact, until recently, you couldn't even find mortgage loans that contained prepayment penalties. But

---

[47]Although it might be the economically smart thing to do.

today, such loans not only exist, they can be excellent choices.

Today's "prepayment penalty" clauses typically allow the lender to charge you a penalty if you pay more than 20% of the outstanding principal balance in any 12-month period of the first 36 months of your loan. If you did make such a large prepayment on your mortgage, under the most common penalty clause, you would be required to pay the lender the lesser of 2% or six months' worth of interest on the amount paid over 20%. Say you obtain a $300,000 mortgage, with a monthly payment of $2,400. Let's also say that, soon thereafter, you get a $90,000 inheritance, and you decide to use it to reduce your mortgage balance. Because that $90,000 is equal to 30% of your loan balance, you exceed the 20% threshold—and that means your lender will charge you $600.

It's easy to avoid this penalty, you say. You simply won't pay off the mortgage prematurely.

But that might not be so simple. What if you want to refinance or sell the house? Doing so, of course, requires you to get rid of (prepay) your mortgage, thus subjecting you to the penalty. (Some lenders will waive the penalty if you are required to move due to a job change or relocation.)

But why tolerate this potential problem? Even though more and more mortgage companies are attaching prepayment penalties to their loans, wouldn't it make more sense to simply avoid a loan that has a prepayment penalty?

Not necessarily. To entice you to accept the penalty clause, lenders will give you a rate that's 0.25% less than what you'd get otherwise—and that savings can really add up. In fact, the difference between 8% and 7.75% for a $300,000 loan is $50 a month! To get those savings, *all you need to do is not pay more than 20% of the balance due during any 12 consecutive month period for only the first three years.*[48]

---

[48]To make this easier to understand, try this: *Just never pay off your mortgage!*

Okay, you're convinced. You agree that a big, long mortgage is best. But how do you act on this advice? It's simple. Just:

1. Go get a new mortgage!

Either refinance, replacing your current loan with a new, bigger mortgage, or get a second mortgage to supplement your existing loan. Which is best? It depends on whether you can get a new loan with better terms than your current loan.

Either way, get the equity out of the house. Your goal is to increase your mortgage balance by up to $100,000. (When refinancing or obtaining a second mortgage, as of this writing, mortgage interest is tax-deductible only for the first $100,000 of new debt. This limit does not apply when you are obtaining the mortgage in order to purchase a home, or to use the money for the purpose of home improvements. Talk with your tax advisor before proceeding.)

2. Invest the proceeds of your refinancing carefully.

Do not spend the money on vacations, furniture, cars, or college.[49] This is your home we're talking about, so you must invest these assets prudently. If you don't know how to do that, hire a professional advisor to do it for you.

3. If you need help with the new payments, let your new investments help you.

Worried that you won't be able to handle the big, new mortgage payments you'll now have? Here's an easy way to solve that problem: Arrange for your new investments to send you a monthly check equal to your increased mortgage payments. If your mortgage costs you 8% and you earn at least that much from your investments, then you can easily generate enough income to help you han-

---

[49]See Rule #11.

dle the new mortgage payments. Over time, you'll probably discover that:

1. Your investments will earn more than what the mortgage is costing you (enabling your account to grow in
   value despite your withdrawals, as discussed earlier);
2. You'll have access to the cash in the meantime if
   it becomes financially necessary (as also discussed
   earlier); and
3. Eventually you won't need this help because as your
   income grows over time, the loan will be easier to
   handle on your own (also as discussed earlier).

So, what are you waiting for? Tip your hat to your spin-
ning-in-his-grave grandfather, and call a mortgage broker
today!

RULE #22 WHEN SEEKING A MORTGAGE, USE THE OLD QUALIFYING RULES.

In recent years the real estate industry has changed the
rules for buying a home. Although these changes have
made it easier for you to buy a home—or a more expensive
home than you'd otherwise buy—it has dangerous implications for your ability to achieve overall financial success.
Therefore, you must ignore what the real estate industry
says you can afford.

When you start shopping for a mortgage—either to buy a
home or refinance—you'll discover two "lending limits."
The first says that your monthly mortgage payment must
not exceed 28% of your income, while the second holds that
your mortgage payment *plus other debts* must not exceed
36% of your income.

These lending limits exist to protect borrowers from
saddling themselves with so much debt that they'll collapse

under its weight. Lenders know that buyers too often borrow beyond their ability to repay the loan, resulting in massive defaults. Although you might think you can afford a $4,000 monthly mortgage payment on a $60,000 income, lenders know better.

The problem is that the two lending limits weren't always 28/36. The limits used to be 22/28. In other words, the monthly mortgage payment for a home owner was once limited to 22% of income, while today's buyers can have mortgage payments equal to 28% of income. Thus, you now can obligate a much higher percentage of your total income to your mortgage than before. This is a dangerous trend, especially considering that taxes also take a higher percentage of your income than ever before. Therefore, if you follow today's lending limits, at best you will be house-rich and cash-poor, and at worst, you will lose your home, destroying your credit record—and maybe your marriage—in the process.

Indeed, there's a lot more to owning a home than a mortgage payment—like insurance, utilities, maintenance, repairs, improvements, and decorating. If you stretch to buy as expensive a house as possible, you won't be able to afford anything else.[50]

You need to set aside money for these expenses, and that means you should not buy as expensive a home as you think you can afford. And that, in turn, means foregoing the current lending limits and sticking with the old limits.

Why has the real estate industry increased the lending limits? Because over the past 40 years, housing prices have grown more rapidly than incomes, and if the limits weren't increased, today too many Americans wouldn't qualify for a mortgage. That, in turn, would put builders, bankers, and real estate agents out of work. Clearly, low lending limits are not in *their* best interests. Be aware that none of these play-

---

[50]And as any home owner can tell you, it's the "other" expenses that will kill you. One of my clients fell in love with a house on a five-acre lot. He met the lending guidelines (barely), but he soon ran into financial difficulties. One reason: He didn't anticipate spending $3600 a year to have the lawn mowed.

ers care whether you can really afford the payments, as long as you sign the settlement papers. If you later default, they won't care: The builder will have already made his profit, the real estate agent has gotten his commission, and as for the money that the banker loaned to you, well, he sold your loan to a servicing company, so the banker has no risk if you default, either. Clearly, the higher the lending limits, the more expensive a house you can buy, and the more money they all make.

That's a big part of the reason why there are so many innovative loan programs available.[51] The real estate industry wants to make it as easy as possible for you to borrow money, because it's in their best interest to do so.

Unfortunately, their best interests can conflict with yours. Therefore, if you buy a home by pushing this lending limit to its extreme, or by using some of the no- or low-money-down loan programs that are available today (because you have to, not because you choose to), you face very real financial risks.

If you want to reduce your risk, keep your total debt payments (including your mortgage) to 28% of income, not 36% as the real estate industry allows. This way, you'll have a much-needed cushion to help you deal with the other financial aspects of your life, such as saving for college and retirement.

All this sounds reasonable enough. But once you start shopping for a house and a mortgage, you'll discover that this advice will force you either to make a larger down payment or buy a less expensive home—neither of which you may want or be able to do. Therefore, you might find yourself tempted to accept the higher loan limits, but if you do, I warn you: You'll regret it later.

Just ask Scott and Cathy. They bought a house based on their combined $70,000 income. Now that Cathy has a little girl, she would like to become a stay-at-home mom. But if she quits her job, the family won't be able to afford the mortgage payments. That's because when she and Scott

---

[51]See Rule #23.

bought the house, they assumed that their household income of $70,000 would remain intact. Therefore, if they want to keep the house, Cathy must keep working.

I don't have much sympathy for Scott and Cathy, because their dilemma is of their own doing. But what if Cathy's decision to leave the workforce was not her own choice? It easily could happen: She might be laid off, become disabled and unable to work, or even die. Since their ability to keep the house is dependent on both their incomes, Scott and Cathy would find themselves in serious financial jeopardy if one income was lost. This is why proper planning is essential—and why you should not buy a home without first creating an overall financial plan.

If they had seen a financial planner before they visited a mortgage broker, the planner would have asked if they intended to have children. This simple conversation would have helped Scott and Cathy understand that it would be foolish to assume that they would always be able to devote as much money to the costs of home ownership as they can today, because the family circumstances are certain to change. If they obligate *today* how their *future* income is to be spent, then they're setting themselves up for big problems later. All this would have led Scott and Cathy to choose a mortgage that is not dependent on their current $70,000 income, and that, in turn, would have meant they would have rejected the 28/36 lending limits for more reasonable—and *realistic*—ratios. You need to do the same.

RULE #23   LEARN THE ROLE MORTGAGES PLAY IN YOUR EFFORTS TO ACHIEVE FINANCIAL SUCCESS.

Mortgage banking was once a solid, staid industry. To get a loan, you went to a bank. Every bank was the same: They offered fixed-rate, 30-year mortgages. And you would send your monthly payment to your bank until you paid off the loan or sold the house.

Today **The New Rules of Money** are in place. Bankers now take a back seat to mortgage brokers, who represent not one bank but dozens, allowing mortgage officers to shop rates and programs on behalf of their clients. Indeed, the mortgage industry now offers dozens of loan programs and introduces new ones constantly. And it is virtually certain that the lender providing your loan will sell it to a loan servicing company, and it's to that company you'll send your monthly payment (until they sell it again, that is).

It's beyond the purview of this book to show you all the new loan programs that now are available. But here are just three examples to show you how innovative the mortgage banking industry has become, and why, under **The New Rules of Money**, your home is now just a place to live, while your mortgage (when used properly) should be viewed as a financial tool that can be a tremendous ally in your overall financial planning:

1. **Believe it or not, now you can borrow more money than your home is worth.**

   Up to 25% more, in fact. This means that a person who lives in a $400,000 home can borrow $500,000. The "loan" is actually two loans, combining a first and second mortgage. The first loan (for up to 100% of the home's current market value) is a traditional loan of your choice—such as a 30-year fixed-rate, a one-year adjustable rate mortgage, a five-year balloon, or other common loan program;[52] the additional 25% will be a fixed-rate second mortgage at rates of 13% to 17% (depending on your credit history). The term of the second mortgage can be as long as 20 years.

---

[52]Interesting how these are called "common loan programs," isn't it?

You can use the money either for debt consolidation or home improvements, reflecting the fact that lenders now realize that both uses represent sound money management.

Here's their thinking: Lenders do not want you to default or enter bankruptcy. Either can happen if you owe a lot of money to credit cards. Therefore, it's in the lender's best interest to help you eliminate your other debt—even if it means lending you more money at the tax-deductible rate of 15% so that you can pay off credit cards that charge non-deductible rates of 18% and 21%. Even though the lender is increasing its risk by loaning you more money, you actually become a lower risk because you now are less likely to default.

Mortgage lenders also like to help people make home improvements: By lending money that you essentially "reinvest" back into the house, the home's value will rise (at least, the lender hopes so). Thus, if you later default, the lender merely sells the now higher-valued house to recoup its money.

Of course, borrowing more money than the house is worth puts you "upside-down"—meaning you owe more on your mortgage than the house is worth. This could present a crisis if later you need to sell (and thus you should not use this strategy unless you plan to live in the house for at least 10 years, and preferably much longer). Still, for those wanting to make improvements, and for those trying to eliminate other debt, this latest loan program is an interesting idea, and one worth considering.

In order to qualify for a 125% loan, you must have an income that can support such payments. Indeed, as with all mortgage loans, qualifying is based primarily on your income, not merely on the value of the house. This makes the 125% loan program particularly attractive for high-income families who do not yet have substantial assets. Many younger workers and those newly married often meet this description.

2. **Another innovative program allows you to borrow against the future increased value of your home, instead of its current value.**

This allows purchasers and existing home owners to add rooms, install a pool, or even completely remodel their new or existing homes, without having to empty their wallets.

If you're looking to buy, you can finance 95% of the value of the house—based not on the house's current value, but the value after all the renovations have been completed. A professional appraiser must estimate what the new value will be, based on comparable properties in the area, and contractors will be paid as the work is completed.

Here's an example: One of my clients, Kris, was looking for a new home. She found an okay house in a great neighborhood. It was small, but listed for only $100,000. She figured that by adding a second floor, a garage, and an in-ground pool, it would be a great home. Unfortunately, the additions would cost another $100,000.

Ordinarily, it would have been impossible for Kris to buy the house and still have enough cash to make all the improvements she planned. But the new renovation programs make that easy: Because the appraiser agreed that the home would be worth more than $200,000 after Kris completed the improvements, she could get the money to do the work simply by putting down an additional $7,500 now. Thus, for this small cash outlay, she is able to install $100,000 worth of improvements!

New loan programs like these can benefit current home owners, too, because they allow you to borrow up to 90% of the estimated future value of the property. For example, if your home is worth $150,000 but you plan to add improvements worth $50,000, you can borrow up to 90% of $200,000. That's $180,000—or $30,000 more than your home is currently worth!

If you're going to seek this kind of loan, keep in mind that spending $50,000 on improvements doesn't necessarily mean your property will grow in value by $50,000. Many so-called "improvements" fail to boost property values, so make sure you consult with a real estate agent and an appraiser before you begin any work.

This warning aside, if you find a fixer-upper with the potential to be the home of your dreams, or if you want to make some changes to your present home but don't have a wheelbarrow full of money, this can be an excellent way to achieve your goal while minimizing your cash outlay.

3. You no longer need 20% down to avoid Private Mortgage Insurance.

Chances are you're paying for it currently, and quite possibly, unnecessarily. To understand why, and to learn how you can stop wasting money, let's review the background about PMI.

When lending money to home buyers, lenders take several steps to make sure they get repaid. They require the home owner to post the house as collateral, and if your down payment is less than 20% of the price of the house, they also require that you buy PMI, which could add $50 to $200 to your monthly payment. This insurance protects the lender in case you default on the loan. Lenders waive the PMI requirement when you put down 20% or more, because home buyers who put so much cash into the purchase are unlikely to default. Besides, if you do default, the lender needs to sell the house for only 80% of its value in order to recover the money it loaned to you.

Few people are able to put 20% down, so they are forced to buy PMI. Others who could manage to scrape together 20% are left cash-poor, with no cash reserves or other investments. Such home buyers face a dilemma: Either pay the 20% or pay for PMI. Most choose the latter.

Today, though, a variety of lenders allow home buyers (as well as those refinancing) to avoid PMI *with as little as 5% down*. This offers you the chance to get into your home with very little cash and, even if you can afford to put down 20%, this eliminates your incentive to do so. (I used to advise clients to put down 20% whenever they could, simply to save the cost of PMI.)

Lenders are willing to waive PMI in exchange for a slight increase in the interest rate, usually ½% to ¼%. Although this slight increase translates to a somewhat higher mortgage payment, it offers several advantages, including:

- Your total monthly payment is still lower than it would have been if you were paying PMI; and
- PMI isn't tax-deductible, but the extra interest you're paying is—which further reduces the net cost of this alternative.

The best news is this: You don't necessarily need to refinance in order to eliminate PMI. Denise bought a $150,000 house 10 years ago, with 10% down. Her monthly payment therefore includes the cost of PMI. But now her mortgage balance is only $123,000 (because she's made 10 years' worth of payments) and the value of her home is $225,000. Thus, Denise now has $100,000 in equity in her home—which is well above the 20% necessary to avoid mortgage insurance!

If you are in a similar situation, and you're still paying for mortgage insurance, all you need to do is get an appraisal to prove to your mortgage company that you've got at least 20% in equity, so you can tell them to eliminate the charge. If they refuse, simply refinance. You can do so for little or no cost, and you could save yourself hundreds of dollars every year!

These are just three examples of how mortgages can now help you with financial and lifestyle issues that go far beyond mere home ownership. Under **The New Rules of Money**, your home mortgage is an important tool to help you achieve financial success.

RULE
#24 DON'T ASSUME PAYING POINTS IS A BAD THING.

With all the mortgage companies bragging about their "no-point" loans, points must be pretty bad, huh?

Not necessarily. In today's world of mortgage lending, paying points just might be the smart way to go. At the very least, you need to consider the idea of paying points.

What exactly is a "point," anyway? One point equals 1% of your loan.[53] Although paying points requires you to bring extra cash to the settlement table,[54] it can make long-term sense. Why? Because points really are nothing more than a prepayment of interest. By prepaying some of your loan's interest, the lender will reward you by giving you a lower interest rate on the rest of your loan.

Peggy wants to borrow $120,000, and her lender offers her a fixed-rate loan at 9%. Unfortunately, that requires a bigger payment than she can afford. What she needs is a rate of 8%.

Well, she can get it by "paying points." In this example, let's say her lender agrees to offer Peggy that 8% rate if Peggy will pay three points.[55] Since she is seeking to borrow $120,000, three points is $3,600. Is cutting her rate by 1% worth paying $3,600?

The answer depends largely on the spread between the no-point rate and the rate with points, and on how long Peggy plans to keep the loan (which itself is largely dependent on how long she plans to own her new home).

Peggy's 9% loan would have cost $965 per month; the 8% loan just $880. Thus, paying three points would lower her monthly payment by $85. Since the points would cost her $3,600, it would take Peggy three and a half years to recover that cost. This simple calculation does not take into consid-

---

[53]Note: One point does not necessarily equal one thousand dollars (a common misconception).
[54]See Rule #25.
[55]The extent to which points produce lower interest rates is something that constantly changes. So this example is not necessarily what will always occur; you might discover that paying three points produces a bigger or smaller reduction in your rate.

eration the after-tax effects of each choice, or the fact that by spending $3,600 on points, Peggy is not able to invest that money elsewhere (all of which makes this a rather complex calculation). On the other hand, this calculation ignores the fact that points are fully tax-deductible when paid to acquire a home[56]—saving Peggy yet more money.

All this complexity notwithstanding, one thing is clear: Peggy should not even consider paying points if she's not going to keep her home (and her loan) for at least three and a half years.[57] Conversely, if she plans to own her home for five years or more, paying those points today will save her a lot of money in the long run.

So the next time you hear mortgage lenders brag about their "no-point" loans, ask them to explain "the point" of their ad.

RULE #25 DO NOT HOLD YOUR NEXT REAL ESTATE SETTLEMENT AT THE END OF THE MONTH.

You've found your dream home, signed the contract, and gotten approval for your loan. All you need now is a settlement date. Would you prefer a date early in the month or near the end—and does it really matter?

Before you answer, consider this: Approximately 70% of all home purchase settlements occur in the last week of the month, and 75% of those close in the last *two days* of the month. People traditionally want to close by the end of the month for one simple reason: Settling in the beginning of the next month would cause you to pay an extra month's

---

[56]Points paid when refinancing are deductible only over the life of the loan, which is not nearly as good a deal.
[57]Of course, if she's not going to keep her home at least that long, she has no business buying a home anyway, as Rule #15 explains.

worth of interest. Naturally, it made sense to avoid this unnecessary cost.

But under **The New Rules of Money**, this is no longer true. In fact, the least expensive time to settle on your home is now in the *first* week of the month, not the last. By settling at the beginning of the next month, you will save money, enjoy better service, and be assured of a smoother transaction. It may sound impossible, but it's true.

Although the reasons are numerous, the first one is obvious: Consider that half of all real estate settlements occur in just two days of each month. Would you want to run a restaurant where half of all your patrons arrive on the same two days? How could you provide high-quality service without burning the food?

Anyone who has ever eaten at a busy restaurant knows how frustrating it is to try to get the attention of a waiter serving too many tables, yet that's exactly what awaits you if you settle at the end of the month. You know that the busy season for accountants peaks on April 14; for florists it's Valentine's Day; toy store owners are busiest at Christmas; and for restaurants, it's Mother's Day. In the real estate settlement industry, the "busy season" is the end of every month!

Therefore, you'll enjoy much better service by settling at the *beginning* of the month instead. Because few people settle at that time, you'll not only be able to pick any time of day you want for your appointment, you also will have the undivided attention of the settlement company's staff. Imagine going to a five-star restaurant for dinner at 5 P.M.—by arriving so early, you'll get your pick of tables and enjoy wonderful service.

Don't worry that closing in the next month will force you to pay extra interest costs. Today, many lenders are so eager to reduce the workload they face at the month's end, *they* now pay *you* to delay settlement by prorating the interest on the loan.

Unfortunately, many real estate professionals continue to perpetuate the myth that consumers will save money if they settle at the end of the month. It's simply not true. So, the next time you buy or sell a house, consider making your settlement experience more pleasant. Check with your lender to see if it offers an interest credit program, and if so, hold your settlement at the beginning of the month. You'll be glad you did.

the new investment strategies

RULE #26 DON'T REFUSE TO SELL ASSETS MERELY BECAUSE THEY HAVE DROPPED IN VALUE.

It's astounding how often people tie their sense of self to the investments they make. If an investment falls in value, they feel like a failure, and they won't sell the asset because doing so would be admitting that they've failed.

If they hold on, they figure, the investment might recover, maybe even turn a profit. If it did, their sense of self-worth would be restored.

Unfortunately, investments don't care how you feel about them. Mathematically speaking, it is twice as difficult for an investment to rise as it is to fall, and you need to understand this simple principle.

Say your $75 stock drops by 50%, to $37.50. In order for a $37.50 stock to climb back to $75, it must gain 100%. So it takes a 100% gain to offset a 50% loss. This is one reason why investments that fall often don't return to their original values—and if they do, it takes much longer.

This is why you must be willing to sell an asset that has fallen in value. "Holding on" conjures up images of clinging to a rope for dear life—and investing need not be so melodramatic. If one of your investments has failed to live up to expectations, or if there are better opportunities elsewhere, *cut the rope.*

RULE #27 STOP TRYING TO BE RIGHT, PART 1.

I remember a call I once got from my client Betty. "I want to buy gold," she announced.

A rather unusual request, I thought. "Why?" I asked.

"Because I think gold is going to rise!" she gushed.

"Okay," I said. "But is it going to rise any faster than the investments you already have?"

"Sure!" she proclaimed. "I think gold's going to hit $500 an ounce!" At the time, gold was trading for about $300. A move to $500 would be a gain of 67%.

"How long will it take for gold to get there?" I asked.

"Not too long," Betty said. "Within five years."

Well, I told her, going from $300 to $500 over five years is an annual return of 10.8%.

"Is that all?" she asked, somewhat deflated. After all, that's no better than what she'd expect from her current investments, and actually a bit worse than she actually had been earning.

Which was my point. When it comes to investing, being right is often not enough. You must be *so* right that *being* right justifies the gamble you plan to make. In most cases, that gamble just isn't worth it, because being right isn't likely to put you any further ahead than if you had simply ignored the whole idea in the first place.

RULE #28 STOP TRYING TO BE RIGHT, PART 2.

My friend John, 35, doesn't save much of his money. Although he earns $45,000, he barely contributes to his company retirement plan, and he has little money in the bank. He figures he doesn't need to save much.

You see, when John does save, he picks highly speculative investments that he thinks will produce super-high returns. So, last time I spoke with him, he owned half a dozen stocks, and he had invested about $1,500 in each one. John figures three will go bust, two might make average returns, but one has *got* to be a winner—the kind of stock grandchildren talk about.[58]

---

[58]As in, "My grandfather bought IBM back in 1952!"

Let's assume John is right. Say that over the next 30 years, three of his stocks bomb, two earn 10% per year, and the sixth hits a home run—quickly doubling in value, then quadrupling and quintupling, eventually settling down to become one of the best stocks of the early 21st century, earning an incredible 20% per year for the entire 30 years.[59]

The results? As John enters retirement at age 65, he finds himself with $408,400. Considering he started with just $9,000, that's pretty amazing. But is it really all that much money?

Not when you contrast John with Mary. She knew she would be unable to pick the next Microsoft—so she didn't even try. Instead, she saved regularly, putting 10% of her $45,000 salary into mutual funds for 30 years. Like John, she got a 4% raise each year, but unlike John, she earned a mere 7.5% annual return on her investments. The results after 30 years? She has $835,000—more than twice as much as John.

Stop trying to pick the one hare. It's no substitute for choosing lots of turtles.

RULE #29 STOP KEEPING SCORE.

Joe, a client worth about $1.5 million, wanted me to look at a deal he was considering. It's a new cable TV operation, he said, and it was being offered to only a few people. He heard about it from his lawyer,[60] who represents the sponsors of the deal.

"How much do they want you to invest?" I asked.

"One hundred fifty thousand," he replied.

"And how much do you expect it to earn?"

"Well," Joe answered, "they're projecting nothing for the first year, and then a 15% return for years two through five. They'd then sell after the fifth year, and investors would receive back their capital plus any profits."

---

[59] If you think 20% a year for 30 years isn't "incredible," consider: No stock has ever done it.
[60] See Rule #67.

"So after six years, you'll have gotten $90,000 plus any profits. How much are they estimating the profit to be?"

"They think they'll be able to sell for twice what it's costing to build," he said.

"Then that's another $300,000. So all told, your original investment of $150,000 would return $390,000 over six years." I did some fast math. "That's an internal rate of return of just under 20%. I can see why you're attracted to this, Joe, but tell me, how risky would you say this investment is?"

"It'll probably be all or nothing," he said. "It's definitely a gamble."

"Would you say that this investment is riskier than your current investments?"

"Much! But actually, that's part of the fun. If it works, I'll make a lot of money."

"And what will that do for you?"

Joe paused on the other end of the phone. "I don't get your question," he offered.

"Here's what I mean, Joe. Let's say you're right, and over the next six years, your $150,000 turns into $390,000—boosting your net worth from $1.5 million to $1.9 million. What will you do with the newfound money? Will you use the money to buy a new house?"

"No, I just moved a year ago. You know that."

"Will you retire earlier than you otherwise would?"

"No."

"Will you buy a new car? Eat out more often, or at more expensive restaurants? Will you do anything that you will not otherwise do anyway?"

"I see your point," he replied. "No, making this profit will not change anything for me."

"You're right, Joe, it won't—especially considering that your money is already earning in the low double digits," I explained. "The difference over six years between what this investment offers and what you'll have anyway, by just doing what you're already doing, isn't all that significant. Do you agree?"

"Yes," he said.

"Then let me ask you this, Joe," I said. "How much extra money would you need to have in six years in order for this investment to produce a *really meaningful* difference to you? I mean, you've just said that having a net worth of $1.9 million wouldn't cause you to retire or buy a new house. What would get you to do that?"

"I might retire if I had $3 million," Joe said.

"Okay, that's exactly what you told me three years ago when I first produced your financial plan," I said. "Now, on that basis, how much would you have to invest in this deal in order for it to return $1.5 million in six years—thereby giving you the $3 million net worth that you'd need so you could retire?"

"I don't know," Joe said. "How much?"

"Based on your projections of how well the investment would do, you'd need to invest almost $600,000. Are you willing to invest six hundred grand—40% of your net worth—into this deal?"

"No, of course not," Joe answered. "That's too much money."

"But that's what it would take, Joe, to make this deal worthwhile for you. Because if you invest $150,000 and it works, it will have absolutely no effect on your lifestyle. Therefore, the investment is pointless and not worth doing. But if you invest $600,000 and it fails—which is quite possible—the effect on your lifestyle would be devastating, wouldn't you agree?"

"Absolutely," he said. "I probably wouldn't be able to retire for an extra 10 years!"

"Then the conclusion is clear, Joe. You should not participate in this investment. Winning won't help you, but losing would hurt. That's a poor combination for an investment."

"But the deal sounds like so much fun," he said. "And it would be neat to pick such a winner."

"Yes, Joe, but investments are supposed to be designed to contribute to your lifestyle—either present or future—or to help you achieve some personal goal. If you're not accomplishing that with your investments—if you're picking investments simply because you think they're going to make money, or if you're leaving your money untouched because you like to watch it grow, or because you want to be able to say you are worth a certain amount (not for any particular reason, mind you, other than you just like the way it sounds)—well then, you're not engaging in financial planning. All you're doing is keeping score."

Keeping score matters only when you play games, and playing games is something you do for fun. And fun is supposed to be an activity whose outcome has no impact on your life. So if you're starting to demand *fun* from your investments, it's time you started a new hobby. Leave your investments alone, and seek fun elsewhere.

RULE #30   KNOW WHEN IT'S TIME TO STOP CLIMBING THE MOUNTAIN.

I was very impressed with Jack and Candy. When I first met them, Jack had already been retired for a year; Candy had always been a stay-at-home mom. They put five kids through college on his working-class salary, and have never received an inheritance. Still, they owned a portfolio worth more than $1.2 million.

"How'd you do it?" I asked. I love to hear rags-to-riches stories.

They looked at each other as if they didn't know, hoping the other would have the answer. "We just saved all our lives," Jack said, rather embarrassed.

"We were careful with our money," Candy added sheepishly.

Careful indeed. Their portfolio consisted of several dozen blue chip and technology stocks, along with a smattering of stock mutual funds. There were virtually no bonds in the portfolio. "You've got a pretty aggressive portfolio here," I observed.

"Is it?" Jack asked rhetorically. "We just recognized that if we wanted our money to grow, we needed to own stocks."

Candy said, "But we were careful never to place too much money into any one investment."

"Well, it's obvious that you've done quite well. So what advice can I offer you?" I asked.

"Now that I'm retired, we'd like to earn more income from the portfolio," Jack answered. Scanning down their list of stocks showed that most of their stocks paid dividends of 2% or less. All told, they were receiving about $20,000 a year in dividend income. Not much to show for a $1.2 million portfolio.

"Well," I started, "we can increase your income easily enough. But it'll require you to sell most of your stocks and replace them with other investments. That means you'll incur some transaction costs and a tax liability. Are you willing to do that?"

"Sure," they replied. "Our investments have done well for us, but we understand that they might not be what's best for us today."

"Okay," I said. "Then let me tell you how we'll proceed." I described for them how we'd replace their pure stock portfolio with one containing all nine major asset classes. And we'd use mutual funds, which have a feature called the Systematic Withdrawal Program, which allows you to receive a monthly income. Through a SWP, they could receive an income of 7% to 8% per year. Through these changes, I estimated that their income would increase to about $75,000 per year, or roughly four times more than their current income.

They didn't look happy.

"You want to put some of our money into bonds?" Candy asked.

"Yes, and real estate, too." I replied. "Also gold, natural resources, and some international securities as well. You need a highly diversified portfolio to help reduce your exposure to the U.S. stock market. This will help the portfolio produce the income you want on a more consistent basis."

"But how much will a portfolio like this grow?" Jack asked.

"Well, anything can happen in any given year," I answered. "But historically, over long periods, portfolios like these have produced competitive returns. Of course, that doesn't mean this will occur in the future. But you shouldn't expect much growth, Jack, because you'll be withdrawing money from the portfolio at the rate of 8% per year. So even if the portfolio manages to earn 10%, you'd have only 2% growth after you get your income."

Now they were looking truly dismayed.

"We were hoping to see the portfolio grow to about $2 million. Maybe we should just leave everything in stocks."

"But if you do that," I reminded them, "you'll be stuck with the same $20,000 income that you get now. The only way to boost your income is to convert the portfolio into investments that produce more income, or to slowly sell some of your stocks and use the proceeds as a substitute for income. But that's a much more aggressive strategy, since a decline in the stock market could seriously undermine your ability to do that."

"But we're used to watching our assets grow in value each year," Candy persisted.

"I know, and thank goodness, too," I explained. "But, Candy, you have to understand that you are no longer in the same situation as before."

"What do you mean?" they asked, almost in unison.

"Well, you two have devoted a lifetime to building and accumulating wealth. You've done an absolutely terrific job at it, too. Few other Americans have been able to save as much money as the two of you did, especially considering that you started with so little.

"But those days are gone. You no longer need to save and accumulate money. You've already done that. Now it's time to start enjoying the money."

They didn't look like they understood, so I continued.

"Look at it this way. It's like you've spent a lifetime climbing a mountain. Well, now you've reached the top of that mountain, and the actions you need to take to stay on top are different from the actions that got you there. If you keep climbing like you've been, you'll fall down the other side!"

This made sense to them, and they are now enjoying their increased income.

RULE #31 STOP FOCUSING ON SAFETY, AND START FOCUSING ON PERFORMANCE.

Why is it that so many people place 100% of their money into bank accounts, Treasuries, EE Savings Bonds, and the fixed account in their company retirement plan? Because they're afraid of losing their money, that's why. This is ironic, because such so-called "safe" investments are about as risky as you can get under **The New Rules of Money**.

How is that possible? Simple: Over the past 20 years, CD rates have averaged 7.3% per year. If you've been in the 33% combined federal/state income tax bracket, you lost to taxes a third of that return, or 2.4%. Thus, you kept only 4.9%.

But inflation averaged 5.2% per year, meaning you lost, in real terms, 0.3% of every dollar you had in the bank. If you kept that up for 20 years, you'd have lost 6% of your money. At that rate $10,000 after 20 years would be worth only $9,400!

This is why many people fail financially. They focus on safety instead of performance. Yet if you are to accumulate wealth under **The New Rules of Money**, you must focus on growing your money in *real* economic terms—after taxes and after inflation—and stop focusing on safety.

RULE #32

AVOID THE "DOGS OF THE DOW THEORY" —THE NEWEST BAD IDEA FROM THE PERSONAL FINANCE PRESS.

A perverse twist on performance rankings has led to a new, popular strategy called the "Dogs of the Dow." It's based on the historical performance of the Dow Jones Industrial Average, which clearly shows that, each year, the previous year's 10 worst stocks of the 30 that constitute the Dow outperform the Dow itself. Therefore, the theory's proponents say, all you need to do in order to secure above-average returns is to buy, each January, the 10 worst stocks of the DJIA.

How do you define "worst"? Simple: They're the ones with the lowest prices relative to their performances. And how do you calculate *that*? Simple again: Just pick the stocks with the highest dividend yields.

Mathematically speaking, it's true: The highest yields always reflect the lowest prices. Say you buy a stock that costs $50 per share, and further say that the company pays you a dividend of $5 per year. Assuming that the price of the stock never changes, your profit is 10%—because you earned $5 on a $50 investment. But if you paid $80 per share, your dividend yield would be only 6.25%.

Thus, the higher the yield, the lower the price. The lower the price, the greater the room for growth. Therefore, this theory holds, by choosing the 10 stocks with the highest dividend yields, you are choosing the stocks with the greatest opportunity for price increases.

Sounds exciting, but it's really nothing new. For years, this concept has been known as the Dividend Yield Theory, but with its new name has come new media attention. And whenever the personal finance press finds some new way to help you get rich quick, they splash it across their covers, knowing that subscriptions will increase.

The Dogs of the Dow Theory is really quite silly, and you

won't achieve great success with this strategy, for several reasons:

1. To bolster their argument, proponents refer to historical data—going back decades—that show that the Dow Dogs made more money than the Dow itself. Therefore, they argue, if you now invest in the Dow Dogs, you will experience the same results. This is nonsense, for as everyone knows (but most prefer to ignore), PAST PERFORMANCE IS NO INDICATION OF FUTURE SUCCESS. ANY ASSERTION TO THE CONTRARY IS A FEDERAL OFFENSE. Just because this theory might have worked for one period of time doesn't mean it will succeed again.

2. I'm not so sure it ever really succeeded, anyway. It's quite possible that the historical data suggest that the Dow Dogs produced above-average returns simply because nobody was actually buying them. It's like saying your sailboat would have sailed faster if you had everyone sit to starboard, because studies clearly show that the starboard side is slicker, and therefore endures less friction than the port side. This is nonsense, because if you had tried this—if everyone on board actually had sat to starboard—*the boat would have capsized!* The same is true on Wall Street: If everyone had bought the Dow Dogs over the past 40 years, those stocks certainly would not have performed as the historical records show. This is the flaw of *static analysis*: The failure to understand that if you had altered the conditions of the past, you also would have altered the outcome. Unfortunately, this is a concept often ignored by investors, advisors, and the personal finance press alike. It's also why you must be skeptical whenever anyone points to back-dated computer modeling to support the brilliance of their latest untested investment strategy.

3. Perhaps the proponents outsmarted themselves: When they discovered the historical relationship between the Dogs and the Dow, they should have kept quiet and

silently invested their own money accordingly. But by telling the world, they've ruined the idea for everyone—including themselves.[61]

4. The rationale for the Dow Dogs theory is flawed. The proponents argue that because the Dogs' dividend yields are out of sync with the rest of the Dow stocks, they will inevitably change to match the rest of the Dow stocks, and for that to happen, the Dogs' prices must rise. Sorry, but it's not true, for there's another way for the dividend yield to fall: The company can cut its dividend! While it's true that boosting a $50 stock to $100 will mathematically cut its dividend yield from 10% to 5%, there's another way to cut the dividend yield, too: Just cut the dividend itself. If the dividend drops from $5 to $2.50, the yield gets cut in half with no change in the stock price. But it seems the theorists forgot about that. Would you care to guess how often a Dow stock's dividend has been cut? Often enough to ruin this idea!

5. Where did the number "10" come from, anyway? Why not 8 or 12? Sounds like David Letterman had a hand in creating this idea. Top Ten lists make for great TV, but I really don't want comedy in my stock portfolio.

6. Hasn't it occurred to anyone that maybe the Dogs of the Dow *deserve* to be dogs? Seymour Goodman of Bear, Stearns has demonstrated that over the past 10 years, the 10 *lowest-yielding* Dow stocks have beaten the Dogs of the Dow (the highest-yielding stocks) *seven times*. Stay tuned: The personal finance press will soon be picking up on this one, and you'll no doubt start hearing about what Goodman lightheartedly calls "the Dow Dandies."

7. Consider the results of a study published in the August 1997 issue of *Financial Analysts Journal*. The authors, Grant McQueen and Steven Thorley, CFA, assistant profes-

---

[61]Ironic, isn't it? If they keep quiet, no one will know how smart they are. But if they tell everyone about it, the theory begins to fail, and everyone thinks they are idiots.

sors of finance in the Marriott School of Management at Brigham Young University, and Kay Shields, an independent financial planner, asked the question, "Does the Dow-10 Investment Strategy Beat the Dow Statistically and Economically?"

Their answer, which took six pages to explain: "After adjusting for risk and transaction costs and allowing for tax disadvantages, the Dow-10 does not outperform the Dow-30."

One day we'll all recall the days of old, when people used to invest in some short-lived fad called the Dogs of the Dow.

RULE #33 PAY NO ATTENTION TO THE DOW JONES INDUSTRIAL AVERAGE...

Assume your town has a population of 20,000, and you're interested in finding out how everybody's doing financially. So you poll just 30 people—the oldest, wealthiest people in town. Will your polling results accurately reflect the finances of the overall population?

Not very likely, I'm sure.

Yet similar results are exactly what you get when you focus on the Dow Jones Industrial Average. The Dow is a group of 30 of the nation's largest companies. A hundred years ago, the Dow accurately reflected the performance of the stock market, because there were few public companies, and all of them were big.

Not so today. With more than 20,000 stocks publicly traded, the Dow no longer is representative of what's going on in the stock market. Why is this a big deal? Because it's the one market indicator you've been watching. Even people who know nothing about stocks have heard about the Dow—because Dan, Peter, and Tom talk about it on every evening's newscast.

"The Dow was up in heavy trading today..." "The Dow lost ground today..." "Dow trading was moderate today..." and so on. Hey, if the three most important men in the news business feel it's important enough to tell us about the Dow each and every day, well, then the Dow must be really important, no?

No.

Dan, Peter, and Tom are telling you about the Dow largely out of habit. Besides, they've only got five seconds to fill you in on the day's activity, so if they were going to tell you about the S&P 500 Stock Index or the NASDAQ, they'd first have to tell you what those are. They simply don't have the time.

Experienced market watchers place little importance on the Dow, knowing that the Dow is not representative of the entire market. Besides, they understand, as you now will, that the Dow consists merely of 30 stocks. These stocks are selected by the editors of *The Wall Street Journal*, not by world-class economists,[62] outstanding portfolio managers with long and distinguished records, or chartered financial analysts. Why do *Wall Street Journal* Managing Editor Paul E. Steiger and his colleagues get to pick what's in and what's out for the Dow? Because *The Wall Street Journal* is owned by Dow Jones & Company.

Exactly how do these gentlemen decide which stocks belong inside the Dow and which Dow stocks ought to be booted out? No one knows for sure. One would assume[63] that they're not making the decision over a beer or two ("Hey, Paul, let's really mess with Lou Gerstetner's head and replace IBM with Anheuser Busch!"). In an ideal world, these two astute market-watchers will replace companies that no longer dominate their industry with companies that do.

For example, few would argue that Wal-Mart is the most important retailer in America today. So, in 1997, Mr. Steiger and his team tossed Woolworth from the Dow, and inserted

---

[62]Some would say, "Thank goodness!"
[63]Or at least *hope.*

Wal-Mart in its place. Three other pairs of stocks were exchanged as well: Hewlett-Packard for Bethlehem Steel, Johnson & Johnson for Texaco, and Travelers for Westinghouse. Nobody had much problem with these changes.

But what's interesting to note is the fact that when the changes were announced on March 17, 1997, the Dow was at 6935. If the Wal-Mart change alone had been made just five years earlier, the Dow today would be over 10,000. That's how powerful an effect one stock can have on the Dow.

But is our economy any different because we say "the market is at 8,000" as opposed to saying it's at 10,000? Most would say that a rose is a rose. But Federal Reserve Board Chairman Alan Greenspan threw the markets into a tizzy when he appeared before Congress in December 1996 to lament "the irrational exuberance" of a market whose recent gains were, in his opinion, simply unsustainable. Imagine how the chairman would feel if the Dow was then at 10,000 —which it would have been had our friends at *The Wall Street Journal* acted a little sooner!

So, when you get home at the end of the day and turn on the evening news, don't let the pronouncements of the Dow's daily performance either excite or perturb you. Because unless your investment portfolio happens to consist of the 30 stocks of the Dow Jones Industrial Average, the performance of the Dow is likely to have little correlation with your investments.

RULE #34 ... AND DISCOVER THE WILSHIRE 5000.

If the Dow Jones Industrial Average takes too small a survey to reflect accurately what's going on in the stock market,[64] then a bigger survey ought to solve the problem. That's one reason why more attention lately has gone to the S&P 500 Stock Index, a basket of 500 stocks.

---

[64]See prior Rule.

And if you really want to gauge the overall stock market, you could look at the Russell 1000, or the Russell 2000. Or even the Wilshire 5000, which contains, by the way, more than 7,300 stocks (don't ask).

Any of these indices would be better indications of what's happening in the stock market, but you won't find them discussed on the nightly news. You could check your newspaper, but many don't carry them, either. Try *The Wall Street Journal, Investors Business Daily, Barron's;* business magazines such as *Business Week, Forbes,* and *Fortune;* or some of the nation's leading daily newspapers, including the *New York Times, The Washington Post,* the *Los Angeles Times,* the *Atlanta Constitution,* the *Chicago Tribune,* and the *Boston Globe.* Better yet, when it comes to news about the market, it's best to ignore them all, because of our next Rule.

RULE #35 FOCUS ON TOMORROW WHEN READING TODAY'S NEWS.

Does the financial news of the day cause you to make investment decisions that often turn into very wrong decisions?

Think back to 1994. It was the worst year in decades for the financial markets—the bond market lost more money that year than ever, the stock market was in the negative, the dollar fell to the lowest level against the yen since World War II, and both gold and real estate fell below the previous year's levels. As a result, many people said, "Things are so bad, I don't want to invest now."

Then came 1995, one of the *best* years ever for Wall Street—the stock market hit new highs almost weekly, the international markets made money, the dollar recovered, the bond market enjoyed its biggest one-year gain in recent memory, and interest rates dropped to their lowest level in more than two years. Things were going so well, you'd have thought that people would say, "Now's the time to invest!" But instead, the masses waited, thinking, "Oh, my goodness, the market is so high, I'm afraid it's going to fall. I want to wait until the market comes down again before I invest."

In other words, people made long-term decisions based on short-term activity. So guess who made the most money in 1995? The people who were invested in 1993 and who stuck with their investments through all the turmoil. This, then, is the key: To achieve long-term investment success, you cannot pay attention to short-term market activity.

People lose sight of their long-term objectives in part because they let themselves be swayed by the news. What you hear on television or read in the newspaper can be misleading for one of two reasons: The information might be conveyed in such a way that it causes you to draw the wrong conclusion, or the information simply might be wrong.

Ask yourself this: How dangerous are the streets of Washington, D.C.?

We hear that Washington, D.C., is the murder capital of the United States, and the local media don't go a day without news of some violent crime in the area. In 1994 the FBI published a report of the most violent cities in the country, based on the number of violent crimes per capita. Can you guess where Washington, D.C., placed on the list?

Our capital city was not even in the top 50.

I use this example to demonstrate the need for perspective. We must make sure that the news we hear does not lead us to draw the wrong conclusions.

There is a rather well-known newsletter writer who predicts the stock market will drop 20%. This scares a lot of people. What most folks don't realize is that this guy has been calling for the stock market to drop 20% ever since the Dow was at 3000. If he was right when he first made the prediction, the Dow would have dropped from 3000 to 2400. At this writing, the Dow is at 8000—and he still says stocks will drop 20%. If he's right, the Dow will drop to about 6500—

leaving it more than twice as high as when he first called for the drop! So even if he's right, he's wrong!

This should tell you that a market drop just doesn't make any difference, for even if you're right in the short term, it doesn't matter in the long term.[65]

Let's assume you have a 10-year time horizon for your investments, and you're debating about when to invest. You think the market is going to drop, so you wonder if you should wait a month or two before investing. Ask yourself this: Back in 1987, would it have made any difference by now if you had invested in August instead of October? Back in November of that year, you would have felt a substantial difference during those couple of months. But 10 years later, that difference has become indistinguishable and irrelevant.

Here's another test: Many people are afraid to invest in stocks and stock mutual funds today because the market is at an all-time high. What these people are really saying is that they like to drive their car by looking in the rearview mirror. Indeed, you can think stocks are high only by comparing current stock prices to the previous ones.

To illustrate this point, answer this question: What do you think the stock market will earn, as an average annual rate of return, over the next 20 years? To give you some perspective, consider that the stock market has averaged 14.2% per year for the past 15 years, and 7.5% since 1946.

So, what do you think? Will the stock market maintain its 15-year pace? Or just its pace of the past 50+ years?

Let's say that stock prices grow only 10% per year for the next 20 years. No, wait. Let's say that stocks will earn only 7% per year—a showing less than half as good as the previous 15 years, and even less than the post–World War II average performance.

At the rate of 7% per year, stock prices still double about every 10 years. That means that the recent Dow of 8000 will become 16,000 in 10 years, and 32,000 in 20 years. Now, com-

---

[65]Unless, of course, you're planning to use the money in the short run, in which case that money shouldn't be in stocks in the first place.

pared to today's level, do you think stocks are too high? Of course not—and it all simply depends on your perspective.[66]

Don't get hung up on the "now." You're not investing for today; you're investing for tomorrow. Keep that in mind when you read today's news.

RULE #36 STAY AWAY FROM S&P 500 INDEX FUNDS...

Investing in index funds is a bad idea, and a lot of unsuspecting people are going to get hurt.

Without question, indexing is hot. In 1997, more than 20% of all the money invested into mutual funds went into index funds. We're talking a number approaching *$100 billion.* By comparison, as recently as 1994, less than 3% of mutual fund deposits went into index funds. Indeed, the largest mutual fund in the world is now the Vanguard 500 Index Fund. It didn't even exist 10 years ago.

How did index funds become so popular so quickly? Because investors love to follow fads. This one is a doozy. It started when someone noticed that, for a certain time period in the late 1980s, the majority of stock mutual funds failed to earn as much money as the S&P 500 Stock Index. This led someone to conclude that it is always so, and based on that conclusion, you ought merely to invest in the stocks of the S&P 500 instead of actively managed stock funds. Besides, this thinking continued, buying the index is a passive activity that doesn't require the services of a professional money manager (instead, you simply buy whatever stocks are contained in the index). By not having to pay the money manager's salary, and by not trading as actively as such managers would require, index funds become cheaper to own than actively managed mutual funds, and this savings translates into still higher returns. Everybody's

---

[66]If stocks grow at 10%, the Dow will be at 64,000 in 20 years; I didn't want to mention that for fear I'd scare you.

endorsement of index fund investing is based on these two arguments.

That's too bad, because both of these arguments are bunk, and if you invest in index funds based on them, you will become, at some point in the future, very disappointed —or worse.

Here, then, is the truth about index funds.[67]

When a person tells me they want to invest in an index fund, my response is, "Fine. Which one?" They always say the same thing: "What do you mean, which one?" Most people don't realize that today there are more than 125 index funds. A dozen were created in 1997 alone. If each is the same, why do we need more than one? How could they all be performing differently? And doesn't the fact that they differ in both makeup and performance suggest that you have to undergo the very investment evaluation that you were trying to avoid in the first place?

I feel your confidence in index funds beginning to weaken.[68]

I know what you want. You want to buy a fund that simply matches the S&P 500 Stock Index. Sorry, but there is no such thing. That's because no index fund is an exact mirror image of the S&P. After all, no fund can be. You see, the S&P—like all market indexes—is just a theoretical concept. A mathematical formula, if you will. It is simply a tool to help observers gauge the performance of the stock market. The eight-member committee[69] of the S&P 500 doesn't actually buy the stocks that constitute the index; they merely create a list of stocks and track them.

And because the index is merely a mathematical theory, it is impossible for a true index fund to perform identically to the index. In fact, let me take that statement a step further: *It is impossible for an index fund to make as much money as the index itself.* That's because the empirical index is not adjusted for commissions or taxes, but index

[67]Got your seatbelt on?
[68]And it's early yet.
[69]Four economists, three MBAs in finance, and one former *Business Week* journalist. *Business Week* is owned by McGraw-Hill, which owns Standard & Poor's, creator of the S&P 500.

investors incur both. Thus, on a net basis, your results will be different from the index's results.

How's your confidence now?

I hope it's still pretty firm, because this last point raises another widespread myth about index investing. This myth says that, because index funds contain passive portfolios with no portfolio manager to constantly buy and sell stocks within the fund, there is no trading, and with no trading, there are no realized gains, which keeps your tax liability low. This has introduced the concept that index funds are "tax efficient."

That's utter nonsense. Although I agree that a low-turnover portfolio[70] is usually better than one with high turnover, it's nonsense to suggest that index funds incur no trading at all. Guess what happens when the S&P Index committee decides to toss out one stock from the index and insert another? Within a day, every index fund will follow suit: They all simultaneously sell the old stock while buying the new one. All this trading occurs not because a given stock has suddenly fallen out of favor, or because another company has exciting news. No, all this trading is done simply because seven men and a woman said, "He's in; she's out."[71]

Guess what happens when everybody buys the same thing at the same time? The price goes up! Guess what happens when everybody sells the same thing at the same time? The price goes down! Thus, index funds become victims of their own game: By engaging in the same strategy at the same time, all the index funds buy for high prices while selling for low prices.[72]

---

[70]Meaning one that does little buying and selling during the year.

[71]At least with a professionally managed fund, the portfolio manager would be buying or selling because of fundamental or technical investment reasons, not just because someone told him or her to. Even having someone "tell the manager to" wouldn't be so bad, if the people doing the telling had their own fundamental or technical reasons for dumping or adding a stock. But investment analysis is not part of the S&P index committee's criteria in creating and maintaining their list (they focus solely on a company's size). It makes you further wonder why people would want to make investments based on the list.

[72]Excuse me, but I thought the key to success was to buy low and sell high, not the other way around.

This is not mere conjecture. *Investment Dealer Digest*'s Jack Willoughby told *U.S. News & World Report* how active portfolio traders exploit this follow-the-index mentality: Knowing that indexers must use whatever money they have to buy whatever stocks are in the index, traders bid up the prices of those stocks shortly before each day's closing bell. This *forces* the indexers—who *must* buy—to pay top dollar to the traders for their shares. For example, when the S&P investment committee added Comerica to the index, the stock's price jumped 6%—for that day only—on trading volume 15 times higher than normal. Clearly, by having to buy the stock immediately, the index funds overpaid significantly for the stock, to the detriment of their investors, while other mutual funds were happy to unload Comerica for a quick 6% profit, to the joy of their shareholders.

And there's another reason index funds tend to pay high prices for their shares: Unlike the Dow Jones Industrial Average, which is an unweighted index, the S&P 500 is a capitalization-weighted index. This means that the biggest companies in the S&P have the biggest effect on the index, instead of everyone having an equal effect. For example, a 10% gain by the S&P's #1 company, General Electric, would have a much bigger impact on the index than a 10% gain by Intergraph Corp., S&P's smallest company. It also means that index funds buy more of the biggest stocks than they buy of the smallest stocks. And the higher a company's stock price gets, the more the index fund will buy it. It sounds bizarre, but it's true: Index funds buy more of a given stock merely because the stock has already risen in value.[73]

Forbes magazine provided an excellent example of this phenomenon in 1997. In a scathing report on index funds, *Forbes* showed that in 1992, Intel was ranked #35 on the S&P 500; its stock made up 0.6% of the index. By 1995, it had climbed to #13, with a 1% weighting, and within a year it was #4, and constituted 2% of the entire S&P 500. This means that when Intel was cheap back in 1995, index funds

---

[73]Silly me. I always thought you were supposed to buy stocks before they rose in value, not afterwards.

bought very little of the stock, but as Intel grew, the index funds bought increasingly large amounts of the stock—at ever-higher prices. This is supposed to be smart investing?[74]

It gets worse. Because index funds tend to hold disproportionate amounts of stock—holding much more stock of big companies than it holds of little ones—it's impossible for you to maintain a balanced portfolio, or to rebalance the portfolio you already have. If you owned a stock that grew in price, your inclination might be to sell some of it. But in an index fund, you can't. Instead, the fund will buy even more—at the new higher prices. This explains why S&P index funds have as much money invested in the 50 biggest stocks as in the other 450 combined. Again, this is smart investing?

The result of all this is that index funds make money only if the biggest stocks make money, because big gains in the little stocks won't make much difference. Thus, index investors were lucky in 1996: six of the S&P's biggest stocks— Intel, IBM, Microsoft, Coca-Cola, Exxon, and General Electric—did very well, and collectively they produced 26% of the index's total gain. Put another way, just 1.2% of the holdings produced a whopping 26% of the profits, while the other 494 stocks in the index earned the rest. But what if those six stocks had done poorly? Do you really want your portfolio's results to be dependent on such lopsided performance?

These problems help blow away the contention that index fund investors enjoy lower taxes than those who invest in actively managed stock funds. Indexers claim that index funds have low turnover, which creates fewer realized gains, which in turn lowers your taxes. This is simply not true. Low-turnover funds (and there are many actively managed funds of this sort, if the idea really appeals to you) do not lower your taxes; they merely *delay* your taxes. While most mutual fund investors pay some capital gains taxes

---

[74]And may Heaven help the indexers if Intel is ever tossed off the list. Immediate across-the-board selling of the stock would instantly decimate its stock price, causing all the indexers to suffer huge losses.

each year, index fund investors tend to pay the bulk of their tax liability all at once—in the year they sell their fund. This isn't a savings; it's only a deferral of the inevitable, and it's not a reason to choose one investment over the other.[75]

Actually, maybe it *is* a reason to choose one over the other—meaning you should choose the fund that is supposedly less tax-efficient. Why? As Rule #75 demonstrates, when you invest in funds that cause you to incur taxes annually, you will pay for those taxes with other money, not with the money in the fund. But if the index fund is accumulating the tax, forcing you to pay all of it all at once when you sell the fund, chances are that the cost will be so great, you'll have no choice but to use some of the proceeds from the sale of the fund to help you pay the bill. The result? You'll have less money in the end, even though you were supposedly investing in a "tax-efficient" fund.

Besides, because of the way index funds operate, you easily could have a capital gains problem *even if you lose money*. Say you buy an index fund when it's $75 a share. Later, a major market correction knocks your shares down to $65. But you hold, confident that the market eventually will recover.

Even though you currently have a loss, you could have a whopping tax liability. Why? Because during the correction, *other* shareholders sold, and to meet the redemption requests, the fund liquidated some of its long-held positions—causing the fund to realize substantial capital gains. As an owner of the fund, you'll pay your share of them, even though you personally did not own the fund when it produced those gains. All this helps to explain why *Forbes* calls index funds "dangerous."

And I'm not done yet.[76]

By now, you're beginning to understand why, if you invest in index funds, you *cannot* do as well as the index itself. Or at least, you're not supposed to be able to. Yet

---

[75] How you doing? Still feeling okay?
[76] Heck, I'm just getting started!

some index funds have earned more than the S&P 500. How can this be possible?

There's only one answer: Despite their claims, these funds are not investing in the stocks that constitute the S&P Index. Or more accurately, they are not investing *exactly* in the S&P. In order to gain some competitive edge against all the other index funds, some are "enhancing" their portfolios. In other words, they are not truly mimicking the S&P Index. Instead, they are hiring a professional money manager to steer some of the fund's assets into other stocks, or steer more money into one S&P stock than otherwise belongs there. By doing this, the fund might make more money than the S&P Index, and it might make less—just like any other stock mutual fund. But by engaging in this type of strategy, isn't the fund abandoning its own principle—that buying and maintaining an unmanaged basket of securities is better than trying to actively manage a portfolio of stocks? Excuse me, but if indexing is such a great idea, why would the indexers be resorting to this tactic?

They're doing this partly because they understand that investors who are willing to accept the risks of the stock market want at least the *opportunity* to beat the market, and as you've seen, index funds deny you that opportunity. And this leads to the most ballyhooed claim of indexers: That index funds make more money than other stock mutual funds. *This claim simply is not true.* In a study of five-year rolling returns since 1981, according to Evaluation Associates, the S&P 500 Index beat the managers of large-stock mutual funds less than half the time, and it beat small-stock funds only once (in the five-year interval 1986–1990). In fact, *Kiplinger's Personal Finance* and *Smart Money* magazines, which were among many in the personal finance press that had previously touted index funds (partly because of their supposed superior performance records) both retracted their positions in the summer of 1996.

Here's an irony for you: Even if indexers are right when they say that most funds fail to beat market indexes, their conclusion—that index funds are the solution—would still be wrong, for the simple reason that index funds *also* fail to beat the indexes. Therefore, if it's true that most funds fail to beat the market, their conclusion does not solve the problem. The correct solution would be to buy one of the funds that *do* beat the market. They're not hard to find, but you won't find index funds among them.

Here's the worst part.[77] The "indexing-is-better" claim fails to acknowledge that *indexing is significantly riskier than investing in actively managed mutual funds*. According to beta calculations, a statistical tool that measures risk, index funds are 6% riskier than growth funds, 10% riskier than growth and income funds, 19% riskier than equity income funds, and a whopping 35% riskier than balanced funds— and the returns earned by index funds do not come close to justifying the additional risk they force you to take.

Since 1991, the stock market has been incredibly volatile—more than at any other time in history. Fortunately, this volatility has been in the typical investor's favor—index funds included. But when the stock market falls,[78] index funds will fall much further than actively managed mutual funds, because index funds are always fully invested in a relatively narrow band of U.S. stocks, while professionally managed funds often invest in other places as well, such as bonds, international securities, or even cash. Although this might reduce a fund's gains in an up market, you'll be grateful in a down market.

One final note:[79] The S&P 500 used to be purely academic, an observer of the game. But today, with nearly a fifth of all the money in mutual funds going into index funds, and with the proliferation of options and futures contracts based on movements in the S&P Index, this particular index has begun to suffer many of the same problems as the Dow Jones Industrial Average.[80] Indeed, while the S&P Index once

---

[77]And you were hoping the worst was over.
[78]That's *when*, not *if*: Historically, the market has experienced a decline of 10% or more, on average, every 22 months—making our current bull market unprecedented in both its duration and in the size of its increase.
[79]Okay, okay, I'm almost done.
[80]See Rule #33.

represented more than 90% of the value of the New York Stock Exchange, it now reflects only 68%, and the figure is dropping steadily.

Therefore, you should now pay less and less attention to the S&P Index—both as a gauge of the investment world, and as an investment itself.[81]

RULE #37 ... AND NEVER CHOOSE INVESTMENTS MERELY BECAUSE YOU THINK THEY WILL BE PROFITABLE.

Investing is now no longer about making money. It's about *managing* money—in both good times and bad. The stock market crash of 1987 and the horrendous bond market of 1994 clearly showed how quickly the markets can now turn, and why we need to show a new appreciation for risk. This is the biggest reason index funds are dangerous:[82] Because they do not offer investors any opportunity to manage their risk.

So, when you invest, you must pay attention to risk, and to learn how to do that, keep reading.

RULE #38 LEARN WHAT "RISK" REALLY MEANS.

In the world of investments, there are many types of risk, and although they differ from investment to investment, they all manifest themselves in the same way: Risk causes investment values to fluctuate.

Thus, investment risk is best discussed in terms of

---

[81]Whew! I feel much better now. Thanks for letting me get that off my chest.
[82]See previous Rule.

volatility: If you invest one dollar today, how much might that dollar change in value? Under what circumstances would that change occur? These are the questions that volatility raises.

The answers are based on the premise that all investments are volatile; there is no such thing as a risk-free investment. Some investments are more sensitive to certain risks than others, and some risks are more likely or more devastating if incurred than others. Therefore, some investments are more volatile than others. The interesting thing about risk is that it works both ways: Investments that have fallen victim to one or more risks can enjoy substantial upside volatility as they put their problems behind them; this is how investment values are able to increase. Risk, then, is not bad; it merely exists. Without risk, investments could not exist. In many ways, risk is like water to a plant: Too little and they fail to grow, while too much could drown them.

To help you put it all in perspective, let's first examine the major types of risk:

Default risk.

The risk that an investment will become worthless.

> UPSIDE:
> Investments that have defaulted often recover, as did New York City's bonds. So did Chrysler. As the investment recovers, its value returns to previous levels, rewarding those who invested while prices were low. Investors who engage in this type of activity are called "bottom-fishers."

Credit risk.

The risk that an investment's financial stability might decline; those that suffer credit risk might ultimately default. The stronger an investment's financial stability, the more valuable it is (a AAA-rated investment is about 25% more valuable than a B-rated investment). However, the stronger an investment's financial stability, the greater its potential losses from credit risk.[83]

UPSIDE:
Low-rated or previously downgraded investments could be upgraded, resulting in an increase in value.

Tax risk.

The risk that investment profits will be subject to taxes, such as the income tax, capital gains tax, intangibles tax, alternative minimum tax, state and local taxes, and/or estate taxes. For an investor in the 28% federal income tax bracket, for example, an investment whose profits are not subject to federal income taxes is automatically 28% more valuable than an investment whose profits are subject to that tax.

DOWNSIDE OF TAX-ADVANTAGED INVESTMENTS:
Investments that are free from taxes typically pay proportionately fewer profits than taxable investments. Furthermore, changes in the law could eliminate the tax advantages that investors were promised or are expecting.

UPSIDE:
None.

Inflation risk.

The risk that an investment's income and principal, when received in the future, will have a reduced purchasing power due to an increase in the cost of living.

UPSIDE:
Deflation might occur, reducing future prices instead of raising them. Cellular telephones are much less expensive today than 15 years ago, as are VCRs and many other products.

---

[83]The bigger they are, the harder they fall.

Interest rate risk.

The risk that interest rates will rise. As rates rise, the value of bonds fall. Interest rate risk affects long-term bonds more dramatically than short-term bonds. For example, a 1% increase in interest rates causes a 10% decrease in 30-year bonds, but only a 4% drop for bonds maturing in five years.

UPSIDE:

If rates fall, bond values rise. Because interest rates are constantly changing, interest rate risk is one of the most important of all risks, and a leading cause of both speculation and losses.

Currency risk.

The risk that foreign currency exchange rates would rise. If that happens, investments you have in that country would fall in value. For example, for a U.S. citizen who invests in Japanese stocks, a 20% rise in the yen would produce a 20% drop in the value of the investments, in U.S. dollar terms. Investments that suffer from currency risk usually also face *political risk*.

Political risk.

The risk that a foreign nation might go to war, or social-ize private industry. Either could destroy your invest-ments.

UPSIDE:

As with interest rate risk, currency and political risks are double-edged swords: Improvements can boost the value of your overseas investments.

Market risk.

The most commonly referred to of all risks,[84] market risk is reflected in the daily price changes of stocks and bonds. Thousands of factors cause market risk.

---

[84]Even though people who refer to it have no idea what they're talking about—and often don't even know that this is what they're referring to!

UPSIDE:

Market risk, or rather investor's changes in perception about market risk, allow investments to rise as well as fall.

Event risk.

The risk that something both unexpected and beyond the control of management will cause an investment's value to decline. Example: The discovery, after decades of use, that asbestos causes cancer. The news led to the failure of Johns-Manville, which manufactured the insulation product.

UPSIDE:

None—not because unexpected good things can't happen, but because such surprises are, well, *unexpected*, and therefore unanticipatable.[85] Most good news, such as a drug company's accidental discovery of a cure for some major illness, certainly would increase the price of the company's stock, but such a discovery is within the nature of that company's business and therefore does not meet the definition of event risk. Such events more properly would be considered *market risk*.

Prepayment risk.

The risk that your investment principal will be returned sooner than you anticipated, particularly if the investment was unusually profitable.

UPSIDE:

None. Be thankful that you got your money at all.

Extension risk.

The opposite of prepayment risk, meaning that your investment principal might not be returned as soon as you expected.

UPSIDE:

None.

---

[85]Is that a word?

Opportunity risk.

The risk that, by having your money invested in one place, you missed the opportunity to invest elsewhere for higher returns.[86]

UPSIDE:

The investment you have might well be better than the alternatives you missed. (Donald Trump once said, "Some of my best investments are the ones I didn't make.")

With this list of risks in mind, let's explore their relationship to—and impact on—a variety of common investments. In the accompanying chart, each investment is assigned a Low, Moderate, or High "Relative Profit Potential."

Low means the investment's design severely limits opportunities for profit.

Moderate suggests that the investment generally earns more competitive returns, but upside reward is still somewhat limited.

High indicates that the investment has unlimited profit potential.

Be aware that merely being able to earn an unlimited return is in no way meant to suggest that a given investment ever has achieved substantial profits, or that it will ever again achieve substantial profits. Many also could argue that grouping so many investments as "High" unfairly —and unrealistically—suggests that they share an equal probability of achieving similar levels of success. That would be an incorrect and unintended conclusion, and such is not the intent of this chart; the "Relative Profit Potential" column merely shows what is possible, not what is necessarily likely. Keep this important disclaimer in

---

[86]Investors who suffer from this can be found wondering, "Should I stay out of stocks and watch them go up, or should I get into stocks and make them go down?"

Asset	Relative Profit Potential	Default	Credit	Tax	Inflation	Interest Rate	Currency/Political	Market	Event	Prepayment	Extension	Opportunity
Cash Equivalents	**Low**	r	r	R	R	R			r			R
U.S. Gov't. Bonds	**Moderate**			R	R	R		R		r	r	r
Muni/Corp Bonds	**Moderate**	r	r	R	R	R		R	r	R		R
Zero Coupon Bonds	**Moderate**	r	R	R	R	R		R	r	R		R
Corporate Bonds	**Moderate**	R	R	R	R	R		R	R	r	r	R
Intl. Gov't. Bonds	**Moderate**		r	R	R	R	R	R	R	r	r	R
Intl. Corp. Bonds	**Moderate**	R	R	R	R	R	R	R	R	R	R	R
Large-Cap Stocks	**High**	r		r		r		R	r			r
Small-Cap Stocks	**High**	r	r	r		r		R	r			r
Intl. Stocks	**High**	r		r		r	R	R	r			r
Real Estate	**High**	r		r		r		R	R			r
Gold	**High**			r		r		R	R			r
Natural Resources	**High**	r		r	r	r		R	R			r
Commodities	**High**	R	R	r		r		R	R			r
Collectibles	**High**	R	R	r				R	R			R

R denotes major risk   **r** denotes minor risk

mind. With this information, choose your investments. For more help on how to do this, read the next Rule.

RULE #39 LEARN HOW TO HEDGE YOUR BETS.

As Rule #38 shows, no investment is risk-free, but all investments are safe from certain risks.[87] Therefore, in order to insure that no single risk can destroy all of your investments, you must make sure that your investments are not sensitive to any single risk, and that means you must invest in a variety of asset classes, not just one. This is called diversification, and it has become the basis for prudent investment management.

An illustration of the benefits of diversification appeared in my first book, *The Truth About Money*. It demonstrated the results of two portfolios: the first invested $25,000 into bank CDs that paid 5.25% per year for 25 years, while the second portfolio consisted of five separate investments of $5,000 each. The results of the second portfolio's five segments were wildly different: The first segment went broke, the second got a return of capital but failed to earn any profit at all, and the third earned a meager 2% annually. The fourth segment, though, managed to produce a 7% annual return, and the fifth was, relatively speaking, a winner. Although it didn't set any records, the fifth segment earned 12% per year, matching the average return of the stock market for this century.

The results: While the first portfolio ended the 25-year period with $96,621, the second, diversified portfolio produced $140,809—$48,188 *more* than the first. This result is possible due to diversification, which owes its success to the fact that the maximum loss of any investment is limited to the amount of the investment, while the maximum

---

[87]Except maybe international corporate bonds, which have never made any sense to me.

gain is unlimited. Thus, the profits from earning 12% on a small portion of the portfolio more than compensate for the complete losses incurred in another portion of the portfolio.

Which sets the stage for Rule #40.

RULE #40 INVESTING IS NO LONGER WINNER-TAKE-ALL. CHANGE YOUR STRATEGY ACCORDINGLY.

Do you suffer from "paralysis of analysis?"

Lots of people do. Fearing that they'll be unable to pick the best mutual fund, many people wind up picking none. This attitude is encouraged by the personal finance press, which, by touting "Hot Fund Picks!" in every issue, give the impression that you had better choose the best fund or risk losing all your money.

But that's no longer the way it is. Today, investing is not a horse race, where you make money only if you pick the right horse. Smart investors today earn a profit by picking *every* horse, knowing that the gains earned by the winner will more than offset the losses suffered by the loser. Think that's impossible? It's not, because when you invest, the most you can lose is 100% of what you invested, while your potential gains are unlimited. This principle is demonstrated every year, for the worst stock of any given year always loses 100% of its value (having gone bankrupt), while the best-performing stock of the year will gain 2,000% or 3,000%. Thus, if you invest equally in the year's best and the year's worst investments, you are certain to have a profit, because the winners' gains will more than compensate for the losers' losses.

This is why professional investment advisors don't merely buy investments for their clients. Instead, they create complete portfolios consisting of representatives from all nine major asset classes. If you choose stocks and stocks fall in value, you might go broke. But if you invest in stocks, bonds, government securities, real estate, precious metals, natural resources, commodities, foreign currencies, and international securities, and stocks then go down, you'll still be just fine.

But maybe you're unswayed by this. I can understand how you might feel. You think you must pick the winner, yet you fear you don't know how. After all, with so many choices, what's the likelihood that you'll pick the #1 fund?

Well, here's a new way for you to think about it. Instead of spending your life *picking winners*, focus on *avoiding losers*. It's a lot easier, and your results will be just as good. To illustrate, let's return to December 31, 1986. At that time, there were 1,150 mutual funds. Say you pick one and hold it for the next 10 years. Will you pick the winner? Not likely. In fact, you are 99.913% certain *not* to pick the winner. You know this, and that's what worries you.

But consider this: Only six funds failed to make money in the 10 years ending 1986, meaning you were 99.478% certain not to pick *them* either. And by avoiding losers, you are certain to make money. The only question is how much. So in truth, the issue isn't whether or not you'll succeed, but the degree of success that you will enjoy. Failure is not even a topic for reasonable conversation.

So don't worry about not being able to pick the fastest racehorse. Under **The New Rules of Money**, you're now playing horseshoes, where just being close is good enough to win.

RULE #41   STOP TRYING TO ACHIEVE INVESTMENT SUCCESS THROUGH STOCK-PICKING.

If you want to make sure you pick the winning horse, all you have to do is bet on *every* horse.

That, essentially, is how successful money managers now

make money. They no longer are worried about picking the right horse, because they know that picking every horse in the race makes winning inevitable. They also know that, in the investment world, unlike real horse races, it's possible for every horse to win. Sure, some win more than others, but on Wall Street, merely finishing the race usually proves profitable.

That's why professional money managers are much more focused on deciding *how much* to bet on each animal, rather than on trying to choose the animals on which bets should be placed. After all, how would you feel if you learned that you picked the right horse, but had placed only 1% of your money on him?

This is why the most critical investment decision you'll make now is choosing how to allocate your money among the many investment opportunities that are available to you.

So if you want to succeed with your investments under **The New Rules of Money**, start learning how to allocate your assets, and stop trying to pick the next hot stock.

RULE #42 BE AWARE OF DIVERSIFICATION'S EVIL TWIN.

The concept of diversification is not new, although the application of it is. Harry Markowitz was the first to relate its benefits, in a paper he wrote as a graduate student in 1952. Although largely ignored for decades, the paper eventually won Markowitz the Nobel Prize for Economic Science in 1990.

Markowitz's paper (which was mostly a series of mathematical formulas) demonstrated that while a diversified portfolio's average *return* will be equal to the weighted average of the returns of its components, the portfolio's average *volatility* actually will be less than the average volatility of its holdings. We know this is possible from our earlier examination of various investment risks:[88] Different investments react differently to various types of risk.

For example, you know that bonds are safer than gold. You also know that inflation, by causing interest rates to rise, causes bond prices to fall. But inflation also causes gold prices to rise. Therefore, during an inflationary period, a portfolio that contains both bonds and gold would decline less than a portfolio that contains only bonds. This is because inflation would cause the bond portion to decline but cause the gold portion to increase, thus reducing the overall losses. Yet the fact remains that gold itself is riskier than bonds. Thus, the two are safer when mixed together than when either one is used separately.

In other words, adding risky investments to your portfolio can reduce the overall risk of that portfolio.[89]

But this simple concept[90] has been distorted by many financial advisors. Although Markowitz was talking about asset class diversification, many investors—and their advisors—have begun to attribute a different form of diversification to Markowitz's theory. This new breed suggests that asset diversification can be enhanced, and in fact, even rendered unnecessary, by *time*.

Indeed, I may have inadvertently contributed to this phenomenon when I included in my first book a series of charts showing that stocks, widely regarded as one of the most volatile of all assets, are in fact quite stable performers over long periods. In fact, I even wrote in Chapter 31 that "the key is not when you invest in the stock market, nor which stocks you buy. The key is *how long* you invest. We can convert something as risky and uncertain as stocks into a safe, predictable investment."

Although this statement is true, it may have led some readers to believe that anyone with a long investment time horizon ought to be invested exclusively in stocks. That was not my point at all. The crescendo was reached in

---

[88]See Rule #38.
[88]Now, go explain to your Aunt Ida why she needs to move some of her CDs into stocks.
[90]Okay, not so simple.

Chapter 45[91] when I wrote, "You can build a portfolio that is safer and more profitable by investing in many asset classes than you can by investing in only one asset class." Still, there may have been too many pages separating those two chapters for every reader to correlate the two.

Regardless of the impact my book may have had (which almost certainly wasn't as significant as I'm making it appear), my broader concern remains valid: Time diversification is now widely used—and often incorrectly so—by individual investors and professional money managers alike.

The problem with time diversification is this: Although it is true that time *decreases the probability* of a loss, it is also true that time *increases the amount* of potential losses. In other words, the longer you hold onto stocks, the less likely it is that you'll lose money. But if you do lose money, it's likely that you'll lose *a lot* of money—far more than if you had only been invested for a short time.

Although you've never considered this (and it's almost certain that your financial advisor never talked about it with you), it's easy to understand why this is the case. Picture Graham, a 35-year-old investor who has $10,000 to save for his retirement. Markowitz[92] would argue that you should invest in a highly diversified fashion. But Graham[93] knows that, historically, stocks have always produced the highest returns. Since he has no plans to touch his money for 30 years, he decides to place his entire $10,000 into a stock mutual fund.

Assuming that Graham's portfolio grows at the average annual rate of 10% (and ignoring taxes for this discussion), his account will grow to $175,000 by the time he becomes an old man.[94] But if, just as he enters retirement, the stock market were to suffer a 20% drop, he'd lose $35,000—3½ times more than his original investment. (By contrast, if that correction had occurred shortly after he had invested,

---

[91]It was a long book, okay?
[92]And my previous book's Chapter 44, thank you.
[93]Having focused on my previous book's Chapter 31, sorry.
[94]Oops, sorry. I mean *older* man.

his loss would have been only $2,000, or ¹⁄₁₇th as great a loss, of course.)

Because his after-correction account value is $140,000, he really has not suffered a loss. He still has far more money than he started with, and to that extent, proponents of time diversification are correct in saying that Graham, by having invested over such a long period of time, had only a very remote probability that he'd incur an actual loss. But time diversification's critics have an equally valid point: By having invested over such a long period of time, any declines in value—*if* they were to occur—would be huge.

This is the Dark Side of diversification. To insulate yourself from this risk, you need to make sure that you are not sacrificing asset diversification in favor of time diversification. Because, with your luck, that asset will drop in value just about the time you need the money most. Don't say I didn't warn you—despite what you may think *The Truth About Money* says.

RULE #43 RECOGNIZE THAT INVESTMENT SUCCESS IS BASED ON TIME, NOT TIMING.

I think I'm setting myself up for another problem (which I'll have to correct in my next book),[95] because readers who stopped at the last Rule might conclude that investment success follows those who diversify by asset class, while failure will befall those who diversify by time.

Actually, neither premise is correct. The real message is that you must now follow *both* criteria if you are to achieve investment success: You must create a highly diversified portfolio, *and* you must maintain that portfolio for long periods.

This is why market timing—the concept of moving in and out of investments as they rise and fall—fails. Market timing

---

[95]Not another one!

is the exact opposite of diversification. Where diversification tells you to invest in a variety of asset classes, market timers put all their money into stocks. Where diversification tells you to hold on to those assets for long periods, market timing tells you to frequently buy and sell your stocks in an effort to capitalize on the momentary fluctuations of the stock market.

Market timing is enticing. One book currently available promises that you can double your money *every two to four months*. Imagine! Double your money every 60 to 120 days! This is the allure of market timers: They offer the promise of such fabulous, quick, and easy wealth that you figure it's worth risking twenty bucks to buy the book and see. Or the $22 to attend the introductory seminar. Or the $295 for the annual newsletter. Or the $2,500 for the complete workshop.

It might be hard for you to believe, but I have never met anyone who has achieved wealth through market timing. But I know of lots of people who have gotten rich selling books, tapes, and seminars about it. Think about it: Let's say you were able to double your money every four months. If you started with $10,000, guess how much money you'd have in 10 years?

You'd have *$5.3 trillion*—enough to pay off the national debt! *In just 10 years!* Assuming you could do this, why on earth would you be wasting your time telling everyone about it? So you could earn the three-dollar royalty from selling a book?

As an investment advisor, I often have much more difficulty convincing someone to invest in a portfolio that will produce—if we're lucky—annual returns that average 8%, 10%, or even (gulp!) 12% over long periods, while guys who claim to be able to double your money in an instant have no problem getting people to throw money at them.

That really bugs me.

RULE #44   STOP TAKING THIS DIVERSIFICATION STUFF TOO LITERALLY.

One final revisit to *The Truth About Money*.[96, 97, 98] My description in Chapter 44 about diversification and asset allocation referred to a study (the one all self-respecting financial planners refer to) that showed that asset allocation—not stock picking—represents 94% of the difference in performance between two money managers. Therefore, as Chapter 44 explained, you need to focus more and more of your attention on asset allocation, and less and less on individual stock-picking. It's the forest vs. the trees, and I repeated this theme in Rule #41.

Well, lest readers of Chapter 44 misinterpret this information, or perhaps merely take it too literally, allow me to elaborate, or at least clarify. The "94% of performance" phrase—indeed the entire notion of diversification and asset allocation—refers not to *annual returns*, but to *volatility*. In other words, I am not claiming that, by carefully allocating your money over a wide variety of asset classes, you are going to end up with more money than if you had merely plunked it all down on 14 Red. I merely am suggesting that, by properly diversifying your investments, you will earn *almost* as much as if you had plunked everything

---

[96]Hey, if everything I said in that book remained true today, why would I need to be writing a *second* one?

[97]And that brings up another point. Long before I ever wrote *The Truth About Money* (did I mention the price is $19.95, at bookstores everywhere?), I was a vocal critic of personal finance books. I still am. The reason? Books get out of date pretty quickly, thanks to a rapidly changing economy, a Congress that's always fiddling with the tax rules, and new research and products that are constantly introduced. So go ahead and read all these books. Just keep in mind that some of the information might be out of date by the time you read it, while others were written purely for the author's and publisher's benefit instead of yours. That's why I'm a much bigger fan of newspapers, newsletters, magazines, radio, and television. While they, too, are laden with self-interest (isn't everything?), at least they're always current (though sometimes also wrong). And when's the last time you saw someone add a footnote to a footnote?

[98]So while I'm at it, I might as well tell you *which* newspapers, newsletters, magazines, and radio and TV shows to read, watch, and listen to. Nah. These footnotes are getting out of hand. Read Rule #47 instead.

on 14 Red, while protecting yourself from the extreme possibility that 14 Red might prove disastrous. But what I am not denying—and this is important—is that, in the end, 14 Red just might have been the more profitable thing to have done.

Although I made this point first in Chapter 39, and again in Chapter 45, some readers might have incorrectly concluded that picking a great allocation model compensates for picking lousy investments. Nothing could be further from the truth. In fact, you must carefully allocate your assets, and then you must select the proper investments for each allocation. Missing on either point could prove as expensive as, well, as picking 14 Red.

If this point weren't true—if the selection of the investments themselves weren't important, or rather, if they were only 6% important—then it would indeed be fine to simply go and pick a bunch of index funds to fulfill your allocation model. But that clearly is not the case, as Rule #36 and *The Truth About Money*'s Chapter 23 explain.[99]

So, to make it all perfectly clear,[100] under **The New Rules of Money**, you now need to devote substantial attention to *both* asset allocation *and* investment selection, not merely one or the other.

And you thought life was going to get simpler.

RULE #45
PUT AWAY THE FORTUNE 500, AND START STUDYING THE FORBES 400.

You no longer make money by examining stocks, which is what the *Fortune 500* is all about. If you want to explore the concept of wealth, you need to study the people who have attained it, and that means studying the *Forbes 400*—the richest people in America.

---

[99]You can read Chapter 23, and the 81 other chapters, too, by picking up a copy for just $19.95—at bookstores everywhere.
[100]At least until further clarification in my *next* book.

You can probably stop with the first guy on the list, Warren Buffett. Without question the most successful investor in American history, Buffett is worth more than $30 billion. How did he do it? By investing in such companies as Coca-Cola, GEICO, Gillette, American Express, The Washington Post Company, Solomon Brothers, and Disney, and holding on to them for decades.

What Buffett does *not* do is actively trade in and out of these stocks. That's market timing, and as Rule #43 explains, it doesn't work. Just look at the members of the *Forbes 400*, the poorest of whom (Oprah Winfrey) is worth $415 million. Twenty-nine attained their wealth through real estate; 34 through the computer revolution; 19 in oil and gas; and 136 via inheritances. But no one achieved their wealth through market timing. No one.

Watch for *Forbes* magazine's next annual listing of the *Forbes 400*. It's fascinating, insightful—and profitable—reading.

RULE #46   MARKET TIMING IS DEAD. BEWARE OF STYLE SELECTION, FOR IT WILL SUFFER THE SAME FATE.

You're a writer in the personal finance press, and the deadline is looming. You need to write an investment story that will show your readers how to enrich themselves. Market timing stories are always good, but that's getting pretty stale lately, and besides, lots of folks like that guy Edelman have really been blasting away at the idea. No, you need something new.

Diversification is a solid subject. The only problem, though, is that diversification never changes from month to month. So, sure, the story will bail you out this issue, but what will you write about next month? Better lay off diversification. No, you need something that's not only new, but something that changes each month. Something that your

readers will like to hear about, but also something that
requires updating. Something to bring them back next
month. That's what market timing used to do for you—
every month, a different stock pick. In June, it's get in the
market; in July, it's get out of the market. Readership was
really solid in those days. That's what you need. Something
like that.

Let's go back to that diversification thing. Your readers
are hearing about it. They're starting to wonder how to
build a portfolio based on it. Trouble is, there's really not
much to it. And now the problem is that all these consumers—your readers—are focusing attention on asset allocation. They're talking in terms of long-term portfolios, for
crying out loud. They used to talk about stock-picking. They
used to gobble up your stories on "The 10 Stocks to Buy
Now!" But this long-term thing is a problem, because it's
leaving you with very little to write about. What you need to
figure out is a way to make forest-looking asset allocators
act like tree-studying stock-pickers. Wouldn't it be great if
you could somehow integrate stock-picking into their asset
allocation modeling?

Hmmm. Pretty good idea. All you need to do is come up
with a story that micromanages the asset allocation concept. But to do that, you need an angle. Let's see. If your
readers do this asset allocation thing correctly, their portfolio will look like a pizza pie, and each slice of that pie will
consist of a different asset class. Your readers, therefore,
are focusing on asset classes, not individual investments. So
they really don't care about stories on Microsoft. And for
each asset class, they simply choose a mutual fund that
invests in that asset class. One mutual fund for the pepper-
oni slice, another for the sausage slice. Because there are
lots of kinds of sausage, the sausage slice will contain samples of every major kind of sausage.

For the portion of their portfolio that's devoted to
stocks, for example, they'll use stock funds, and those stock
funds will contain some large companies, some medium-
sized companies, and some small companies. Within each

of those sizes will be some growth companies and some value companies. They will do this because, on Wall Street, every dog has its day—so at various times, some types of companies are going to do better than other types of companies. Because the winds change pretty frequently, your readers ought to have all of these types of companies in their portfolio all of the time. That's about the only way they'll really be sure they own the right asset at the right time—which is the whole point behind asset allocation, anyway.

Wait! Your readers probably don't realize any of this. They've only recently been introduced to asset allocation itself. They don't yet realize that stock funds can differ dramatically from each other. They don't realize that every stock fund's portfolio manager has his or her own way of picking stocks and of managing a portfolio. That each has a style all his own.

What we need, then, is a story about how to build a portfolio based on investment styles. Style management. That's it. That's the ticket!

Of course, it's really next to impossible to manage a portfolio of mutual funds based on style management. Oh, sure, there's a lot of newfangled software out there that tracks the investment styles of mutual funds, and Morningstar and other mutual fund rating services publish the investment styles of the mutual funds they track. But there are three problems with the whole idea. First, most mutual fund managers are constantly changing the investments that are inside their portfolios. So even if they tend to be a mid-cap growth manager,[101] that doesn't mean they won't sometimes invest in a large-cap value stock if they think it represents a good opportunity.

Second, investment managers have been known to change their minds. They are not obligated to stick with one style forever, and if their particular style falls out of favor,

---

[101]Meaning they tend to invest in medium-sized companies that are usually fairly young, and which, it is hoped, will one day be worth a lot of money—as opposed to *value* companies, which tend to be older and already *are* worth a lot of money.

you can be pretty sure that their style will change. Because if they don't change it, the next manager will. After all, fund managers change teams more often than baseball players. There isn't a relief pitcher in the league who's going to throw to the batters what they've been hitting all night. He's going to do things differently. And that's the biggest problem of the investment-style tracking software. All it really does is show you how a fund has been managed so far, and like investment performance itself, there's no assurance that this same investment style will continue into the future.

And the third problem is that, according to a study published in *Financial Analysts Journal,* 40% of all mutual funds are misclassified. So you can't be sure that your "small cap" fund is really buying small growth companies.

But none of these problems really matter. Because your readers don't know it—and you're not about to tell them. Instead, your story will focus on this HOT! NEW! idea called *style management.* It sounds cool. You'll have no trouble coming up with fresh stories built around this theme every month. You can focus on a certain asset class, or a certain style within that asset class, or a certain fund within that style within that asset class, or...

Sure, it's bogus. But who cares? You milked market timing stories for 10 years, and the whole indexed funds thing is still going strong....

Heck, if you're lucky, you'll be able to write about *this* for 10 years. By then, some other HOT! NEW! idea will come along. Let's get to that keyboard.

Don't you just love being a reporter in the personal finance press?

RULE #47 STOP LOOKING FOR TIPS. SEEK EDUCATION INSTEAD.

Media coverage of personal finance can be grouped into six types. The first, of course, is the personal finance press, represented by such magazines as *Money, Kiplinger's Personal Finance, Smart Money,* and *Worth.*

The second is the general media. Publications in this group range from daily newspapers to such targeted magazines as *Good Housekeeping.* Shows like *Good Morning America, Nightline with Ted Koppel,* and *Oprah* also fit into this group. While it's not their sole focus, they often cover personal finance.

The third group is the business press, including *The Wall Street Journal, Investors Business Daily,* and *Barron's* newspapers; technical and professional newsletters such as *Kiplinger's Washington Letter* and *Kiplinger's Tax Letter;* as well as magazines such *as Business Week, Forbes,* and *Fortune.* CNBC, and PBS's *Nightly Business Report* and *Wall Street Week* also are in this group.

The fourth, the trade press, produces everything from daily fax reports to monthly magazines, and are read by— and often are available only to—Wall Street professionals. These publications include *Financial Analysts Journal, Registered Representative, Dow Jones Investment Advisor,* the *Journal of Financial Planning, Inside Information,* and many, many more.

The fifth group consists of books, like the one in your hands. These are, shall we say, numerous—and written sometimes for consumers and sometimes for professionals.

The final group consists of the 300 or so investment tips newsletters, each containing current buy/sell recommendations for its readers, with subscription prices ranging from $49 to $1000 or more per year.

Is anything from any of these groups any good? Absolutely. Much of what's produced is outstanding—and like anything else, much of it is garbage, too. How do you know what to read, and what to ignore?

It's really very simple. Read, watch, and listen to everything you can, but pay attention only to those that *educate*. When you come upon something that *recommends,* you must:

1. *evaluate* the reasoning behind the recommendation,
2. *confirm* that you understand the reasoning, and then
3. decide if you *agree* with the reasoning.

Only if you complete all three steps should you act on the recommendation.[102] Often you'll have to turn to a second, third, or fourth source for help with these steps.

If, for example, a story or news show is explaining interest rate risk, pay attention, because the education will be valuable. But if they start telling you that interest rates are going to drop, you must:

1. Learn why they think interest rates will decline.

Too often predictors don't explain themselves. You must dismiss any recommendation that is not supported. If the rationale is provided, then you must...

2. Confirm that their reasoning makes sense.

Don't merely accept what they say; make sure their position is supportable. Here's an easy way to tell: After receiving their position, repeat it—in your own words—to a spouse, friend, or coworker. As you are explaining their position, you'll quickly decide if you feel like an idiot saying whatever it is you're saying.[103] If your coworkers don't laugh you out of the building, then...

---

[102]And if you do implement the recommendation, you obligate yourself to a fourth step, which is to *review* its status periodically.

[103]As in, *"Interest rates will soon decline by a half point because Alan Greenspan got married last year, and his new bride, Andrea Mitchell, works for NBC News, and she needs a scoop."* When reading this, it might actually seem plausible, but when you repeat it to someone else, you'll realize that it's complete lunacy.

3. Decide if you agree with it.

Keep in mind that something isn't necessarily right simply because it isn't stupid.

Note that when it comes to *education* and *recommendations*, most media do a little of both: They have great stories that can teach you a lot, but they also run sensational pieces like "Hot Funds to Buy Now!" and "Retire Before You're 40!" that have little value other than to attract readers, listeners, or viewers.

Of course, people *do* buy these publications and tune to radio and TV for the hot tips, which has led one prominent figure in the field to accuse some in the media of "financial pornography." He has a point: Nobody buys *Playboy* for the articles, and nobody watches *Wall Street Week* for its in-depth look at Social Security. They want to know about the next hot stock. You must make sure you are differentiating the one from the other.

Are the media wrong to offer recommendations? I'll dodge that bullet, thank you. But I will say this: The media is a business, and their job is to attract readers, listeners, and viewers. *Money,* for example, does that pretty darn well, with 10 million readers, so it's obviously doing something right. But consumers who understand which stories are which are going to be a lot better off than consumers who don't understand the difference—let alone those who don't even understand that there *is* a difference.

You'll discover that it's an evolutionary process. You start by reading one magazine. No problem. It's definitively written, clear, and concise, with no chance of a misunderstanding. Its explanation as to why interest rates are about to drop is very convincing. You're happy, secure in the knowledge that interest rates are headed south. Until you read a second magazine, which persuasively argues for a hike in interest rates. Now you're confused. So you turn to a third, hoping it will break the tie. Instead, it says interest rates are irrelevant, that you ought to be looking at stocks, not bonds, anyway. Now you've been exposed to three attitudes, each of them intelligently offering their opinion. Then you start to understand: They are, indeed, merely *opinions,* not facts.

So you reread the first two articles, this time focusing not on *what* they are saying about where interest rates are headed, but on *why* they are saying it. You discover something you weren't expecting: Both publications agree on what causes interest rates to move, and on the financial implications if rates indeed move. They differ on only one point: Whether the rates are going up or down. Then you realize that they haven't got a clue, any more than you do.

That's when it hits you: It's not that they aren't any better at this than you are. *It's that you are just as good at it as they are!* So, for the very first time in your life, feelings of intimidation about personal finance start to fade away. You're beginning to feel ready to make the call: Do I really want to be in a government bond fund right now? You don't turn to the magazines for the answer. You rely on your own judgment.[104]

But you know you don't have enough facts. Or enough knowledge. So you continue reading. While you keep subscribing to the magazines that got you started, you need more as you begin to feel they're a little too basic, so you turn to the business press. You are surprised at how easy they are to read, and how good they make you feel. Then you start to listen to radio talk shows about money, and you start buying books like this one. You even start sharing what you've learned, buying copies for your family and friends[105] to help them discover what you've learned.

What you've learned is that the field of personal finance is an art, not a science, and there is no "one" answer to any situation.

---

[104]*Smart Money* magazine tries to get this point across to its readers by running something called "FACE OFF: Buy/Don't Buy." Each month, they pick a stock and invite two esteemed money managers to discuss it. The first expert explains why you should buy now, while the other tells why you should sell. One of my own newsletter's readers once complained to me that *Smart Money's* "FACE OFF" was of no value, because it never really answers the question of what to do with the stock. I'm afraid he's missing the point that *Smart Money*—and I—are trying to make.

[105]Hint, hint.

It's fun to run across people who are going through this process. One of the first callers to my radio show, Mike, said, "When I finished reading *Money* magazine, I knew exactly what to do. But then I picked up *Kiplinger's*. Then I turned on Louis Rukeyser. Now I just don't know *what* to do."

Keep on doing exactly what you're doing, I told him. You'll figure it out. When you've taken it as far as you can, turn to a financial advisor for help.[106] Somewhere along the way, you'll start to ask, "Who wrote the story I'm reading? What's the background of this TV show's guest?"

In fact, I find this part of your development very intriguing. When people call my firm to inquire about hiring us, they ask us plenty of questions: How long have we been in business? What are our credentials, expertise, education, management style, and philosophy? What kinds of investments do we recommend? Do we personally invest as we recommend our clients invest? Will we provide references? How are we compensated? These are all very good questions, which we encourage and are happy to answer.[107]

Indeed, you should ask questions like these of any advisor you're considering to hire. But what gets me are the multitudes who throw five grand at some stock because it was touted by a magazine, or radio or TV show, or some Web site. It never occurs to them to ask about the author or guest's background and credentials, or whether they have a conflict of interest.[108] Indeed, are they telling me to buy the stock merely because someone paid them to say so? Do they own the stocks they're touting? How pertinent to my own situation is the advice they're giving?

Such abuses abound. The U.S. Securities and Exchange Commission recently fined one newsletter publisher $300,000 for running outlandish ads claiming that you could have turned $10,000 into $39 million by following his advice.

---

[106]I don't care how many health and fitness magazines you read, you'll never be able to perform your own surgery or prescribe your own drugs.

[107]For more on how to choose a financial advisor, read Part 12 of *The Truth About Money*.

[108]All registered investment advisors must disclose all conflicts of interest to their clients. Not so for the media, which is protected by the First Amendment.

Another sinner printed an ad that claimed his advice would have produced a profit three times higher than if you had used a buy-and-hold strategy. Independent auditors proved he was lying.

It won't take long for you to be able to tell who *educates* and who merely *recommends*. The same is true for financial advisors themselves: Don't hire a stockbroker, insurance agent, lawyer, accountant, or financial planner who merely tells you what to do. Make sure they explain why they want you to do it—and make sure you understand the explanation and agree with it.

If you don't understand what they're telling you— whether it be the media or your personal advisor—cancel your subscription.

RULE #48 AVOID THE GOVERNMENT'S NEW INFLATION-ADJUSTED BONDS.

For years financial advisors (me included) have complained that bonds are bad bets for most investors, largely because of inflation. After all, why would you want to invest in something that pays a fixed income, when we live in an increasing-cost society?

The solution seems simple enough: Create a bond where the interest you earn increases with inflation. That is exactly what the administration did with the 1997 introduction of inflation-adjusted bonds. But not only is the concept itself mediocre, the administration's method is downright poor. Consequently, you need to avoid these new investments. Here's why:

The current yield at this writing for a 10-year Treasury is 6.5%, but the yield of the inflation-indexed bond is only 3.625%. If you're wondering why the indexed bond's rate is so low, you're asking the wrong question. You should be wondering why the ordinary Treasury rates are so high.

Because the yield on a bond never changes, the income a bond pays will be eroded by inflation. Therefore, investors demand higher rates in anticipation of that future problem. Hence, 10-year Treasuries pay 6.5%.

But such front-loading isn't necessary for indexed bonds, because the rate will rise with inflation. Therefore, the initial rate for the indexed bond is only 3.5%—and it rises as needed, on a pay-as-you-go system.

That's the first problem with indexed bonds. The ordinary bond buyer gets the higher rate right now—without waiting for the inflation everyone expects—while the indexed bond buyer must wait for inflation actually to occur. Not until inflation has cumulatively grown 85% will the indexed-bond buyer's rate catch up with the rate enjoyed by the ordinary bond buyer. Assuming 4% annual inflation, that will take about 16 years (including compounding)—on a bond that matures in just 10 years! Tell me again why indexed bonds make sense.

It gets worse. Because indexed-bond buyers start by earning less than ordinary bond buyers, they are in the awkward position of actually *hoping* for high inflation—because high inflation eventually will cause their bonds to exceed the 6.5% rate paid by ordinary Treasuries. That's like asking the skipper to aim for the iceberg. Do you really want to return to the economic environment of the 1970s?

I can imagine the conversation at home: "Hey, honey, my indexed bonds are way ahead of them fixed-raters!" The retort: "And a loaf of bread is 12 dollars!"

If the government succeeds at eliminating inflation, buyers of indexed bonds will be stuck with low-paying paper. If the government fails to eliminate inflation, buyers of indexed bonds might be the last to sink with the ship—but sink they will. Heads, you lose, and tails, you're thrown out of the game.

It gets worse. Everyone who has endorsed inflation-adjusted bonds has assumed that inflation only goes up. But inflation also can fall, and when it does, the interest paid by these bonds also will fall. Thus, investors buying indexed bonds are placing themselves on an interest-rate roller coaster: Because the bonds pay interest semiannually, investors won't know whether their next interest check will be more or less than the one they just got.

In fact, they might not get any interest at all. If the inflation rate drops enough, the interest payment could fall below zero. If that happens, not only will the investor get no interest currently, but future interest payments will be reduced until the shortfall is eliminated. Tell me again why indexed bonds make sense.

It gets worse. The government says buyers of indexed bonds can sell their bonds prior to maturity. But considering that the interest rate (a) is less than ordinary Treasuries, (b) might be less than what it was when the bond was originally issued, and (c) might be lower in the future, depending on what happens with inflation, the market for these new securities is quite limited. That means people who need to sell their indexed bonds may have considerable difficulty doing so.

It gets worse. Ask any investor to explain how indexed bonds work, and they'll tell you that the interest rate rises with inflation. That's simple enough. Unfortunately, it's also wrong. Not only might the interest rate fall, as described above, the truth is that the Administration has created an extremely complex design for these bonds, and when you read the next paragraph, you're not going to like it.

Here's how the bonds will work: Say you buy a $10,000 indexed bond paying 3.5% interest. That means you earn $350 in the first year, and you must pay taxes on that income. Assuming a 28% federal tax bracket, that's $98, leaving you with $252. Let's say inflation rises 10%. The way the government designed this thing, the bond's interest rate does not change. Instead, the *value* of the bond will increase 10%. Thus, you will earn 3.5% on $11,000. That's $385, less $108 in income taxes, leaving you with $277. The effect is the same as though the government had increased the rate itself, rather than the principal value. If there's no difference, what's the point? Good question, and the answer will annoy you.

By increasing the value instead of the rate, you now own

a bond worth $11,000. That means you have a profit of $1,000. Guess what! The Treasury Department calls this profit an "Original Issue Discount" (investors call it *phantom income*), and that means you must pay income taxes on the increase. Since your bond grew by $1,000, you owe another $280 in taxes. But you netted only $277 from interest! Thus, if we have high inflation (which is what you indexed bond buyers are hoping for, remember?), you would be forced to pay taxes on money you don't have. Tell me again why indexed bonds make sense.

It gets worse. The Treasury Department is issuing these bonds in denominations of as little as $50. Forget investors —the government is targeting unsophisticated, unsuspecting consumers. Just wait until they find out that their annual tax bill on these bonds is more than the income they received from the bonds.

It gets worse. The entire concept of inflation-adjusted bonds is based on the premise that bonds are broken and need to be fixed. This premise holds that bonds suffer from inflation risk, and the prescription is an indexed bond. That cure, though, will kill the patient.

Think about it: No investor is happy earning a 3.5% annual return over 10 years, but that's what indexed bonds offer. The fact that the rate is "inflation-adjusted" merely confuses the issue, because the proper goal for any investor is to "earn an effective return," not merely to "beat inflation."

The proper prescription, then, is not some complex, government-devised solution, but plain old everyday stocks. Stocks, and their brethren stock mutual funds, offer the best chance for ordinary families to create wealth over the long term, and indexed bonds will prove to be a poor alternative, just as ordinary bonds have proved. If the idea of investing in stocks makes you nervous, get over it, for these new indexed bonds will lead you to financial failure with far more certainty.

Canada, Great Britain, and others have tried indexed bonds, and their results have been underwhelming. Our government is discovering the same thing: As of this writing, those who bought these new bonds when they were introduced in 1997 have lost 4% of their money, while those who bought ordinary 10-year Treasuries have gained 5%. But the news isn't all bad: By selling these low-yielding bonds, the government is saving half a billion dollars a year in interest. That's great for us taxpayers, but it's terrible for us investors.

As your financial advisor, my advice to you is this: Don't buy inflation-indexed bonds.

RULE #49 DERIVATIVES ARE HERE TO STAY, SO GET USED TO THEM.

What in the world are derivatives, and why have they been in the news? Should you worry about them, or are they just headaches for big institutions and program traders? Well, guess what: You probably already own derivatives and you don't even know it.

A derivative is an investment whose existence is based on another investment. For example, there are two ways to buy a stock. You can buy it outright today, or you can buy the right to buy the stock later. This second method is done via stock options. Buying options gives you the right to buy the stock in the future—but you can't have the right to buy a stock unless the stock itself exists, and therefore, options are derivatives, meaning their existence is based on (*derived from*) something else.

Another, more common, example of a derivative is a Zero Coupon Treasury Bond. You buy a zero at a discount from its face value. For example, you pay $5,000 today, and at maturity you get $10,000. Instead of receiving interest between now and then, the bond increases in value.

Zeros are a popular and safe way to save, but the interesting thing is that the federal government does not issue 30-year Treasuries that don't pay interest. Instead, brokerage firms buy Treasuries from the federal government, and then split them in two: The half that pays interest is sold to one investor, and the half that grows until maturity (the zero part) is sold to another investor. That's how you are able to buy 30-year zeros even though the government doesn't issue them. Zero coupon bonds, in essence, are derivatives.[109]

Today, derivatives have gotten a bit exotic. In addition to the dull and boring stock options and zero coupon bonds, new derivative products are based on esoteric mathematical computer models based on the movement of currencies, interest rates, or the prices of securities that are rolled into other securities.

For the most part, the derivatives market is new and untested. We do not know how some of these investments will fare, say, during a stock market crash, if interest rates rise, if high inflation returns, or if some nation suffers political instability or war. That uncertainty translates into substantial risk for investors in these instruments.

The derivatives market got a taste of what can happen in a rising interest rate environment when Federal Reserve Board Chairman Alan Greenspan raised rates six times in 1994. Because an increase in rates creates a domino effect on the derivatives market, major corporations that were engaged in derivatives for one reason or another lost billions of dollars. Although Congress and federal regulators have expressed concern, Wall Street and the White House believe that additional regulation is not necessary.

Because of the negative publicity that derivatives have received, many people shy[110] away from these products. But what you probably don't realize is that you currently own derivatives. You'd be amazed at how many mutual funds engage in derivatives trading. Indeed, derivatives are now an integral part of the financial marketplace.

Get used to derivatives. They are another example of **The New Rules of Money**.

---

[109]They're also a terrible investment, which I covered in *The Truth About Money*.
[110]*Run* is probably a better word.

RULE #50

STOP PARTICIPATING IN DIVIDEND REINVESTMENT PLANS.

What once was an innovative, unique, and affordable way for consumers to participate in the then-closed world of stocks is now an antiquated and outdated idea, and those who continue to participate are frozen in a time that the rest of us have long since left behind.

I'm talking about Dividend Reinvestment Plans, or DRPs.

To understand what they are and why they have such a secure place in the investment world, you first need to understand the world that led to their development.

After World War II, it didn't take long for America to begin the long climb to prosperity that we're still enjoying. During the war, virtually every American put their money behind the war effort, by buying U.S. War Bonds, the predecessor to today's EE Savings Bonds. These investments provided the United States with much of the money it needed to finance the war, and for their patriotism investors were rewarded with a competitive, guaranteed interest rate.

After the War, the nation immediately began to see a change in the economy. For the first time since the Depression of 20 years earlier, people once again were starting to make money by buying stocks. But as much as you might have wanted to participate in the new bullish economy, your ability to do so was impeded by several barriers to entry.

For one thing, you didn't have much money—a prerequisite for investing in stocks. Oh, sure, you could have borrowed money to invest, but that's what caused the Crash of 1929—a point still very much on everyone's mind. Why not just buy one share of a $20 stock? You could afford it easily enough, but the brokerage environment made it prohibitively expensive. You see, prior to 1975, brokerage commissions were regulated, and therefore all brokers, regardless of firm, charged the same rates.[111] Commissions were based on two factors: The number of shares you were trading and the price per share. The more shares you traded, and the higher the price of the stock, the lower the commission on a per-share basis. Indeed, the total commission to trade 1,000 shares of a $100 stock was only $460, or 46 cents per share, while someone trading 100 shares of a $20 stock would pay $65, or 65 cents per share.

Notice I'm using the word *trade* instead of *buy*. That's because stock commissions are charged whether you're buying or selling. Since you don't realize any profits until you sell a stock you've previously bought, you therefore pay commissions twice—once to buy the stock, and once to sell it.

Therefore, as a percentage of his investment, the buyer of those 1,000 shares would need to see his stock rise 0.92% just so he could break even. The buyer of those 100 shares, meanwhile, would need a gain of 3.25%—3½ times more than the big investor. Therefore, it was easier for a wealthy person to become wealthier than for a poor person to become wealthy. Perhaps this is the origin of the phrase, "It takes money to make money."

To make matters worse, there were minimum commission costs, meaning the fee to buy one share could be the same as the fee to buy 100 shares. Consequently, on a percentage basis, the buyer of just one share would have to see his stock double in value just to break even! The odds certainly were against small investors, and as a result, those who didn't have the cash to purchase large quantities of high-priced stocks were effectively cut out of the stock market.[112]

In case that wasn't enough to dissuade small investors from buying stocks, the stock exchanges added yet *another* penalty: Anyone trading in "odd lots" (meaning anything other than 100-share increments, called "round lots") were

[111]May 1, 1975, the day the U.S. Securities and Exchange Commission deregulated stock commissions, is known as May Day. It deregulated brokerage commissions and allowed for the introduction of discount brokers.
[112]And that meant most Americans. One hundred shares of a $20 stock represented a $2,000 investment—more than the annual income of most families at that time.

assessed ⅛ of a point each time they traded. In other words, if you wanted to buy one share of a $20 stock, they'd charge you $20.125—plus the commission. And when you wanted to sell that $20 stock, they'd give you only $19.875—minus the commission. So, round-trip, you'd lose an extra 25 cents per share, making profits that much harder to achieve.

If all this wasn't enough, there was one last obstacle: Dividend income—the source of half or more of the profits for many stocks—was of little benefit to long-term investors unless you used the money to buy yet more shares, thus compounding your returns.[113] Assume you own 1,000 shares of a $20 stock. Further assume the stock pays a 3% annual dividend, which is 60 cents per year. With your 1,000 shares, your dividend is $600, which you can use to buy 30 more shares. Thus, next year, you'd have 1,030 shares, which would produce a dividend of $618, allowing you to buy another 31 shares, which increases next year's dividend even more, letting you buy yet more stock next time. Do this for 40 years, and you'll become downright wealthy— which is how most rich people get that way (and how children of rich people stay that way).

But if you bought only one share, you'd get a dividend check for just 60 cents. What, may I ask, are you supposed to do with that? You can't reinvest it because the stock costs $20—plus commissions and odd-lot charges. So you merely pocket the change and in 40 years, you're still earning 60 cents in annual dividends. So much for getting rich in the stock market.

Because of the insidious combination of minimum fees, odd-lot charges, and the inability to reinvest dividends, it was virtually impossible to make money in stocks by buying only a few shares at a time. Since that was all you could afford, you had little choice but to stay out of stocks, and watch the rich get richer.

Until the idea of a Dividend Reinvestment Plan came along.

---

[113]It's a myth that most stocks make money simply through price appreciation. Dividends account for as much as half of a stock's profits.

Recognizing that millions of Americans were effectively prohibited from buying their stock, this remarkably innovative program was specifically designed for the masses. Instead of forcing consumers to buy their stock from stockbrokers, companies could sell their stock directly to the public—in any increment and with no commissions. Furthermore, instead of sending dividend checks to its stock owners each quarter, each company would allow the shareholders to reinvest their money back into the stock, so they could accumulate more shares. To solve the problem that the dividend might not be large enough to buy an entire share of stock, each company would allow them to buy partial shares—as little as $\frac{1}{1000}$ of a share! Thus, even those owning just one share would be able to reinvest their dividends, allowing them to compound their returns just like the rich boys! Indeed, that 60-cent dividend would be enough to buy 0.03 additional shares. Thus, after one year, the small investor would now own 1.03 shares, while the investor who bought 1,000 shares would own 1,030 shares. On a percentage basis, the small investor was now doing just as well as the big boys—in fact, because the small investor paid no commissions, he was really doing even better!

This program, which came to be known as a Dividend Reinvestment Plan, was a wonderful opportunity for small investors. But it was not created by Corporate America strictly out of goodwill. There are several important reasons why this idea made good business sense:

1. Many stock owners are active traders who buy and sell stocks on the slightest news. Active trading creates volatility in a stock price, and this can prove very distracting for a company's management, which would rather focus its efforts on long-term growth. DRP investors, who are investing for the long term, are more stable and loyal shareholders than ordinary stock traders, and this allows management to focus less on the company's stock price, and more on its business.

2. If there's one thing stock owners hate, it's a *volatile* stock price. The more people you have owning your stock, the more stable the stock price will be (because the less impact by any one trader). So, by inviting small investors to own your stock, you expand your stockholder base, which in turn reduces volatility and makes everybody happier.

3. If there's one thing stock owners love, it's a *rising* stock price. The only way to get the price to rise is to increase the number of buyers. By definition, those who participate in DRPs are regular buyers of your stock. That helps the price rise, and makes everybody happier.

4. Companies love DRP investors, because it's a lot cheaper for the company to issue dividends in the form of additional shares than to pay those dividends in cash.

5. While institutional investors, such as banks, insurance companies, and pension funds, are solely interested in a particular stock for its profit potential, individual investors also are consumers, and they tend to buy the products of companies whose stocks they own. A person who owns Exxon stock is more likely to buy Exxon gasoline, for example, and therefore having a large number of DRP investors helps to increase your company's market share. In fact, many companies give shareholders discounts or free samples.

With all these advantages, it didn't take long for other companies to follow suit. Today, more than 1,000 companies offer DRPs, and millions of Americans participate in them. There are several books on the market devoted to DRP investing, and even a couple of newsletters, too, and the personal finance press touts their advantages warmly. As a result of all this media focus, most of the investing public has now become familiar with DRPs.

Just in time for you to forget all about them.

DRPs are dinosaurs, an idea that, while innovative in its day, has become antiquated and ineffective compared to the most powerful and important investment vehicle of the 20th century: Mutual funds. Here's why you need to cancel your DRPs:

1. One of the keys to successful investing is diversification, but DRPs tend to be offered only by the largest of companies. Indeed, according to a study by the American Association of Individual Investors, companies that offer DRPs had an average market capitalization[114] in 1996 of $1.6 billion, while non-DRP companies had an average market cap of just $82 million. And DRP companies averaged $1.3 billion in sales, while non-DRP companies averaged only $67 million. Clearly, those who limit themselves to DRPs are investing in only a narrow segment of the stock market. This wouldn't be too big a concern—if it weren't for the fact that big companies tend to have less growth than small companies. Indeed, according to AAII, the average five-year sales growth of DRP companies was 6.3%, while non-DRP companies grew 12.6%—or nearly twice as much. Clearly, by the time a company offers a DRP, its greatest years of growth are likely behind it. Many mutual funds, however, allow you to invest in small companies, during their greatest growth years.

2. DRP investors tend to be too narrowly focused, failing to understand that there's a big investment world stretching beyond their field of vision. For example, one of the most popular choices for DRP investors are utility companies. Not only have utilities traditionally been considered to be among the safest stocks, they also pay some of the highest dividends on Wall Street—making them ideal for DRP investing. But if you ask a person which power company they are using for their DRP, 99% of the time it'll be their local power company. New Yorkers tend to DRP into ConEd, Virginians DRP into Dominion Resources, and

---

[114]Market capitalization refers to the size of the company. You merely multiply the share price by the number of shares outstanding. The bigger the company, the bigger its market cap.

Floridians rely on Florida Power and Light. Being a fan of your hometown team is fine for sports, but investing your money in a company merely because of where you live is a very poor investment strategy. As AAII's senior financial analyst John Bajkowski puts it, "An investor should purchase and hold a company with a DRP only if it is still an attractive investment when considered against other investment opportunities."

Bolstering this point is a study from Columbia University, which found that, of those who own stock in one of the seven regional "Baby Bell" companies, investors overwhelmingly invested in shares of their local phone company. Maryland residents, for example, buy Bell Atlantic, while those in Chicago buy Ameritech. Clearly, everyone thinks "their" Baby Bell is better than the other six—and, just as clearly, everyone can't be right! Yet investors prefer to invest in their "home town" stock, as though they're rooting for the football team. If familiarity is a good reason for considering a stock, said *Business Week* in a review of the study, then investors should be as willing to reject it as to invest in it. Investing in a company simply because you know of it is a poor decision. [115]

3. By bypassing the brokerage world, investing in DRPs, by definition, means you are investing on your own. You must do your own research, and you will be unable to rely on a professional advisor to assist you. By contrast, most mutual fund investors enjoy the advice and assistance of a professional advisor.

4. Once you select the DRPs you want, you must work with them via mail. If you're going to participate in a dozen or so DRPs, as most would argue you should (for diversity), expect to get a lot of mail.

5. All this requires you to do a lot of record-keeping. Each time you send in money, and for each quarterly dividend

---

[115]Which helps explain why you should not invest in the stock of your employer. See Rule #85.

you reinvest, you create a separate "trade lot." You must maintain itemized records of all these transactions, for eventual reporting on your tax return. If you fail to maintain the proper records, you could incur a much higher tax liability than otherwise necessary.

6. One of the biggest advantages of DRPs—the ability to buy them without commissions—now rarely exists. Many DRP investors have failed to notice that companies are starting to introduce fees into their programs, such as a $1.50 or $3 charge to reinvest your quarterly dividend. Others are assessing this fee for each deposit you make. While many consider this small fee to be merely a nuisance—and quite reasonable compared to stock commissions—these fees actually are deadly, and indeed destroy the entire point of investing in DRPs. Consider: If you invest $50 monthly into a DRP that charges $3 each time, you'd invest $600 in a year—and your account would be reduced by $36. That's equivalent to a 6% commission—twice what brokers would charge. To make up for that, your stock would have to grow 6% for you to break even!

7. Meanwhile, stock commissions have long since been deregulated. Today discount brokers allow you to purchase any amount of stock for one fixed price, often for as little as $29, regardless of how many shares you're buying or the price of those shares. Furthermore, the New York Stock Exchange dropped its odd-lot fee in 1990, further easing the burden on small investors.

8. The DRP's other claim to fame—the ability to give you fractional shares for your reinvested dividends—also is no longer unique. Many brokerage firms now perform this same service for you, for free. And mutual funds, of course, have been doing this for decades. Clearly, DRPs' competitors have narrowed the gap.

Indeed, mutual funds are now best. Thirty years ago, you couldn't buy a fund without paying a commission as high as

8.5%. But today, thousands of mutual funds are available at significantly reduced fees or even commission-free.

Mutual funds offer a variety of other benefits and services as well. Although DRPs allow you to invest systematically each month through automatic check debiting,[116] you can do that with mutual funds, too. Mutual funds offer other advantages, too, such as free check-writing privileges, greater investment flexibility, and professional management of your investments. Mutual funds also maintain complete tax records for you, so you don't have to track your cost basis or trade lot data, either. DRPs offer none of these benefits.

You can research and invest in mutual funds on your own, if that's what you like to do (as you must do with DRPs), or you can seek assistance from financial advisors if you prefer. But few advisors will counsel you on DRPs. So if you insist on dealing with DRPs, you're on your own.

There is no question that DRPs once were an exciting innovation that opened the door to stocks for millions of Americans. But today they are as advanced as Henry Ford's Model T—although marvelous in their day, you don't want to be driving one on today's investment superhighway.

RULE #51 STOP PAYING COMMISSIONS AND CHOOSE ASSET MANAGEMENT FEES INSTEAD...

Neil's son was a new stockbroker. "Dad, I've got a fabulous hot investment for you! Can I sign you up for a hundred thousand?" Bruce asked.

"A hundred thousand dollars?" Neil replied. "How much is the commission?"

Bruce paused. "Four percent," he said.

---

[116]With an ACD arrangement, your bank account is automatically debited each month for a prearranged amount. You simply need to remember to record the transaction in your checkbook.

"That's four thousand," Neil said. "Of the four grand, how much do you get?"

"Well," Bruce said, "I work on commission. The payout, based on my commission grid, is 28%."

"So how much does that work out to?" Neil asked.

Bruce pulled out his calculator. "Twenty-eight percent of $4,000 is $1,120," he said.

"And how much of that will you pay in taxes?" Neil asked.

"About a third," Bruce responded.

"Leaving you with how much?" Neil continued.

"About $750," Bruce said.

"Great," said Neil. "How about I send you a check for $750 and we'll call it even?"

I love this story, because it speaks volumes about the brokerage business. But the joke is rapidly becoming obsolete, because the financial industry is moving away from commissions—with all the problems they bring—and toward asset management fees.

Without question, asset management fees now are the most popular way to compensate financial advisors. Unlike commissions, which are based on transactions, asset management fees are based on the size of your assets. That's the first reason consumers like them: They eliminate commissions. Second, and perhaps more importantly, asset management fees put the advisor on the same side of the table as the client. The client obviously wants the assets to increase in value. Since the fee is based on the size of those assets, the more the assets grow, the more money the advisor makes. The client doesn't mind, because it means the client is making more money, too.

The result: Consumers feel that asset management fees eliminate worries over conflict of interest, because advisors who make bad recommendations will suffer along with the client.[117] Asset management fees therefore give advisors plenty of incentive to do a good job for their clients.

---

[117]Though obviously not nearly as much.

Advisors like asset management fees, too, because fees provide a steady stream of income without the advisor having to worry about selling something new to his clients.[118]

So when you are looking for an advisor, ask how he or she is paid. Don't be surprised to find—and you might even want to demand that the method of compensation be in the form of—an asset management fee.

RULE #52 ...AND REALIZE WHY STOCKBROKERS SOON WILL BE EXTINCT.

The problem with asset management fees (see Rule #51) is that they are far too low for stockbrokers, who are used to earning much higher compensation. Compare the 4% commission that brokers typically earn against the 1% (or less) annual asset management fee, and you see the problem: Brokers face a 75% cut in income when moving to asset management fees.

To see the effect, let's return to Rule #51's Neil and his son, Bruce. Whereas Bruce would have generated a gross commission of $4,000 by selling his dad that $100,000 investment, he'd gross only $1,000 by giving Dad an asset-managed account. With a 28% cut of that revenue (the firm keeps the rest), Bruce would earn just $280—before taxes! Of course, Bruce would continue to receive that same $280 every year (plus more as the account grows in value), but that won't help him make this month's mortgage payment.

This is not a problem for Bruce if he already manages several hundred million dollars, but it's a crisis for him if he's new to the business. This explains why Merrill Lynch

---

[118]Of course, asset management fees are really commissions, because they are based on the size of the account. (Real fees are based on time or a flat rate, not on how much money you invest.) Still, asset management fees are regarded as a benign form of commissions, because the advisor is paid to manage the money, not just move it around.

(with $500 billion under management) is not in danger of going broke, but why many of its brokers are. At one large brokerage firm, for example, where each broker sells an average of $10 million worth of investments per year at an average 4% commission, the average broker's pay exceeds $100,000. If the brokers instead earned a 1% fee for this same business, their first year's gross would be only $25,000—and there's a whopping big difference in lifestyle when a person earns $25,000 instead of $100,000.

Still, asset management fees are both popular with and beneficial for consumers,[119] and the brokerage community knows it has no choice but to convert its legions of stock-brokers into financial planners. Most of them already have started trying to make the transition. Merrill Lynch now calls its stockbrokers "Financial Consultants" and sells financial plans for $250. Smith Barney offers financial plans, too. So does Dean Witter.

But dangers lurk for the public. A 15-year veteran stock-broker is not suddenly a financial planner merely because a new title appears on his business card, or because he's now able to sell computer-generated "plans" that are prepared by the home office—or because he's moved from com-mission-based compensation to asset management fees.

This is why the big brokerage firms find themselves in a quandary: Its customers want the comprehensive advice and skills of a professional financial planner, and they like the low cost and objectivity offered by asset management fees. But many of the firm's stockbrokers don't like the idea. Often, stockbrokers consider planning to be mere window dressing, and they've been doing fine without it for years, selling investments for fat commissions. Besides, if they move to asset management fees, their incomes will be reduced *sharply*.

Still, some stockbrokers around the country have made the transition successfully, and more are doing it all the time. The result is that today you can find at any given bro-kerage firm many highly talented, professional advisors

---

[119]How often does *that* happen!

who are competent in all areas of personal finance, including taxes, insurance, mortgages, and wills and trusts—as well as investment management. But it's also still true that this planning professional's cubicle could be next to one occupied by an options-trading, cold-calling cowboy.

From a consumer's perspective, things are improving. The big brokerage firms are encouraging their stockbrokers to move toward asset management fees, and most have endorsed financial planning as their new business model. Merrill Lynch, which once prohibited its stockbrokers from becoming Certified Financial Planners, for example, now encourages its brokers to obtain the CFP and other professional designations.

Still, there have been some missteps in the brokerages' efforts to change each broker's mentality from product-pusher to that of consultative advisor. For example, some brokerage firms that now offer financial planning actually have *sales quotas* for them—requiring that their stockbrokers sell a minimum number of financial plans every month, whether or not their clients want or need one. It seems these firms are treating financial plans as just another product to sell, like a muni bond. And Merrill Lynch goofed big-time when it introduced its Financial Advantage Service in 1997. Merrill promoted the service's asset management fee as "an alternative to commissions…a unique way to manage all your finances for one annual fee…no commissions on transactions." What Merrill failed to highlight was the fact that, under the FAS client agreement, the brokers still would receive commissions for selling certain investments. Needless to say, Merrill was widely criticized after the *Washington Post* broke the story in June 1997, especially when the *Post* quoted a Merrill spokesman as saying, "This account has not been marketed by us as the best option for every customer."

So the metamorphosis continues. Stockbrokers are a dying breed, and like dinosaurs before them, they one day will be extinct. Or will they? Dinosaurs, some argue, became smaller, swifter, and more agile, and today are called birds. Whatever the answer, the effect on you depends on whether you choose to maintain an account at a brokerage firm and, if you do, whether your advisor is a traditional stockbroker or a member of the new generation. That distinction makes all the difference: Just as the best hospital is irrelevant if your surgeon is a klutz, it now matters less which brokerage firm you use and more which advisor you hire at the firm.

As Donald Marron, CEO of PaineWebber, told *USA Today,* "We are talking to our brokers and saying, 'You grew up in this business being a transactor, in which you did trades for clients and charged a commission. Now you have to switch from that to being an asset gatherer.'" Clearly, not all of the nation's brokers are going to get the message, but your success could well depend on whether yours does.

RULE #53   LEARN HOW TO SPOT THE NEW SCAM ARTISTS.

Have you ever come across a bucket shop? Or been tangled up with a boiler room operation? If you don't know what I'm talking about, I'm glad to hear it, because that means you haven't fallen victim to the latest variation of crooked stockbrokers who are determined to separate you from your money.

Industry insiders know all about the "boiler rooms"[120] where "cold-calling cowboys"[121] wearing telephone headsets "dial for dollars."[122] If you answer their call, they'll say you need to act fast because they've got "the" hot deal for you. These people are slick. Too often your money disappears, and usually so do they—federal regulators and police can't catch up with these guys, because as soon as the complaints start to surface, they shut down their operations and reopen elsewhere under a different name.

---

[120]So called because of their "high-pressure" sales tactics.
[121]a.k.a. salesmen…
[122]…who make their sales pitch over the telephone.

One of my clients fell victim to this type of scam, but luckily recognized something was not right before it got beyond her control. Stacy received a call from a woman who identified herself as being with a company in New York. She wanted to know if Stacy had any IPOs or ISOs. Stacy explains: "She sounded very legitimate. In my ignorance, I asked her what she was talking about. She said, 'Initial Stock Offerings.' I said, 'No, I've got a financial advisor and I deal with him on all of those things.' She said, 'Tell me some of the investments you own.' So I gave her a couple of names."

Stacy then requested more information from the woman so she could show her advisor. A packet arrived the next day via Federal Express, showing that the firm's IPOs[123] posted gains of 153% in less than six weeks. That same day, Stacy got another call—this time from someone else in the woman's company. This caller, a man, acted "real pushy" and said Stacy was wasting time and needed to act fast. He told Stacy, "We're going to issue this stock tomorrow, and it's going to come out at $7 per share, and by tomorrow evening it's going to be around $17, and you're going to miss out unless you buy it now." Two days later, the same person called to tell Stacy that the stock went to $20 and that Stacy, in her stupidity, missed out. He tried to pressure Stacy into opening an account, and even resorted to chewing her out, saying, "What's wrong with you? You don't have any financial sense at all!"

The next time the man called he *really* bullied Stacy, until Stacy agreed to open an account. Stacy says, "I told them at least four times that I did not want to buy stock; that I never buy anything over the phone. The man told me, 'In order to open an account, you have to buy some stock. We don't make anything on it; we only make $40.' Then he put the woman back on the phone, and she said, 'I need your Social Security number,' which I gave her." Stacy also gave the

---

[123]Initial Public Offering. This refers to a stock that is being sold to the public for the first time. The woman's use of the phrase "Initial Stock Offering" is an indication that a scam is occurring, because although it sounds legitimate, there is no such thing.

woman the name of her bank, which she felt was okay because the woman didn't ask for her account number.

Then the woman told Stacy, "We're issuing 200 shares of stock to you, and it'll be $4,000." When Stacy practically yelled into the phone that she didn't want the stock or want an account opened, the woman hung up the phone. Stacy, annoyed and frustrated, thought it was all over.

The next day, Federal Express delivered a letter advising Stacy that she had purchased 200 shares of stock and to please remit $4,040. "When I called the firm, I was livid," Stacy recounts, "and they told me they had never received a complaint like this before and that certainly it would be taken care of."

Fat chance. The next day Stacy got a call from the same guy saying she owed $4,000 for the stock and that she had reneged on the stock purchase.

After that conversation, Stacy called me to see if she had any liability. Fortunately, because she had called them to cancel the transaction (which she said she never authorized in the first place) and because she had never sent them any money, she had no liability.

Stacy actually handled herself pretty well, although she made two errors, one fundamental and one strategic.

Her fundamental error was in giving them personal information, including her Social Security number and bank information. *Never give information about yourself to people you do not know.*

Her strategic error was that she acted as any reasonable, prudent person would act. After receiving a solicitation, she requested more information, with the intention of consulting her advisor before making a decision. The problem is that Stacy wasn't dealing with reasonable people! She was talking to a bunch of crooks, and consequently, none of her "reasonable actions" would prove effective.

There is only one way to stop telemarketing crooks: *Stop talking to them.* Hang up the phone. Don't fret that your mom taught you never to be rude to people. Mom never said you had to be polite to robbers.

Here are some warning signs to help you spot a con artist:

1. **The original call came from New York, even though Stacy lives in Maryland.**

   Legitimate brokers don't solicit clients from across the country.

2. **The sales pitch was aimed at her emotions.**

   They started with vanity: "I'm calling you because you're special." Then they moved to greed: "We can make you rich." When that didn't work, they moved on to intimidation: "You are stupid!"

3. **They refused to take "no" for an answer.**

   Honest cold-callers will politely end the call, while crooks know the longer you stay on the phone, the more likely you will eventually give in. (It also explains why insults work so well. If you're about to hang up, calling you a jerk is sure to keep you on the line, if only so you can yell something back. This gives them the chance to apologize, saying they've had a bad day, been under pressure, family problems, etc.—anything to keep you on the line.)

4. **They bragged about their prior performance and promised future results—saying the new stock would open at $7 and rise to $17 in a day.**

   That's against the law. Think about it: If the deal was so good, why would they want *your* money? (They'd keep all the stock for themselves!)

5. **They said they wouldn't make any money on the transaction (only $40!).**

   Are they working for free? Beware of anyone who claims they don't earn anything or that you don't pay anything.

6. **They used an overnight delivery service (in this case, Federal Express) instead of the mail.**

   By avoiding the U.S. Postal Service, they avoid charges of

mail fraud. Insist that people write to you via regular mail, and if they complain that time is too short, remind them that the post office offers overnight delivery. Remember: These guys are sharp; they know what they're doing, and they know you don't.

If you receive something you don't understand or believe is fraudulent, do what Stacy did: Call the company and speak with a manager to reject the sale or clarify it. Never pay the invoice. If you do, odds are good you will never see your money again. Don't ignore it, either, for silence can be interpreted as consent. Therefore, it is critical that you make your opposition known.

If you find yourself talking to a cowboy and you just can't bring yourself to hang up on them (thanks to a civilized upbringing), try these answers:

1. **"Thanks, but my brother is a broker, and he has all my money."**

   This stops most cold-callers, who figure you're getting plenty abused already.

2. **"Thanks, but I'm a stockbroker myself."**

   This won't work all the time; the most brazen will try to get you to sell their deal to *your* clients!

3. **"I work exclusively with _____. I'd like him to review your offer. Please send him your information at _____."**

   By letting them know that you're already associated with a professional advisor, you build yourself a wall they can't climb over. To anything they say, just keep repeating the sentence, "I never do anything without first consulting my advisor."[124]

---

[124]If you don't have an advisor of your own whose name you can use, feel free to use my name and address (12450 Fair Lakes Circle, Suite 200, Fairfax, VA 22033). I'm probably the only guy around who *likes* getting cold calls. (I love to hear about their latest scams, so I can warn you!)

4. "I work for the NASD. What is your CRD number?"

If you want to play hardball, this will knock them right out of the park; I've never had any cold-caller stay on the line after hearing this one. The National Association of Securities Dealers (NASD) is responsible for licensing and regulating stockbrokers, and word that it[125] is poking around is always enough to send the crooks diving for cover. The Central Registration Depository maintains the backgrounds and disciplinary records for all licensed stockbrokers.

To get a copy of your broker's CRD file, call the NASD at 1–800–289–9999. You also can contact your state securities regulators or the North American Securities Administrators Association at 202–737–0900. When contacting any of these groups, you'll need as much information as possible, including the broker's full name, firm, and address.

---

[125]Or the U.S. Securities and Exchange Commission; use "the SEC" instead of "the NASD" if you like.

your family, money, and the law

RULE
#54A TALK WITH YOUR KIDS ABOUT YOUR WILL.

RULE
#54B TALK WITH YOUR PARENTS ABOUT YOUR INHERITANCE.

There are two subjects never discussed at the dinner table. One of them is money.[126] This must not continue, for more than ever, money is a family affair. Just look at the factors involved:

People are living longer than ever.

A 65-year-old can expect to live to 82, while an 85-year-old can expect to live to 91. My grandmother, now 100, says she never expected to live this long.[127]

Such long life expectancies virtually assure that your kids will become involved with your personal finances. Your adult children will help you pay your bills, manage your savings and investments, prepare your taxes, arrange for insurance, apply for Medicare and Social Security reimbursements, and help you secure and pay for long-term care services. Your kids have a vital interest in all this, not just because they love you, and not just because they want an inheritance, but because if your affairs are not managed properly, you will run out of money, and *they'll* have to support *you*. Indeed, for the first time in our nation's history, wealth in many families is not transferring from father to son—it's going from daughter to mother.

---

[126]You know what the other one is.
[127]We're glad she has.

The costs of raising a family have never been greater.

If you are 65 today, it's quite likely that your grandparents never even attended school, while your grandkids are submitting their homework via e-mail. In the weeks before the new school year began, your parents had to buy you a notebook for 50 cents. Today, your grandkids are buying a notebook *computer* for $2,500. Whereas you carried your lunch with you to school, today's school kids leave the campus for McDonald's.

The good news about our advanced society is that our standard of living has never been better. Our homes are warm in winter and cool in summer. Food is always fresh and plentiful. Medical attention is readily available.

The bad news is that all this costs a lot of money. Houses are bigger and more expensive. Although your parents did have a telephone, your kids have three phone *lines* going into their house. You grew up with one TV; your kids have a TV *and* VCR in every room—and a satellite dish on the roof. Your family didn't own a car, but your son's family needs three of them.

All this helps explain why 75% of women are in the workforce, and why, among the nation's 54 million married couples, 55% are dual-income families. Because Americans are marrying later and having children later, it is increasingly likely that your children will be trying to pay for their kids' college costs at about the same time they're getting ready to retire.[128]

This is why grandparents spend more money on toys than parents do, and why grandparents start more college savings funds than parents. It's not that parents don't want to do these things; it's that too often they cannot afford to.

Yet, despite such intense interfamily relationships, there is a remarkable lack of communication about finances between the generations. The grandparents assume their kids need help with putting the grandkids through college,

---

[128]I see this in my own family. My oldest brother will be 65 when his youngest child is a college freshman.

but it's never directly discussed. Instead, the grandparents simply open a custodial account for each grandchild. They forget that they're investing the money into the same type of low-risk asset they use for themselves, and they don't realize that the college planning needs of an eight-year-old are vastly different from the interest income needs of a retiree. They also never stop to consider that putting money into the child's name could destroy that child's ability to qualify for college grants or other financial aid.[129]

The kids, meanwhile, have not discussed with Mom and Dad what their parents' wishes are regarding heroic measures in the event of a terminal illness. Does Mom want to be taken off life support and be allowed to die naturally, or would she prefer medical intervention? What about related medical decisions, including the administration of hydration, a feeding tube, ventilators, or CPR? How does Dad feel? What if you don't want heroic measures, but your children are unable to let go? Arguing about such things in an emergency room at 4 A.M. is not ideal.

Sit down with your family today and have the conversation you should have had a long time ago, because without question, the very worst five words you ever could utter about your parents, children, or grandchildren are, "If only I had known."

RULE #55 START GIVING MONEY TO YOUR KIDS NOW. DON'T WAIT UNTIL YOU'VE DIED.

Are you expecting an inheritance? Most people expect to receive some sort of inheritance, large or small. In fact, 62% of baby boomers say they expect to get an inheritance within the next 20 years. But not everyone has made their plans known—parents have not told their children what they plan to give and children have not inquired about what

---

[129]See Rule #9.

they will receive. That being the case, how can we be sure that the money is being put to its best use?

The 87-year-old mother of a client of mine exemplifies this point perfectly. Genevieve has $1.7 million in investments that she doesn't touch. Social Security and her deceased husband's pension cover her modest living expenses.

When I asked what she planned to do with all her money, Gen said, "I'm just holding on to it. When I die, it'll go to my boys [my client and his brother] to help them get along."

Since her "boys" are 67 and 63, I found this quite interesting. Her *grandchildren* range in age from early 30s to mid-40s, and they're busy having kids of their own. I pointed out to Gen that life expectancy tables project that she'll live to age 94. "If you plan to leave your money to your children," I told her, "they will have to wait seven years. Then, your will must be probated, and that'll take at least one more year." All told, I explained, her elder son could be 75 years old before he received any inheritance; the younger could be 70 or more. Some of her grandchildren could be nearing age 50, and many of her great-grandchildren would be out of college by then.

I offered her an idea: Why not start to give them the money now?

Suddenly, it occurred to Gen that her grandchildren and great-grandchildren could use the money now, to help them pay off college loans, buy homes and cars for their growing families, as well as to begin saving for the future.

Why hadn't this idea occurred to her without my help? There are many reasons, of course, but I think one of them has to do with longer life spans. You see, when she was born in the early 1900s, the life expectancy of Gen's parents was about 50 years. That means Gen received her inheritance when she was in her early 30s. Without giving it any thought, Gen assumed the same would prove true for her kids.

Of course, today people live much longer. By the time Gen passes on, her kids will be well beyond their major spending years. But her thinking is frozen in the early 1900s: It hasn't occurred to her that life expectancy tables now suggest that all the money she plans to give her children will get to them years after they need it most.

For this reason, parents with adult children should consider gifting some of their money to their kids and grandkids today—but, of course, only if doing so does not hurt the parents financially.

If you (a) are in your 80s or beyond, (b) have money you'll never use, and (c) have adult children and grandchildren to whom you plan to leave all your money anyway, then consider giving some of it to them now. You'll discover the joy of helping them spend it! Watch your grandchildren go to college, buy a car, or build a home! Help your great-grandchildren learn how to ride a bike or travel abroad with the money you've provided!

Parents who are concerned that their kids will squander their gifts can take comfort from a study done by First Interstate Bank. They asked Baby Boomers around the country what they would do if they were to receive an inheritance or large gift. The results:

- 26% said they would use the money to pay off debts;
- 25% said they would use the money for their children's college education;
- 20% said they would save it for retirement; and
- 14% said they would use it to purchase a home.

All these responses sound very reasonable to me.

The topic of money must no longer be taboo at the kitchen table.[130] Children should let their parents know their financial needs and plans. If they don't know you want to buy a house, how can your parents or grandparents offer to help with the down payment? And parents must recognize the realities of inheritances: We're living longer than ever, and if we leave money to our children upon our death, they

---

[130]See Rule #54.

are likely to be in their 60s or 70s when they receive it. Their time of greatest financial need will have come and gone.

One of the most important of **The New Rules of Money** is that times are changing. Therefore, you need to change with them. Talk with your parents or children, and put the family's money to its best use: For the benefit and welfare of the entire family.

RULE #56 MAKE SURE YOUR HEIRS KNOW HOW INVESTMENTS WORK BEFORE THEY INHERIT THEM.

Lisa was in my office, describing her financial picture. In addition to her house, two bank accounts, several IRAs, a variety of mutual funds, and a retirement account at work, she owned several thousand shares of Johnson & Johnson stock.

"When did you inherit the stock?" I asked.

"How did you know I inherited it?" she replied, somewhat surprised.

"It's obvious," I said. "You do not own any other individual stocks, yet this is worth more than all of your other assets combined."

I was right, of course. Lisa was displaying classic symptoms of what I call *inheritanitis*, and I knew the conversation was only going to get worse.

"My dad died two years ago," she said. "Mom died in 1992. Dad had worked for Johnson & Johnson before the war, and he bought the stock sometime around then. He never sold it, and it split several times over the years." Splits indeed. The stock was worth $132,000.

"Would you consider selling it?" I asked, as if I didn't know the answer.

"SELL IT!!?" she exclaimed, right on cue. "My father would turn over in his grave! This stock was precious to him. I will *never* sell it!"

Here we go again, I thought. Another victim of inheritani-tis. This is an extremely common affliction among middle-class Americans, whose working-class parents somehow managed to accumulate significant—and often substantial— wealth during their lifetimes. Lisa was treating the stock her father had left her with the same emotional attachment as Grandmom's necklace that her mom had given to her. Indeed, Lisa thought the stock was an *heirloom*.

She couldn't be more wrong. In one of the most impor-tant of **The New Rules of Money**, Lisa needed to under-stand that she must not continue to own an inherited stock *merely because it was inherited*. After all, it's just a financial asset. Her father knew that. To him, the stock was an invest-ment—nothing more, nothing less. He bought it because he hoped it would grow in value, and that the profits would help his family financially. But then he went to war, and the stock certificate sat for years, ignored and forgotten, in some bank's vault.

Later, when he returned home and started his life anew, he left the stock alone. In the ensuing years, he'd often think of selling the stock. It had grown nicely—in fact, too nicely. Selling the stock would cause him to incur a huge tax on the profit, called a capital gains tax. The tax would be so large, in fact, that it would be more than what he *earned* in a whole year. He couldn't bear the thought of paying so stag-geringly high a tax, so he didn't sell. The stock sat. And con-tinued to grow. And the pending tax bill grew with it. Every time he thought about selling, the tax consequences just froze him. So he never sold.

Instead, Lisa inherited the stock. By now, it had been in the family longer than most relatives, including Lisa herself, so she began to attribute much sentimental value to the stock. "I can remember Daddy reading the newspaper after dinner, remarking at how well the stock was doing," she recalled. Sometimes, he'd show her the stock listing in the business pages. She was too young then to understand what Dad was showing her, but it was an important memory for her. That stock was part of her childhood.

Helllllloooooooooo!

Such sentimentality is hogwash. That stock wasn't part of Lisa's childhood. It was part of a net worth statement. Stock certificates are like dollar bills. They are money—rich people's money. If Lisa's dad had left her $132,000 in cash, she'd have had no trouble converting it to something else in an instant. But because this particular form of money has a name, *Johnson*, and a traceable history, like a genealogy of sorts, Lisa has come to regard the money like a little brother. *Sell my little brother?* Impossible. *Daddy would roll over in his grave.*

In truth, Daddy would roll over in his grave if he discovered that Lisa *wasn't* selling the stock. He wanted to sell the stock for years, so that he and his family could enjoy the money that the stock represented, to get a little more pleasure out of life, to make life a little easier. The only reason he never sold was because of the taxes he'd have to pay. But Lisa doesn't have that problem. When she inherited the stock, her "purchase price" is deemed to be the stock's value as of the day her dad died—not the date her dad had originally bought the stock.[131] This is called a "step-up in basis," and it means Lisa can sell the stock *without having to pay any taxes!*

If Dad were here today, he'd have only one comment: *"What on earth is she waiting for!?"*

Indeed, Lisa needs to sell the stock, for two reasons. First, the dividend it pays is negligible. If she never sells, and instead passes the stock to *her* children when she dies, the only benefit she'll have gotten from the stock is the dividend—all 1.5% of it. I can hear her Dad now. *"She could get more income from a savings account, for goodness sake. What's wrong with that child!?"*

Second, Lisa is taking a huge risk to leave such a large portion of her assets in just one security. I have nothing against Johnson & Johnson. It's a big, successful company. But so were Eastern Airlines and Studebaker. Neither is

---

[131]She could choose instead the date of six months following her dad's death, if that date's price would result in lower taxes.

around any more. When institutional money managers and mutual funds invest billions of dollars for their clients, they never place more than 5% of a client's assets into any one security, for safety. Lisa, who currently has 65% of her net worth tied up in this one stock, is being wildly aggressive with her investments. She would be much more prudent to manage her money like the professionals do—diversify![132]

These are exactly the reasons why I want her to sell the stock. But she resists, worrying that she'll somehow betray her father. Intellectually, she knows selling the stock would be the prudent thing to do. She just can't seem to bring herself to do it. She's got a mighty bad case of inheritanitis. Fortunately, I have the cure:

"Lisa," I explain to her, "I understand why you feel an emotional attachment to this stock. Don't you suppose that you might feel just as attached if it were a hundred shares instead of two thousand?"

After all, I explain to her, Dad didn't buy 2,000 shares of Johnson & Johnson. He had bought only 100 shares. The rest were obtained via stock splits over the years. So, I suggest that she keep the same number of shares that Dad had originally bought, and convert the rest into something else that would be safer, more appropriate, and possibly even more profitable for her.

She agrees. She will keep the original 100 shares, which satisfies her need and desire to stay connected to Dad. The rest will be used as the basis for a new portfolio.

The problem in this case is obvious: Dad never explained to Lisa why he bought the stock and why he hadn't sold it. If she understood his motivations, she would have had no problem dumping the stock.

There is a lesson here for both donors and recipients. Before you bequeath investments to your children, you must tell them that they will be free to sell any investment they inherit as they wish. And when you receive investments through an inheritance, do not treat them as family heirlooms.

---

[132]See Rule #41.

RULE
#57 DO NOT NAME MINOR CHILDREN
AS BENEFICIARIES OF YOUR
LIFE INSURANCE POLICIES.

If you think naming your kids as beneficiaries on your insurance policies means they will get the money, think again.

If you have children under 18, you've probably made a common mistake with your life insurance policies: You've named your minor children as the policy's *secondary beneficiaries* (having named your spouse as the primary beneficiary).

You made the choice when you applied for the policy, and it made sense to do so. After all, the coverage is intended to protect your spouse and pay for your kids' future college costs. So it seemed logical to name your spouse as the primary beneficiary and, to protect against the unlikely (and unthinkable) event that both you and your spouse might die, you named your kids as the secondary beneficiaries.

Indeed, your life insurance agent (or benefits officer at work) didn't object, so what's the problem?

The problem is that your life insurance agent (and benefits officer at work) are not trained financial and legal advisors. So they don't know—just like you don't know—that kids under 18 do not get inheritances, even if they are named in the policy as the secondary beneficiaries.

Instead, the money will go into the registry of the court, and the judge will name a guardian of the money for the kids. Even if your wills name a guardian for the kids, the money must get its own guardian. Naming a guardian of the money in your will isn't enough, either, because life insurance proceeds go directly to beneficiaries named in the policy.[133] Although you might have named a guardian for the kids in your will (and you'd better, or the court will decide that, too!) it's the policy and not the will that controls the insurance proceeds.

---

[133]Unless the children are under age 18. See *The Truth About Money,* page 522.

Since you named your minor children as beneficiaries, any insurance proceeds beyond $5,000 (in most states, children cannot directly inherit more than that) will be turned over to the court, which will appoint a financial guardian to manage the assets. And it doesn't stop there: Most distributions will then have to be approved by the court. Worse, there is no assurance that the court will appoint as financial guardian the same person you named as the children's guardian.

Chances are, after a year and thousands of dollars in legal fees, the life insurance money will be placed into a guardian account for the kids (until they turn 18, which typically is the latest age that a court may place money beyond the reach of a child). But once they're 18, the kids get the money—and they just might choose a sports car over college, despite your intentions.

What's the solution?

In your will, establish a trust for the child, and name *the trust* as the secondary beneficiary. You can even set up the child's trust inside your own living trust. That avoids probate as well as a court guardianship proceeding—and you get to determine the age you want your kids to receive the money. (You may decide to withhold the funds from them well beyond age 18.)

A second, simpler option is to designate as the insurance beneficiary a custodian for an account established under either the Uniform Gifts to Minors Act or the Uniform Transfer to Minors Act. The insurance money will go directly into the UGMA/UTMA account, which will be managed for the benefit of your kids by the custodian you've named. This custodian can be the same person who's serving as the child's guardian, and distributions can be made at any time for the child's support and education. It's easy to set up a UGMA or UTMA account; any financial advisor, bank, broker, or insurance agent can help you. Be aware, though, that in many states, the money can only be held in UGMAs/UTMAs until the kids turn 18 or 21, while the trust described above allows you to withhold money as long as you wish. To determine whether a UGMA/UTMA or a trust is the better course, first decide whether you object to giving an 18- or 21-year-old unrestricted access to an inheritance.

Protecting your family through life insurance is a smart thing to do, but you need to make sure you handle the policy properly, or your plans could be thwarted. Don't name your kids as direct beneficiaries. That may be the easy thing to do, but it could prove very costly.

RULE #58 DO NOT OWN YOUR OWN LIFE INSURANCE POLICIES.

One of the most attractive features of life insurance is that the death benefit is exempt from income taxes. However, this does not mean the proceeds are *tax-free:* Without proper planning, insurance proceeds could be subject to estate taxes.

Insurance death benefits are considered part of the estate of the person who owns the policy. Even if the policy does not name you as the owner, any incidence of ownership—such as paying the premiums, directing who the beneficiaries are, or borrowing against the policy's cash value—could cause the Internal Revenue Service to regard you as the policy owner. If that happens, the policy's death benefit will be considered to be part of your estate and it will be taxed accordingly.

This doesn't seem logical. After all, you didn't get the money—your beneficiary did. Why, then, is the death benefit placed into your estate? It's simple: From the IRS's point of view, life insurance is an asset, one you gave to your heir, and therefore, like all your assets, it is part of your estate—even though you never reap any benefit!

There's an easy way to eliminate this problem: Simply name someone else as owner of your policies. You also can name some*thing* else—such as a trust. Although this is easy, there is some fine print involved. First, if you die within three years of transferring ownership of your policy to another, the IRS will add the death benefit back into your estate as though you had never transferred it out.[134] Second, if your insurance policy has accumulated more than $10,000 in cash value, simply "changing" the owner to another person or trust could have gift tax consequences.[135] To make sure you're not ignoring the details, be sure you talk with qualified legal and financial counsel before you act. Otherwise, most of your insurance proceeds could be benefiting the IRS instead of your heirs!

RULE #59 DO NOT TITLE ASSETS JOINTLY BETWEEN GENERATIONS.

Parents must not allow their children's names to be added to their assets, such as the house, car, or investment and bank accounts. It's understandable why many families do this. After all, the kids are helping Mom and Dad with their affairs, running to the store for them, picking up a prescription. The kids even might be paying their parents' bills, or balancing their checkbook. Besides, the kids are going to inherit everything anyway, and if you don't add their name to the property, they'll just have to go through probate, which is a very expensive and time-consuming process. Adding a child's name to the account avoids probate, so what's the harm?

Today, plenty. Under **The New Rules of Money**, titling

---

[134]This three-year look-back period does not apply if a different owner is named at the time you purchase the policy.

[135]You are permitted to give up to $10,000 to any one person in any one year with no gift tax problem. If your policy's cash value exceeds $10,000, you could incur a gift tax, and with gift tax rates as high as 55%, that's quite a problem! (See Rule #68.)

assets between the generations is a big mistake, for several reasons:

1. **Adding a child's name to an asset of the parent may convert that child from *heir* to *owner*.**

   Why is this significant? Because heirs do not pay capital gains taxes on appreciated assets, while owners do.[136]

2. **Naming the child as co-owner places the assets at risk.**

   As a co-owner, the child often has unrestricted access to the asset; the child actually could "steal" the money from the parent—though the "theft" would be quite legal. This problem certainly will never happen in your family, I'm sure, but these other problems might: By naming a child as an owner, the asset becomes subject to the claims of that child's creditors. The asset also could be attached in a lawsuit filed against your child. Or it could be listed as a marital asset if your child faces a divorce, and half of it or more could be awarded to a former son- or daughter-in-law that the parent will never see again.

3. **By listing one child as a co-owner on your assets, you accidentally—but effectively—disinherit your other children.**

   If a parent has three children but adds just one to his or her bank account, that child becomes the sole heir to that account—even if the parent has a will that says all three children are to inherit everything equally. Why? Because jointly held assets pass to the survivors directly; the will is irrelevant. Thus, the one child whose name is on the account or deed for convenience gets it all. If that child tries to "do the right thing" by redistributing the asset to his or her siblings, massive gift taxes[137] could be incurred.

---

[136]See Rule #68.
[137]See Rule #68.

For all these reasons, assets must never be titled between generations. If you haven't done it in your family—either between yourself and your parents, or yourself and your kids—don't. But if you have, talk with an estate attorney to see how you can correct the problem.

But wait. If the kids' names aren't added to the accounts, doesn't this mean everyone is stuck with probate? Yes, until you read the next Rule.

RULE #60 FOLLOW THE NEW RULES THAT LET YOU SKIP PROBATE QUICKLY AND EASILY.

Traditionally financial advisors and estate attorneys would routinely recommend that their clients establish Revocable Living Trusts to pass assets to their children. Unlike joint titling of assets, which raises all the problems listed in the previous Rule, living trusts allow you to avoid capital gains taxes, skip probate, and insure that your assets are distributed as you intend.

But living trusts can be a bit cumbersome. You'll pay an attorney several hundred to a thousand dollars or more to draft the trust, and then you've got to retitle all of your assets into the trust itself. It's usually not a big deal, but it can be a bit of a hassle.

Now there's an easier way.

It's called "Transfer on Death," or TOD registration, and it's now available in every state. Similar to the "Payable on Death," or POD, provisions that have been in place for bank accounts for years, TODs allow you to reregister your brokerage and mutual fund accounts to show the names of your heirs.

Unlike a joint registration, where the presence of the child's name would legally constitute co-ownership, a TOD registration has no such problem. By registering the asset as "John Jones TOD Johnny Jones, Freda Jones, and Alice

Jones" (or whatever paperwork your mutual fund or broker requires), you are simply stating that Johnny, Freda, and Alice are to inherit the asset upon John's death. This not only enables everyone to avoid probate, but it avoids capital gains taxes that have accumulated as well.[138]

This is not to suggest that TOD registration is the best course of action for your family. Revocable living trusts offer a variety of additional benefits that may make them preferable, such as keeping your affairs private and within the family, and making it harder for disgruntled heirs to complain. Revocable trusts also enable you to direct how you want your assets to be managed during your lifetime should you become incompetent. For each of these issues, revocable trusts are superior to TOD registrations.

Still, TODs are quick, easy, and free—and a new and better alternative to jointly titling assets between the generations.

RULE #61 FORGET ABOUT GETTING MARRIED. FOCUS INSTEAD ON *BEING* MARRIED.

I received a letter from a reader of my first book, *The Truth About Money*,[139] thanking me for helping him get out of credit card debt. When he got married in 1994, he had little money, so he charged both his wedding and honeymoon expenses to Visa—raising his balance to more than $9,000.

If you are planning a wedding, please do not spend more money than you have. And that applies to the parents as well as to the bride and groom.

Let's face it—weddings are expensive. According to *Bride's* magazine, the average wedding in the United States costs $15,000. In the Washington, D.C., area, according to *Washingtonian* magazine, the average is more than $27,000.

---

[138]Would you *please* see Rule #68 already?!
[139]At a bookstore somewhere.

You don't have to let a wedding send the newlyweds or their parents into financial ruin. All you need to do, quite simply, is scale down. Easier said than done, for sure. After all, the parents of the bride are thinking, "This is my baby girl. I want her to have as beautiful a wedding as my best friend's daughter did. In fact, ours will be even grander." And the bride herself is envisioning all the fairy tales she read while growing up, and she wants a wedding that even Cinderella would envy—a gorgeous white gown, full orchestra, and flowers overflowing the church.

I'm not saying you should forget all that and elope instead. Rather, I merely caution you not to spend more than you can afford.

Let's put this into perspective. Say you invite 200 guests at $50 per person[140]—that's $10,000 just for the reception. Add the costs for the wedding dress and veil ($1,000), band ($2,000), photographer ($2,500), liquor ($2,000), limo ($250), invitations ($600), rehearsal dinner ($1,500), clergy fee and licenses ($250), and more (such as accommodations for out-of-town relatives), and it's easy to see how the bills can add up to $20,000, $30,000, or even $40,000—for an event that will last just four hours!

Many people who cannot afford this expense incur it anyway. They take out home equity loans, borrow against their company retirement plans, or charge the wedding to credit cards. This is financial irresponsibility. And if you are demanding that your parents do this for you, then you are being just plain rude. Are the 240 minutes of fun worth the destruction of someone's financial future?

Being in debt is no way for a bride and groom to start their marriage. Keep in mind that money is the biggest cause of divorce in our country. Why create such stress on your marriage for no good reason? It occurs to me that many of the people who overspend on their wedding are more concerned with *getting* married than with *being* married.

I'm not trying to destroy the Big Day. I just want every-

---

[140]If you think that cost is too high, you haven't shopped banquet prices lately!

one involved to take a deep breath and put the wedding into perspective. It should be a beautiful event, one that you and your family and friends will remember forever—but it shouldn't mean you will be *paying it off* forever.

RULE #62 IF YOU'RE GETTING MARRIED OR ARE NEWLY MARRIED, GET READY FOR A WHOLE SET OF NEW RULES.

Congratulations! You're married—or about to be. And with all the incredible changes that it brings, some of the most important involve money.[141]

Because money is one of the leading causes of divorce,[142] your marriage's success could well be determined by the financial rules and habits that you and your spouse establish. Although this topic may seem mundane, seemingly innocuous questions such as who pays the phone bill are fraught with emotional charges, reflections of your upbringing, and definitions of masculinity, femininity, power, and self-respect, and therefore carry incredible implications for your marriage.

With the two of you sitting at the kitchen table, write down the answers to these questions. When you're done, exchange answers.

1. How much and what kind of debts do you have? Make a list of all your debts, including for each:
   A. The name of the creditor;
   B. The amount of money you owe each creditor;
   C. The minimum monthly payment for each debt;
   D. The term of each loan (meaning when it will be paid off); and
   E. The interest rate each loan is charging you.

---

[141]Surprise!
[142]Or is it the lack of money?

2. Are you behind on any payments? Have you ever missed a payment? Have you ever been turned down for credit? If yes, explain.

3. Has a creditor ever contacted you? If yes, provide details.

4. What is your annual income?

5. Do you plan to work full-time until retirement age? If not, and if you are working full-time presently:
   A. What changes do you plan to make?
   B. When do you plan to make them?
   C. What will it cost to execute these changes?
   D. How will you pay for it?
   Specific and detailed answers are required.

6. Do you expect your partner to work full-time until retirement?

7. What percentage of the family's total household income do you expect to contribute?

8. Which of the two of you will be responsible for paying the bills each month?

9. How much of *your* income are *you* willing to devote to the household's monthly bills? Express your answer in both a dollar amount and as a percentage of your income.

10. How much of *your partner's* income should *your partner* devote to the household's monthly bills? Express your answer in both a dollar amount and as a percentage of your partner's income.

11. How much of *your* income are *you* willing to devote to savings and investments? Express your answer in both a dollar amount and as a percentage of your income.

12. How much of *your partner's* income should *your partner* devote to savings and investments? Express your

answer in both a dollar amount and as a percentage of your partner's income.

13. How much in credit card debt do you think is acceptable?

14. Would you be willing to use *your* income and assets to pay off the debts *your partner* accumulated prior to the marriage? If yes, what percentage of *your partner's debts* would *you* be willing to pay?

15. Should your partner be willing to use *his or her income* and assets to pay off the debts *you* accumulated prior to the marriage? If yes, what percentage of *your* debts should *your partner* be willing to pay?

16. Do you plan to maintain a bank account in your name only?

17. Does it matter to you if your partner maintains a bank account in his or her name only?

18. Should the two of you maintain a joint checking account? If yes:
    A. Should money be contributed to it by you, by your partner, or both?
    B. What percentage of income, should you or your partner contribute?
    Be specific with your answers.

19. Do you have or plan to obtain credit cards in your name only? If yes:
    A. How many cards?
    B. What is or would be your total credit limit?

20. Does it matter to you if your partner maintains credit cards in his or her name only?

21. Should the two of you maintain joint credit card accounts? If yes:
    A. Which of you will use these accounts?
    B. Will the money to pay the charges made on these accounts be contributed by you, by your partner, or both?

      C. In what amounts, and in what frequency
         will these contributions be made?
Be specific with your answers.

22. How many children do you want to have?

23. How soon do you want to have your first child?

24. When your first child is born, will you or your partner
leave the workforce to be a full-time parent? If yes:
      A. For how long?
      B. Which one of you will do this?

25. Are you willing to relocate to another city?

26. Is it your intention to relocate to another city?

27. If you got a windfall of a "significant amount of
money," how much would that be?

28. What would you do with that windfall? Be specific.

Don't bother looking in the back of the book for the correct answers; they aren't there. In fact, there are no "correct" answers—except maybe for Question #13. No, what's much more important is that your and your partner's answers *match*. Don't be surprised if they don't at first. That's expected. But, hopefully, your answers will not be so far apart that, through conversation and compromise, you can't reach understanding and agreement.

Don't worry if your agreements, which sound perfectly natural to the two of you, seem unconventional to others. Among my firm's large number of clients, I have seen hundreds of systems in use—from the couple who invests 100% of her paycheck, using his to pay for all of the family's expenses, to the couple whose husband abdicated complete control of the family's finances to the wife ("I tell him what I'm doing with the money, he gets mad and won't talk to me for two days, and then we both forget all about it—and we've been doing that for 42 years.")—and I can assure you that the system that's *best* for the two of you is the system that *works* for the two of you.

How do you define "what works"? Your system is working if:

1. The bills are being paid on time.
2. You are not increasing your debts; ideally, you are reducing them.[143]
3. You are saving money regularly.
4. Neither of you feels that you have been given undue responsibility for the family finances.
5. Neither of you feels that the other is failing to live up to their financial responsibilities.

One thing you're likely to discover as you begin to meld your finances together is one immutable fact: You are going to have to change how you handled your finances before you got married. Being married is very different from being single, and this wondrous lifestyle change demands an equally tremendous change in how you approach personal finance.

So be aware of this: *Being unwilling to change* will prove deadly to your marriage. If you can't agree on these important questions, or if these questions provoke anguish, dismay, or conflict, then it's highly likely that there are serious matters afflicting your relationship. It's something you might want to think about before you get married.

RULE #63 STOP GIVING YOUR CHILDREN AN ALLOWANCE.

Long gone are the days when Mom would hand her child a nickel for milk money at school, or 50 cents for the Saturday matinee. As any parent raising children today can tell you, kids are a lot more expensive than they used to be.

And kids are going to get even more expensive. If it costs

---

[143]Except for the mortgage, of course. See Rule #21.

you $7.50 to send your kid to the movies today, then it's going to cost your kids $24 to send *their* kids in 20 years, assuming inflation rates remain unchanged.

That's why you need to stop giving your kids an allowance—both to enlist their help in your fight to control costs, and to begin teaching them how money works.

Instead of giving your kids an allowance, hire them. Pay them when they do chores or perform some previously agreed-upon assignment. Just a few points to consider when you do this:

1. Don't overpay them.

If you're going to move someone from welfare to employment, they should be able to earn more money than they were before. Otherwise, why should they bother working? But don't overcompensate them, either. Earning as little as 10% more than they were earning before is more than enough.

2. Make certain you are not engaging in bribery.

You shouldn't have to pay your kids to take out the trash. A household requires everybody's participation to make the place work. Reserve paychecks only for those tasks that are truly worthy of compensation.

3. Do not make all of their compensation performance-based.

Most people work at occupations where doing a great job doesn't result in an increase in income. Teach your kids that doing a great job is often itself the reward—they shouldn't always assume that better performance will result in increased income, either immediately or at all. Of course, if you'd rather teach your children that they'd be foolish to work at any job that doesn't reward performance, go right ahead—but make it clear to them that that is the lesson you're teaching.

4. Teach them about the responsibilities that go with money.

They should be taught to tithe a portion, save a portion, invest a portion, and enjoy a portion.[144] The opportunity to earn money brings with it certain obligations—to their church and community, to their family, to their future, and to themselves! Make sure your child learns that money itself is unimportant; it's what money can do that counts. Through this process, your kids will begin to learn about value and how to assign different values to different things. This will teach them that life is about choices, and how making choices affects them and those around them.

This raises an important point: Once you show your kids how easy it is for them to save money, and how quickly money is able to grow if left alone, you will probably find it difficult to get your children to spend *any* money at all. Although you'll find their propensity to save refreshing and relieving (and somewhat amazing), encourage your kids to find enjoyment in the things that money lets them do. After all, those who only amass money, like Ebeneezer Scrooge prior to his reformation, have little enjoyment of life, and those who fall in love with money indeed fall victim to the root of all evil. Be sure you teach your kids how to love what money can do, not money itself.

5. Withhold taxes.

Sure! Their first employer certainly is going to withhold taxes, so you might as well get them used to it. This will teach them that they cannot count on spending everything they earn, and if you're really clever, you'll set aside the money you're "withholding" and add it to their savings and investments. When they express regret at

---

[144]*Savings* should be defined as money they will spend in a short period, perhaps several months to a year or two, while *investments* should be money they are not planning to spend until college or their first car.

not having accumulated quite enough money to buy a major item, like a car, despite years of savings, you'll be able to produce this additional windfall. You'll not only look like a hero, but you'll have taught them both the benefits of delayed gratification and the time value of money.[145]

When should you start teaching your kids about money? A lot sooner than you think. Studies have shown that children make their first *assisted purchases* (meaning a parent is guiding them through the process) at age three, and their first *unassisted purchases* as early as age five. And they make *a lot* of purchases: According to *Business Week,* kids under 14 spend $20 billion of their own money every year, and they influence another $200 billion in spending. If you don't believe me, ask yourself: Who chose the cereal the kids eat in the morning? It certainly wasn't their Mom. Look at the brand of clothes and shoes the kids are wearing, and the toys you bought them for Christmas. Do you really think *you* made those decisions? Your kids have a very active role in much of the family's daily spending, so you might as well make it official.

Let the 10- to 13-year-olds do the food shopping. Give them the list and the cash, and watch how they perform. Go with them in case they get overwhelmed or stuck. But don't overrule them. If they want to buy tons of ice cream, let them. They'll soon regret the decision when the family runs out of food later in the week. With a little practice, they'll soon be doing fine at this—and spending on junk food probably will go down.

Meanwhile, 14-year-olds and up should help you prepare your tax returns. Worried about letting your kids see how much money you make? Get over it (and read Rule #54). Getting your kids involved with the grittiest of economic realities will give them a huge boost in their efforts to achieve financial success.

---

[145]And you thought you didn't even know what that was.

Your kids are not learning about money in school. If they don't learn about it from you at home, how will they ever get this information?

RULE #64 IF YOU HAVE MONEY OR KIDS, YOU SHOULD SIGN A PRENUPTIAL AGREEMENT BEFORE YOU (RE)MARRY.

Prenuptial agreements, also known as premarital agreements, once were used only by the sensationally wealthy. When Jackie Kennedy was negotiating her prenuptial agreement with Aristotle Onassis, she reportedly demanded $20 million up front. Yet today premarital agreements have become useful to those with, shall we say, more modest means.

Prenuptial agreements often are used to protect children from a prior marriage from becoming disinherited. Before you remarry, you each disclose all your assets and obligations, and you each promise to waive any rights to the other's property at death (or divorce). This enables your assets to pass to your children from your prior marriage.[146]

(If you are already remarried, you probably have a will that says your children are to inherit your assets. But if you think that means your kids are protected, think again. If your new spouse survives you, your plan may be sabotaged, because a surviving spouse may claim property from your estate—even if your will or trust says otherwise. Almost every state has a law that entitles a surviving spouse to a portion of the estate unless that right is expressly waived in a valid agreement. To solve the problem, many turn to a Qualified Terminal Interest Property, or QTIP, Trust. This trust allows your surviving spouse to

---

[146]This waiver usually applies only to property you had in your name prior to the marriage.

enjoy access to the assets during his or her lifetime, but the assets revert to your kids upon your spouse's death.)

Premarital agreements also are helpful if you want to ensure that your assets remain within your bloodline. For instance, say your child inherits your assets upon your death, and later, the child marries and divorces. It is quite possible—even probable—that your assets could be distributed to nonfamily members. You can avoid this problem by placing your assets in a trust and requiring your child to sign a prenuptial agreement with his or her intended before he or she can receive any assets from the trust. It might sound gruff, but it will help ensure that your assets, such as heirlooms or real estate that have been in the family for generations, indeed stay in the family.

Prenuptial agreements must be drafted with care, for they are likely to be challenged when significant assets are at stake. Accordingly, separate legal counsel should represent each party to the marriage.

Prenuptial agreements don't necessarily indicate a lack of commitment to a future mate. Under **The New Rules of Money**, they can be a reasonable step to avoid disappointments or further trauma to children when they lose a parent.

RULE #65 IF YOU ARE FACING DIVORCE, YOU MUST NOW FOCUS YOUR ATTENTION ON THE MONEY, NOT YOUR EMOTIONS.

Divorce is a tragic event, and too often people going through divorce become completely engrossed in the emotional issues, causing themselves to ignore the long-term financial effects of their settlement decree.

The key is to meet with a financial planner before the divorce settlement. As noted by *The Wall Street Journal*, "Pre-divorce financial planning probably makes sense for just about everybody. While a good attorney will know about many of the tax and other financial aspects of a set-tlement, lawyers often suggest that clients sit down with a financial pro to map out their long-term needs." In fact, said the *Journal,* couples who have done proper planning usually reach a settlement faster and with fewer legal fees than those who don't plan.

Here are some key points that can help you plan:

1. Draft your divorce decree carefully,

because most agreements cannot be changed later. It is critical that you think about your needs beyond the next five years.

2. Be sure you understand the difference between child support and alimony.

The former is for the support of children, and most juris-dictions have guidelines to determine the appropriate amount. The latter is more discretionary, and largely up to the judge.

FOR CHILD SUPPORT:

- If you *pay* child support, you get no tax deduction for doing so.
- If you *receive* child support, the income is tax-free to you.
- Child support ends when the child reaches adult-hood, unless otherwise agreed.

FOR ALIMONY:

- The payer receives a tax deduction.
- The receiver must include it in their gross income for tax purposes.
- Alimony ends when the recipient remarries, unless otherwise agreed.

Therefore, it's often in the payer's best interest to call payments "alimony" instead of "child support," and it's usually in the recipient's best interest to receive child support instead of alimony. Although this can create an inherent conflict between the divorcing couple that must be resolved, the bigger crisis arises when one spouse is aware of these distinctions and the other is not.

3. **Make sure your decree requires your ex-spouse to buy and *maintain* insurance**

if you are the recipient of alimony or child support. Securing life and disability insurance policies will ensure that payments to you will continue even if your ex dies or becomes disabled. Also, make sure you are the owner of any such policies. This way you will receive regular statements showing that policy premiums have been made and that the policies remain in effect. It also renders your ex-spouse unable to make changes even though he or she is paying to keep the policies in force.

4. **If you are the economically dependent spouse, you are entitled to some of the other's retirement and pension plans.**

For most people, the two biggest assets they have are their home and their pension or retirement plan. Everyone focuses on the home, but many ignore the ex's company benefits. Basically, workers must give their ex-spouse a share in their pension or retirement plan, or they must give up something else to keep it.

Keep in mind that an ex-spouse keeps his or her rights to the pension or retirement plan even if he or she later remarries. That's because the pension or retirement plan is property acquired during the marriage, and the non-pensioned spouse gets half of whatever was accumulated during that time.

5. **When divvying up your 401(k) or other retirement plans, don't ignore taxes.**

It's very common for a spouse to withdraw money from a retirement plan as part of the divorce settlement, and give the money to the ex, assuming that the ex must pay the taxes. But guess what? That's not how the IRS sees it. If you withdraw money, *you* could owe taxes.

In order for your ex to be responsible for the taxes, you must complete a qualified domestic relations order. The QDRO is kept with your divorce decree or court-approved property settlement, and it must include the name and address of the plan participant and alternate payee; the name and account number of each retirement plan affected; the amount to be paid by each plan to the alternate payee; and the number of payments or the period covered by the QDRO. It should further specify that a QDRO is being established under the state's domestic relations laws and Section 414(p) of the Internal Revenue Code.

Both of you can avoid taxes by having the QDRO specify an amount that is to be rolled over from one's 401(k) or pension plan to the other's IRA. If the money is transferred directly to the IRA, neither spouse will incur any taxes at all.

Make sure you get this right, or you could suffer a huge tax bill that should have been paid by your ex-spouse.

6. Don't let the spouse who handles the investments determine how the investments are split.

The assets should be split equally, meaning each spouse gets half of each asset, based on the number of shares owned—not merely half of the current value of the combined portfolio. If the husband handled all the investments, he'll be more likely to know which of them are worth more than the others.

One client came to me four years after her divorce. While married, her husband had handled the family finances, and when it came time to divorce, he agreed to split their $200,000 portfolio in half. She thought she owned $100,000 worth of investments—but when I examined her portfolio in detail, I discovered that it consisted almost exclusively of highly speculative tax shelters and limited partnerships—most of which had long since gone bust.

It turned out that while the divorce decree required the assets to be split equally, the husband's lawyer had arranged for the split to be based on "original cost" instead of "current market value." The husband, knowing each investment in detail, kept the stocks, bonds, and mutual funds for himself, and gave his soon-to-be–ex-wife the other half of the investments—knowing that her "half" consisted of assets that were by now virtually worthless. So, although they split $200,000 worth of investments equally (based on original cost), he got investments that were currently worth $100,000 and she got investments currently worth almost nothing.

Even if your ex is not acting as deviously as this guy, make sure you factor in the effects of taxes and transaction costs when calculating the value of assets. For example, a $10,000 Certificate of Deposit is worth more than $10,000 in stocks, because in order to sell the stocks, the owner will have to pay transactions costs or capital gains taxes. If you're not financially savvy, the best step (although not necessarily the most cost effective) is to demand that all investments be sold and the net proceeds split according to the divorce decree.

7. Don't ignore inflation.

If an income stream is part of your negotiations, make sure the income will keep pace with the cost of living. Payments should be adjusted for inflation over time, based on changes in the Consumer Price Index or other independent gauges.

8. Protect your credit.

You must understand that when people hold joint credit cards, mortgages, auto loans, or lines of credit, both parties are equally liable for the debt. I have seen several instances where he discovered halfway through the divorce proceeding that she was supporting herself on their joint credit cards—which she had no intention to pay. If you have any joint credit cards or other lines of credit, close them as soon as you feel that the marriage might end, and open new credit card accounts in your name only. Many a separated spouse has been financially ruined by a soon-to-be-ex's spending.

9. Should keeping the house really be your primary goal?

Many people facing a divorce are determined to keep the house. But in reality, you probably can't afford it.

One recent caller to my television show said her husband had left her. "He's demanding the house," she said. "What do I need to do so that I can keep it?" With some prompting, she explained that, four years ago, they bought a $300,000 house. It has a $240,000 mortgage (costing about $2,000 a month). Her income was $65,000; his was $54,000.

I gave her the bad news: Neither of them was going to get the house. Or, more accurately, one of them might get it, but the one who did would not be able to keep it. And therefore she shouldn't even try.

You see, their ability to buy the house was based on their combined income of nearly $120,000. By cutting her household income nearly by half, it'd be virtually impossible for her to keep the house—a fact she'd learn a few months *after* the divorce was settled. Then she'd find herself forced to sell it anyway—except that because she'll have already paid her ex-husband half the value of the house, she'd be footing the bill for all the fix-up and selling expenses—including the real estate agent's 6% commission and any capital gains taxes.

"Don't try to keep the house," I told her. "That house was part of your marriage, and your marriage has ended. Your ability to keep the house has ended with it."[147] If your ex-spouse really wants the house, I told her, turn that fact into a negotiating weapon to win other, more financially valuable concessions.

---

[147]Sometimes I can be really blunt.

That's hard to hear, but a message that needs to be heard. If you plan to divorce, be prepared for a new lifestyle, for it is unlikely you'll be able to maintain the lifestyle you had while you were married. Keep your emotions from controlling your actions, and focus intellectually on the economic realities of your new life, and the new rules that go with it.

RULE #66 WANT TO TRANSFER ASSETS TO YOUR KIDS? DON'T ASK YOUR ADVISOR FOR HELP.

Ask older Americans, and chances are they'll say they plan to leave all their money to their kids. But since 50% of older Americans will need long-term care at some point in their lives, many retirees will go broke before they die—before they have a chance to give their money to their kids.

Indeed, the average cost of a nursing home is $50,000 a year, and Medicare does not pay for it, nor does your health insurance. Therefore, rather than watching a lifetime of accumulated assets be erased by long-term care costs, many Americans seek to preserve the family's wealth by engaging in the strategy known as "asset shifting."

Through this strategy, healthy parents give all their money to their kids; thus, by the time they enter a nursing home, the parents will already be broke—making them eligible for Medicaid, the federal insurance plan for the poor.[148]

Although this can be an effective strategy for protecting your children's inheritances, the notion is fraught with moral and ethical problems—not the least of which is the

---

[148]Make sure you understand the difference between Medicare and Medicaid. Medicare is the federal health insurance plan for the elderly. Everyone over 65 is entitled to Medicare benefits, but Medicare does not pay for long-term care costs. Medicaid, the joint federal/state health plan for the poor, does. So, to get the government to pay for your long-term care costs, you must qualify for Medicaid, and to do that, you must be poor.

fact that asset shifters who can afford it have transferred the cost of their care from themselves to the taxpayers.

Thus the ethical debate: Do middle-class Americans have the right to transfer their assets to their children, thus shifting their long-term care expenses to taxpayers?

Medicaid was designed to protect the truly needy in our society, not to serve as a middle-class tax dodge. If your parents have money, do you believe that they should use that money to pay for their own care, or should they asset shift to protect your inheritance?

If the ethical problems don't dissuade you, maybe this will: Asset shifting is now a federal crime, and professional advisors who help you can be punished with fines and prison terms!

My advice: Do not engage in asset shifting as a way to protect yourself and your family from the costs of long-term care. The better route—the more practical, ethical, economical, and now *legal* solution—is to buy long-term care insurance. Buy it now, for yourself and your parents, before long-term care is necessary.[149] If you wait until the care is needed, it'll be too late.

RULE #67 DO NOT TURN TO LAWYERS FOR FINANCIAL ADVICE.

You're being sued. You need to write a will. You are about to be divorced. You are planning to start a business.

To whom will you turn for professional advice?

If you said a lawyer, you obviously didn't think this was a trick question. No matter, because you're right: You do need an attorney. Not just any attorney, but a litigator for lawsuits, an estate attorney for your will, a divorce attorney if you split up, and a corporate attorney to help you launch that new business.

---

[149]To learn how, see Rule #81.

The law is very complex today, and attorneys now specialize, just as physicians do. It's a foolish client who engages in legal matters without competent legal advice—and it's an equally foolish client who relies on that legal counselor for financial advice.

Lawyers are trained in the law, not in personal and business finance. Often lawyers are as unaware of the financial implications of a decision as you are. That's why you need to see a financial expert at the same time you see the attorney, and that's why my firm's planners and I routinely work with our clients' lawyers and accountants. When they don't have one, we offer referrals or rely on our own in-house experts.

Whom should you see first? Assuming all parties are competent, it doesn't really matter, because we all know when to refer you to the other. As a financial planner, I'd suggest[150] that it probably makes sense to see the financial advisor first, because no matter what the issue is, it often comes down to the money. Because we're good at identifying the issues, we can point you to the right type of specialist, whether it's a retirement plan specialist, third-party administrator, independent trustee, valuation expert, appraiser, mortgage broker, real estate agent, psychologist (!), accountant, or, yes, an attorney.

---

[150]With complete objectivity, of course.

This page intentionally left blank
for lawyer jokes

the new
tax rules

RULE #68

DON'T REFUSE TO SELL APPRECIATED ASSETS MERELY BECAUSE YOU DON'T WANT TO PAY TAXES.

My client, Rudy, needed my help. Not for him—he is a successful architect in Washington, D.C.—but for his mother, Debbie, age 77. A widow in good health, Debbie lives alone in a small apartment in Chicago. Her sole income is Social Security, about $800 a month. Her only assets are some savings and whatever items are in the apartment. Oh yes, and $2.4 million in stock.

It turns out that Debbie's deceased husband had spent his career with one company, and had accumulated about 34,000 shares of the company's stock by the time he retired in 1982. Most of the stock was purchased for a fraction of its current value. Like so many others, this particular stock does not pay a dividend. Thus, for all its value, Debbie receives no income from it. But every morning at breakfast, she looks at the stock's price in the newspaper.

Rudy is worried because his mom needs more money to support herself. So, during a visit to see her son and his family, Rudy brings her by to see me. After listening to Rudy, I ask Debbie if she shares his concern. "Would you like to have more income than you receive?" I ask.

"Why, sure," Debbie replies. "My rent has gone up, and the utilities are higher, too, and it costs a lot to fly out to see my grandchildren. A little more income would be nice."

Then Rudy asks me the big question. "How much income do you suppose my mom can receive?"

"Well," I say slowly, "she's earning about $800 a month now. With a few changes, we can probably increase her income to about $135,000 per year."

"A hundred and thirty-five thousand dollars a year!" Rudy yells, almost falling out of his chair.

"Well, yes," I say, adding quickly, "but that assumes we do not erode principal. If your mom is willing to spend down her assets, then we can probably boost her income to about $200,000 a year—and maybe even more."

Debbie says nothing, but Rudy is clearly agitated. "Did you hear that, Mom? You'd be able to get out of that little apartment! You could travel! Eat out! Go to the theater! Mom, you love going to the theater—you and Dad used to go all the time!"

Debbie smiles, and turns to me. "And how do I get all this income?" she asks. Debbie speaks softly, like you'd expect from a kindly old grandmother who's lived through a Depression and four wars, including the War to End All Wars. Yet you know that behind the face is a mind as sharp as steel tacks.

"You'd have to sell your stock, ma'am," I say, feeling as though I'd just admitted to running over the family cat.

"But if I do that, I'll have to pay taxes, won't I?" I'm not telling her anything she doesn't already know. Clearly her son has had this conversation with her before.

"Well, yes, ma'am, you would," I answer.

"And how much would the tax be?" I feel like a student being grilled by his professor.

"I've already factored the taxes in," I parry, attempting to dodge the question. "The income you'd get of $135,000 would be net of taxes." I'm referring to the tax cost of selling the stock, not the tax cost for receiving the annual income. I'm trying to keep the numbers simple, and to accentuate the positive. I know I'm failing on both counts.

"But how much is the tax?" Debbie asks again, unyielding. I almost expect her to say, "Drop and give me twenty!"

With nowhere to hide, I give in. "Worst case, about $625,000, I figure. Assuming a zero basis in your stock, which is unlikely. So the actual capital gains tax probably would be somewhat less than that, maybe $500,000." It's a weak attempt to turn a horrendous number into merely a terrible number. It doesn't work.

She's smiling now, knowing she's won. With her final

words on the subject, she drives her sword into my spreadsheet. "I can't afford that," she says quietly.

The three of us talk for another 45 minutes, but nobody says anything new. The bottom line is that Rudy's mom cannot bring herself to pay a $625,000 tax bill, which is what would happen if she sold the stock, even though doing so would allow her to earn a six-figure income by investing the remaining proceeds. She prefers to see the glass as half empty, and there's no way for me to overcome that attitude.

Especially when she stirs in a tablespoon of martyrdom. "If I sell, I lose $625,000," Debbie says, "and my children [Rudy and his two sisters] will inherit only $1.8 million. But by leaving the stock alone, they'll get the entire $2.4 million."

No they won't. If she were to die today, owning the stock as she does, she'd lose about $750,000 to estate taxes. The kids would get only about $1.7 million. Besides, Rudy chimes in, "We don't care about the money, Mom! Tamara, Nicole, and I just want to make sure you're okay!"

She is unfettered by this. "I'll just start to give them some of my stock now," she says. "That way, I won't be worth so much when I die and the estate tax will be much less."

No, it won't. For two reasons. First, she will discover that it's impossible to lower the value of her assets merely by making gifts. That's because under gift tax law, gifts of more than $10,000 to any one person in any one year are taxable, requiring the completion of a gift tax return. Therefore, even if she gives the maximum per year to Rudy, his wife, Rudy's two sisters, the sisters' husbands, plus their collective six children, that'd be a total of only $120,000 a year. But if the stock grows by just 6%—and its annual growth rate has been much better than that for decades—it will increase in value by about $150,000. So even if Mom gives away as much as she's allowed, her net worth will still go up. She wouldn't have solved the problem at all.

Besides, if she gives the stock to her kids while she's still alive, they'll simply have to pay the capital gains tax that she is trying to avoid. That's because recipients of gifts retain the donor's cost basis, while an heir receives inheritances with a stepped-up basis.[151]

But if she's that concerned about taxes, then I have the ultimate answer: A Charitable Remainder Trust. With a CRT, the stock could be sold without anyone paying capital gains taxes. She then would be able to receive income for life from the proceeds, and, by combining the CRT with a life insurance trust, still leave everything to her kids and grandkids tax-free. The best part is that she'd be making a substantial gift to the charity of her choice, which in turn would give her a healthy tax deduction for the charitable donation—which would help offset the income taxes she'd owe on the large income she'd be receiving.[152]

Rudy's eyes are wide open, but his mom is unmoved by this fancy advisor talk. I've used all my weapons, even hauled out the big artillery: I tried explaining to Debbie that having her entire net worth tied up in just one stock is extremely dangerous. What if something happens to the company, or to the economy?[153] But I lose anyway. That's because I'm arguing facts, while she's arguing attitude. Attitude always wins.

Two days later, she returns to her small apartment in Chicago, and at breakfast, she looks at the price of the stock in the newspaper.

And that's too bad.

RULE #69 STOP THINKING YOU KNOW WHAT'S IN THE CURRENT TAX CODE.

I would be wrong to say that you don't know anything about the tax code.[154] You likely know quite a bit about tax law.[155] The problem is that most of what you know is out of date,

---

[151]See Rule #56.
[152]Humph. Who says financial advisors can't do neat stuff?
[153]See Rule #87.
[154]Maybe not.
[155]Maybe not.

because Congress changes part of the code each and every year. So, although you came across a particular rule or situation at one time or another, it doesn't mean that that rule is still in effect today.

Sometimes the changes come with much publicity and fanfare, such as the Tax Reform Act of 1986. But more often the changes get little public attention. Consequently, many people adopt attitudes and strategies about money that are, quite literally, obsolete.

Here are just a few examples of the changes that have occurred in the past several years:

- If you plan to claim your newborn child as a dependent, you now must obtain a Social Security Number for the child first.

- If you deduct business expenses, you now need receipts only for expenses that exceed $75 (up from $25).[156]

- Spouses who do not earn an income now are entitled to make an IRA contribution of up to $2,000—but beware: The deductibility rules have not changed since they were changed in 1986.[157]

- Unreimbursed long-term care expenses now qualify for the medical expense deduction. That means they are now tax-deductible if your total medical expenses exceed 7½% of your adjusted gross income.[158]

- Long-term care insurance premiums also are now partially tax-deductible—maybe. To get the deduction, you've got to meet stringent requirements. First, only a certain portion of your premium is eligible for the deduction, based on your age. For example, a 50 year old may deduct up to $375, even though the insurance might cost more than $500.[159] But a 65 year old

---

[156]Because the IRS can't resist making exceptions to exclusions, you still need receipts for lodging expenses regardless of the amount.

[157]Huh?

[158]*Adjusted Gross Income* means your income minus certain deductions. The amount of income tax you pay is based on your taxable income, not on your actual income.

[159]See Rule #81.

can deduct up to $2,000, which is more than enough to buy a basic policy. Still, these deductions are available only if your total medical expenses exceed 7½% of your AGI.

- Life insurance benefits that are received prior to death are now tax-free. Not that you want them.[160]

- If you have medical expenses in excess of 7½% of your adjusted gross income, you now can withdraw money from your IRA to pay for them, without incurring the 10% premature withdrawal penalty. And some people who have separated from employment now also can withdraw money from their IRAs without penalty to pay for health insurance premiums—regardless of whether they've incurred medical expenses.

As important as these changes are, they're nothing compared to the changes created by the newest tax legislation: The Taxpayer Relief Act of 1997. This massive law—with 225,000 words—includes:

- 36 retroactive provisions;
- 114 changes effective immediately;
- 69 changes effective January 1, 1998;
- 5 changes effective later (as much as 10 years later!);
- 285 new sections of the tax code;
- 824 amendments to the tax code;
- $151 billion in tax cuts, the most since 1981; and
- $56 billion in tax increases.

I have examined the new law in great detail. My overall conclusion: The Taxpayer Relief Act of 1997 is as arrogant a name for legislation as I've ever heard. In fact, I grade the law a D. Why? Because it fails to help you if:

- you have no children;
- you have children, but they are adults;

---

[160]Because if you are getting life insurance proceeds while alive, it means you are dying.

- you do not own a home;
- you own a home but do not plan to sell;
- you are already retired;
- you are not saving for retirement; and
- you do not own investments.

So who does the law help? Supposedly, under the new law, you'll be better off if:

- you have children under 17;
- you have children attending college;
- you are selling your home;
- you sell investments.

The problem is that although the law claims to help the people described above, in many cases it won't, thanks to little known and tricky rules buried into the law. Therefore, I'm sorry to say, chances are you'll be very upset once you learn the details of the new legislation—which I'm going to share with you here.

Also, be aware that the new law is extraordinarily complex. Congress and the president have ignored all their previous promises of simplicity. Therefore, in order to enjoy the tax savings offered by the new law, you will find it extremely difficult to conduct your own tax planning or even to prepare your own tax return. Indeed, Congress might as well have titled the new law, "The Financial Advisor's Job Security Act of 1997."

I am particularly disappointed because a very large portion of the law's complex language is completely unnecessary. It is most unfortunate that the congressional tax-writing committees continue to ignore opportunities to keep the rules easy to understand and simple to follow.

Here then is a review of the major sections of the code that affect your personal finances.[161]

---

[161]As with all the information in this book, this information is intended to serve an educational purpose only. As individual circumstances will vary, please do not act on any of the information you see here without first consulting your own advisor.

Tax Credits: Money or Nothing?

Tax credits are highly coveted by astute taxpayers, because they are much more valuable than tax deductions. That's because one dollar in credits saves you one dollar in taxes, while one dollar in deductions saves you from nothing to a maximum of 40 cents. Because they are so valuable, tax credits also are very hard to get, and until now, they've been flat unavailable to most taxpayers. This is why the three new credits offered by the new law have gotten so much media attention. So, let's look at them in detail.

1. The Child Tax Credit.

In 1998, for each of your dependent children who are under age 17, you get a $400 tax credit. In 1999 and beyond, the credit is $500.

- **If you are married,** you lose some or all of the credit if your adjusted gross income is $110,000 or more.

- **If you are single,** you lose some or all of the credit if your adjusted gross income is $75,000 or more.

2. The Hope Scholarship Tax Credit.

Starting in 1998, you get a tax credit of up to $1,500 per student for each of the first two years of college.

- Actually, you must spend $2,000 each year to get each year's credits. Expenses for meals and lodging do not qualify in meeting the $2,000 figure.

- Expenses must be paid in 1998 or beyond and cannot be used to cover academic periods in 1997 or earlier.

- To be fully eligible for the credit, married couples must have an income of less than $80,000 ($40,000 for singles).[162]

---

[162]Also, in case you need to know, you lose eligibility for any year in which the student is convicted of a drug felony. There's nothing funny about this, so why are you laughing?

3. The Lifetime Learning Tax Credit.

An additional tax credit is available for qualified educational expenses, including expenses to acquire or improve job skills.

- You get a 20% credit for the first $5,000 you spend. This increases to $10,000 after 2002.
- **If you are married,** you lose some or all of this credit if your adjusted gross income is $80,000 or more.
- **If you are single,** you lose some or all of the credit if your adjusted gross income is $40,000 or more.
- Half-time students are eligible.

Also, note that expenses must be paid after June 30, 1998, and must be applied to expenses incurred after that date.

It's hard to argue with provisions that provide dollar-for-dollar tax relief. But I do argue, because these don't do that. Why not? Because a huge number of taxpayers who try to claim these credits will find their savings wiped out by the Alternative Minimum Tax.

The what?

Let me explain. The Alternative Minimum Tax was created in the 1980s to prevent rich people from completely avoiding income taxes. You see, back in the '80s, the tax code was filled with exotic exemptions, exclusions, deductions, and credits that enabled you to reduce your taxes substantially—sometimes even to the point where you'd pay no taxes at all. To take advantage of these loopholes, though, you needed to earn (and invest) substantial sums of money—money you likely don't have. As a result, the only people who benefited from these schemes were *rich people*, and Congress hates rich people. So, to make sure rich people weren't able to avoid income taxes altogether, Congress created the Alternative Minimum Tax.

Here's how it works: you first prepare your tax return, taking advantage of all the fancy exemptions, exclusions, deductions, and credits you're entitled to (or which you've maneuvered yourself into). If you've done proper tax planning, you've minimized your taxes or even avoided them completely. But thanks to the AMT, you have to redo your taxes, using a different set of tax forms—the AMT forms—and under the AMT, you're not allowed to claim as many of the "tax preference items" (as the fancy loopholes are called) as you did on your regular return. If the AMT calculation shows you owe more than you owed on the regular tax forms, you must pay the higher amount. Thus the name: the AMT makes sure that you pay an *alternative minimum tax*.

Through the AMT, not only do you not get to take advantage of all the fancy tax-saving strategies you worked so hard for, but your tax return is more complicated than ever (and more expensive, too). Essentially, you have to prepare your taxes twice—once normally, and once again for the AMT. Since only rich people have been affected by all of this, nobody but rich people have cared about the AMT—and nobody cares (at least on Capitol Hill) if rich people are unhappy.

The problem is that Congress hasn't changed its definition of "preference items"—and tax credits are still on the list. Thus, anyone who claims the Child Credit, the Hope Scholarship Credit, or the Lifetime Learning Credit now must do their tax return *again,* to determine if they are subject to the AMT. You'll almost certainly have to hire a professional tax advisor, because few mortals are able to calculate the AMT on their own. Not only will this cost you more money and aggravation, but you're likely to lose some or all of the tax credits you thought Congress was giving you in the new tax law.

"But the AMT shouldn't affect me!" you say. *"I'm not rich!"*

Oh, yes, you are—at least as far as Congress is concerned. Taxpayers with incomes as low as $41,350 will fall under AMT scrutiny. As a result, in some cases, those who think the new credits will cut their taxes by $2,000 will discover that the AMT makes them pay back $1,500 of the savings.

This is supposed to be Taxpayer Relief?

Before you start complaining, consider those that the law ignores, such as childfree couples, and those whose children are already grown, not attending college, or who already incurred college debt. Still others are left out, too, including those whose children have won academic or athletic scholarships and who therefore are not spending money on college. The law seems to unfairly penalize those whose children are achievers.

All these groups will say that the credits should have been made available for everyone, not just for certain groups of people who behave in a certain way. And the final argument is that the credits don't go far enough—Congress should have made them far more generous, and with far fewer and less complicated restrictions.

Grade: D. Which just proves that no matter how hard you try, you just can't please everyone. Or, when it comes to taxes, you can't please *anyone*.

The Capital Gains Tax Is Lower, But More Complex

Unless you've been riding alongside the Mars Rover, you've heard by now that the capital gains tax has been reduced to 20% from 28%. Well, what you've heard is wrong. Or, more accurately, incomplete.

Thanks to the new law, there now are not one, not two, not three, but *nine* capital gains tax rates, and to make matters worse, there are lots of conditions, exceptions, and exclusions. The actual tax rate depends on a combination of how long you own the asset, what type of asset it is, what your ordinary income tax bracket is, and when you bought or sold the asset.

Welcome to your first lesson in "How to Create a Really Complex Tax Code." Here is the truth about capital gains, but let me warn you: This is going to get messy.

- **If you own an asset for 12 months or less,** the gain is taxed at the same rate as you pay for everything else. In other words, there is no capital gains tax cut for "short-term capital gains." This part of the law is not new.

- **If you own an asset for more than 12 months and up to 18 months,** the gain is taxed at 28% (even if your ordinary tax bracket is higher) or 15% (if your ordinary bracket is 15% or lower). These are now called "mid-term capital gains."

- **If you own an asset longer than 18 months,** the gain is taxed at 20% (even if your ordinary tax bracket is higher) or 10% (if your ordinary bracket is 15% or lower). These are now called "long-term capital gains."

- **If the investment was sold between May 7 and July 28, 1997,** you can use the 20% rate if you owned the asset more than 12 months. Don't ask why.

- **If you buy an asset after December 31, 2000, then hold it for at least 5 years,** the gain will be taxed at 18% (even if your ordinary bracket is higher) or 8% (if your ordinary bracket is 15% or lower).

- **If your ordinary tax bracket is 15%,** you can use this lowest rate as of 2001, **but if your ordinary tax bracket is 28% or higher,** you can use this lowest rate only for assets you purchase after 2000 (effectively giving the lowest-bracket taxpayers a five-year head start. So much for fairness.)

- **Exclusion for gains from collectibles.** This means that gains from selling your baseball cards (like you're going to declare those gains anyway) will be taxed at 28%. And they created **an exception to the exclusion:** Certain coins and bullion do indeed qualify for the lower capital gains rates, even though they are collectibles. Naturally, certain other coins and bullion are excluded from the exception to the exclusion. Are you following all this?

- **Exception for gains that result from depreciation of investment real estate.** If you don't know what depreciation is, then you don't own investment real estate, so you needn't fuss over it. But if you do own investment real estate, start fussing—because profits attributable to depreciation will be taxed at 25%, not the more favorable 20% rate.

- **Another exception, this one for gains on small business stock.** Casual investments in stocks and stock mutual funds don't count, but if you somehow do qualify (you probably won't), the tax is just 14%. Remember: It's the *trade* date that determines the holding period, not the settlement date. And naturally, there's an **exception to the use of the trade date for most installment sales.** After May 6, 1997, you can use the dates you receive each installment sale payment to establish eligibility for the lower capital gains rates, instead of the trade date.

I give this part of the law a grade of B. The rate reduction is nice (though no financial planner worth his fee will ever defend any capital gains tax higher than zero), but the array of rates, dates, exceptions and exclusions is dizzying. Couldn't Congress have accomplished its goal with far fewer variations?

Selling Your Home?
The Tax Is Simpler—But Not Lower

The best way to begin understanding the new law is to forget everything you knew about the old law, because the new law is *completely* different.

If you sold your principal residence (*read*: your home), on or after May 7, 1997, the gain is taxed under the new capital gains rates, with one twist: the first $500,000 (for married couples; $250,000 for singles) of gain is excluded from the capital gains tax.

This means:

- Anyone who sells a home is entitled to the $500,000 exclusion—not just those 55 and older. You can use this new exclusion even if you used the old $125,000 exclusion. Pretty cool.

- The home must have been your primary residence for at least two of the five years before the date of sale. You do not have to live in the home when you sell it. The old law was three-in-five. Cool.

- You can claim $500,000 even if just one spouse owns the home, though both must meet the two-in-five rule. If you do, even divorced or separated spouses can use the exclusion—even if they've moved out. Very cool.

- You can use the new $500,000 exclusion every time you sell your primary residence (but no more than once every two years). The old law let you use the exclusion just once, and only up to $125,000. Under the old law, if you only used, say, $75,000, you forfeited the other $50,000. Now, you get to use the full $500,000 every time you sell your home. Extremely cool.

- The exclusion will be prorated if unforeseen events, such as a job change or illness, make you unable to meet the two-year time requirement.

- If you signed a contract to sell your home between May 7 and August 5, 1997, you can choose (a) the old law's option of deferring the gain, (b) the old law's "age 55 or over one time exclusion" option, *or* (c) the new law's $500,000 exclusion—whichever works best for you. Totally cool.

- Only one piece of fine print: If you converted rental property to a principal residence, you can't use the new $500,000 exclusion on gain attributable to depreciation taken after May 6, 1997. No biggie.

The bottom line from all this: Assuming that your gain is $500,000 or less, you now can rent your next home or buy a less expensive home, without incurring any capital gains tax—*regardless of your age.*

Grade: B. The new law makes life much simpler—which is supposed to be one of the goals of tax reform. The old law required you to consider such factors as your age, marital status, the price you paid for the house you sold, the price you pay for the replacement home, and other considerations. But none of these details matter anymore. With the new law, you can sell your house whenever you want and choose to buy or not buy a replacement house—it doesn't matter, because for the overwhelming majority of Americans, the results will be the same: You will not pay a capital gains tax when you sell your house.

So why am I not awarding this an A? Because while the law has made your life simpler, it isn't fairer. Yes, the $500,000 exclusion *sounds* a whole lot better than the old $125,000 exclusion, but it's really not that much of an improvement. That's because most houses in this country are worth less than $150,000, meaning that the typical homeowner never will accrue a gain of more than $125,000—let alone $500,000. By this notion, Congress could have created a $5 million exclusion! It wouldn't make any difference, because if no one has such a gain, then "excluding" it doesn't cost Congress any money to "give" it to you.

But there's a flip side Congress hopes you don't notice: you still get no deduction if you sell your house for a loss. Congress argues that this is only fair, since it is giving up the tax of your home's profits. But in truth, it's not fair at all, because very few people have huge gains when they sell their house, while *lots* of people have big losses, thanks to the weak real estate market of the past 10 years.

If Congress truly wanted to be fair about it, they would have treated home sales like all other assets—taxing profits while letting losses be tax deductible.

So, the new law contains a neat trick: Congress gives us a deal we really can't use but that doesn't cost it anything, while denying us a deal we could have used but that would have cost it a fortune. So, for its foxlike cleverness, Congress loses its grade A. That'll teach 'em.

One final observation. Under the old law, the only way

for those under age 55 to avoid taxes when selling their house was to buy a more expensive replacement home. The new law has eliminated this requirement: Taxwise, all home sellers (regardless of age) can buy any replacement home they want, regardless of price. In fact, sellers don't even have to buy *any* replacement—if they wish, they instead can rent for the rest of their lives, with no tax problem.

Will this create a problem in the real estate market? Since sellers no longer have a tax incentive to "buy up," the upper end of the marketplace could soften significantly as the low end replace their homes with other low-end homes, and the upper end, too, replace theirs with new low-end homes. This could be very bad news for the upper end of the real estate market, and we're not convinced that lawmakers (or the real estate lobbyists) considered this potential problem.

New Rules for—and Types of—IRA Accounts

Talk about confusing! There are now five types of IRAs—deductible, rollover, nondeductible, Roth, and Education—and each has its own eligibility rules and conditions for assessing or waiving taxes and penalties. Which should you use? Let's look at each one.

1. THE DEDUCTIBLE IRA

This is the one you know and love, and it remains largely intact. For those who qualify, contributions are tax-deductible, and the profits grow tax-deferred. When you withdraw the money after age 59½, the profits are taxed at your ordinary income tax rate. Withdrawals prior to age 59½ are subject to taxes plus a 10% penalty.[163]

The new law claims to let more people contribute, but the claim is overblown. To wit:

---

[163]There is an exception to the penalty for early withdrawals, a process known as Substantially Equal Periodic Payments, but it's dumb and no one uses it. Forget I mentioned it.

- **If you are married** and your household income is $50,000 or less, you will be able to fully contribute to a deductible IRA starting January 1, 1998. (The old limit was $40,000.) After 1998, the limit will rise just $1,000 per year through 2002, then jump to $60,000 in 2003, $65,000 in 2004, $70,000 in 2005, $75,000 in 2006, and the new ceiling will top out at $80,000 in 2007.

- **If you are single** and your household income is $30,000 or less, you will be able to contribute to a deductible IRA starting January 1, 1998. (The old limit was $25,000.) The limit will rise just $1,000 per year through 2002, then jump to $40,000 in 2003, $45,000 in 2004, and the new ceiling will top out at $50,000 in 2005.

As small as these increases sound, they're actually even smaller, because inflation will erode their value over the next 10 years.

Starting in 1998, a nonworking spouse will be able to contribute up to $2,000 even if the working spouse is covered by a retirement plan, provided all the other requirements are met.

2. THE ROLLOVER IRA

These rules have not changed: When you move money from a company retirement plan to an IRA, it goes to a rollover IRA rather than to a deductible IRA. Why? Because you took the deduction when the money was initially contributed, and Congress doesn't want you to get a second deduction just for moving the money. The rollover IRA's withdrawal rules are identical to those for the deductible IRA.

3. THE NON-DEDUCTIBLE IRA

You're familiar with this one, too. People who are not eligible to contribute to the deductible IRA are permitted to place money here instead. You don't get the tax deduction for making the contribution, but the profits will grow tax-deferred, with withdrawals of the profits taxed as ordinary income. But don't do this—and to see what you should do instead, read Rule 77.

4. THE ROTH IRA

This is new, and quite interesting too, though not as great as it first appears. Named after the U.S. senator from Delaware who sponsored the bill, this new IRA can be used beginning in 1998. Like the non-deductible IRA, you can contribute up to $2,000, and while you don't get a tax deduction for doing so, the money will grow tax-deferred. But unlike the regular and non-deductible IRAs, withdrawals from the new Roth IRA will be completely *tax-free,* provided:

- You leave the money in the account for at least five years after making the first contribution and
- You reach age 59½ (with exceptions for death or disability).

Thus, someone who contributes at 54 years old or younger will be able to withdraw the profits tax-free at age 59½, while those 55 and over will have to wait five years. Also:

- You will be able to withdraw your original contributions at any time without penalty;
- Unlike deductible and non-deductible IRAs:
  —You are not required to begin making withdrawals by age 70½, *and*
  —You are permitted to continue making contributions after age 70½.

To be fully eligible to contribute to a Roth IRA, your adjusted gross income must be $150,000 or less if you're married, or $95,000 if you're single.

So far so good? Okay, then, consider this: If your adjusted gross income is below $100,000, you are permitted to move your existing IRA accounts (both regular and non-deductible) to the new Roth IRA without incurring the 10% penalty; the tax, though, will still be due. If you agree to do this and make the transfer in 1998 you can pay the tax that's due over four years.

Should you?

In a word, no. But thanks, Senator Roth, for the offer.

Actually, in keeping with the spirit of the tax law, allow me to offer our own exception to this advice: *No,* do not transfer your existing IRA to the Roth IRA *unless* you can afford to pay for the tax you'll owe out of earned income. Here's why:

Your current IRA is growing tax-deferred. When you make withdrawals at retirement, the income will be taxable. That's version (a). Here's version (b): You withdraw the money now, pay the tax that's due over the next four years and move the remaining assets to the Roth IRA, where you will later withdraw the balance tax-free. If you compare (a) and (b) on a spreadsheet, you'll discover that, at retirement, there isn't any difference: You'll end up with the same amount after taxes, regardless of whether you use version (a) or (b). And, of course, that has to be true, for if moving to the Roth IRA would save you money, Congress wouldn't let you do it!

But while version (b) doesn't save you money, it does increase revenue for the government. That's because moving money to the Roth IRA now causes you to pay taxes today instead of paying those taxes years from now, and Congress is happy to collect the cash sooner rather than later.

So what, you might be saying. *I don't mind giving Congress the revenue now, provided I don't increase my costs.* But you could be, because although moving to the Roth IRA means future withdrawals are to be tax-free, this will prove true *only if the rules don't change*. It's quite possible that you could unwittingly find yourself moving to the Roth IRA today (incurring a tax) only to find yourself forced to pay taxes again later because a future Congress needs the money.

Also, note that I said the spreadsheet calculations reveal no difference. This assumes that your tax bracket never changes. This is not necessarily a valid assumption, and if your future tax bracket is higher than today's bracket, then moving to the Roth IRA is a winning strategy, but if your future bracket is lower than today's, moving to the Roth IRA is a loser. At our firm, we never gamble on such things as future rates of return, inflation rates, interest rates—or tax rates, so I'll leave that speculation to your crystal ball.

So, based on all this, why are we endorsing the idea of moving to the Roth IRA *if* you can afford to pay for the tax out of earned income? Because it would allow you to move the full value of your IRA from an account where it will one day be taxed to an account where it will not be taxed. Assuming Congress plays fair (which is what I'm assuming), that's a pure winner. But to pull that off, you must have enough income to be able to pay the increased taxes you'll incur over the next four years.

For example, say you have $100,000 in your current deductible or non-deductible IRA. Moving that money to the Roth IRA will force you to incur a tax of as much as $40,000 (not counting the state income tax liability; unlike the feds, your state will *not* let you pay over four years!). That means you must come up with $10,000 per year for four years. If you can cover that cost with your salary and other income, or by adjusting your expenses, then moving to the Roth IRA is a great idea—but the Roth IRA is not a good idea if you must sell other assets or liquidate other investments in order to pay the taxes that will be due.

A final note: Although non-deductible IRAs still are permitted, there's no reason to contribute to them, since the Roth IRA is basically the same thing, only better (since withdrawals from the Roth will be tax-free while withdrawals from non-deductible IRAs will be taxable).

So, that covers what to do with your existing IRAs. But what about future contributions? To which account should you contribute in 1998—a regular IRA or a Roth IRA?

The answer: *neither*. The best place to invest is your company retirement plan, because doing so will enable you to contribute far more than just $2,000. Besides, in many companies, employers match some or all of your contributions, further boosting your profits. And all the money you contribute will give you a current tax deduction, something you don't get from the Roth IRA ('tis better to get a tax break today than a tax break tomorrow. A bird in hand...)

- *If you are eligible* to participate in a company retirement plan, do so to the maximum extent you are permitted—but only to the extent that such contributions are tax-deductible. (Do not place after-tax contributions into your company retirement plan.) Then place $2,000 into the Roth IRA. After that, continue investing for your retirement with a variable annuity.

- *If you are **not** eligible* to participate in a company retirement plan, then invest $2,000 in the Deductible IRA. After that, continue investing for your retirement with a variable annuity.

Got it?

5. THE EDUCATION IRA

This new non-deductible "IRA" (it ought to be called an IEA) allows you to contribute up to $500 per child per year, beginning January 1, 1998. A married contributor (meaning the person investing the money) must have an adjusted gross income of less than $150,000, while singles must earn less than $95,000 to make the full contribution. What's the point? This:

- You can withdraw the money tax-free if you use it to pay for college.

- If the child doesn't need the money for college, you

can transfer the account to another child of the same family.

- If the child doesn't attend college, you must withdraw all the money from the Education IRA—paying taxes and that 10% penalty in the process—when the child turns 30.

Ever see a child facing a plate of vegetables he doesn't want to eat? That's my take on Congress's attitude regarding the Education IRA: It didn't want to offer a tax break for education, but us taxpayers weren't about to excuse Congress from the table. So, while we weren't looking, Congress slipped the veggies to the dog, hiding under the table. Then, with much bravado, Congress proudly presented to us the empty plate, with a broad grin, saying, *"Here! Look what a good job I've done!"*

Not exactly. The truth is that the Education IRA, as written, stinks[164]—and you should stay away.

For one thing, the law has big loopholes that will have to be closed. For example, it appears that anyone can open an Education IRA for any child—despite the fact that the law imposed income limits on the child's parents. (Thus, it appears, nonqualifying parents simply can ask a grandparent, brother-in-law (or, for that matter, an independent trust company) to open the account for them. But that might go against the spirit of the law, putting you in trouble with the IRS. The law also isn't clear about whose Social Security number is to be used on the account—a detail that can be very important when making withdrawals. I'd wait until they clarified the rules—and the intent—before opening an account.

But there's an even bigger, more complex problem: The Education IRA is not compatible with other college planning strategies. Use it and you lose other, better, opportunities. To understand why, realize that the proper way to approach college planning is, first, to con-

---

[164]Blunt enough for you?

tribute as much as possible to the effort, and, second, to end up with as much money as possible. Naturally, the more you save, the more you're likely to have in the end. And of the four ways you can save for a child's college—saving money in your name, saving in the minor's name (under the Uniform Gift to Minors Act), participating in tuition prepayment plans, and using the new Education IRA—the worst is the Education IRA. Here's why:

1. If you contribute to the Education IRA, you cannot also contribute to a tuition prepayment plan. And the pre-payment plan lets you put away much more than the Education IRA.[165]

2. The Education IRA lets you invest only $500 per year. By contrast, you could invest unlimited amounts into a UGMA account—and since the UGMA's first $1,300 of earnings enjoy special tax breaks, you could invest $10,000 or more with the same tax benefits as the Education IRA—but by having so much more invested, your ending value will be far greater.[166]

3. If you withdraw money from the Education IRA to pay for college, you can't also take the Hope Scholarship Tax Credit or the Lifetime Learning Tax Credit for that same student in that same year. This is the ultimate scam: Congress creates two new features to the tax code—the education tax credits and the Education IRA—and brags about how both of them will help parents with college planning, knowing that no parent will actually be able to use both benefits for each child.

To summarize, I don't like either the tuition prepayment plans or UGMA accounts (as you know from reading Rules 9 and 10). Yet both of them, I must admit, are bet-

---

[165]Not that you want to contribute to a tuition pre-payment plan. See Rule #10.
[166]Not that you want to contribute to a UGMA account. See Rule #9.

ter than the Education IRA. Therefore, the Education IRA must be reeeeeeaaaaaaalllllllly bad. And it is. Stay away.

NEW PENALTY-FREE WITHDRAWALS PERMITTED

Starting January 1, 1998, for all but the Education IRA, you now may make penalty-free withdrawals for college or to buy a home.

For college:

You may withdraw an unlimited amount, and use the money for yourself, your spouse, your child or grand-child.

For home-buying:

You may withdraw up to $10,000 for yourself or your spouse, child, grandchild or "ancestor," provided the recipient is (a) a first-time home buyer (defined as someone who has not owned a home in the past two years, not necessarily someone who has never owned a home) and (b) hasn't ever received more than $10,000 from such withdrawals, regardless of source.

I am unimpressed by these new provisions, because any use of retirement assets for anything other than retirement is certain to haunt you in later years. Never use your IRA for anything other than retirement. Period.

SPECIAL NOTE REGARDING DEDUCTIBLE AND NON-DEDUCTIBLE IRAS AND COMPANY RETIREMENT PLAN ASSETS

Two of the four notorious "Goldilocks Rules" have been repealed. The first, the 15% penalty for withdrawing "too much" money from your IRA and company retirement plan, had been "temporarily" repealed through 1999 by previous legislation. The new law now makes that repeal permanent.

The other Goldilocks Rule repealed is the 15% "too little"

penalty for having accumulated too much money in your IRA or retirement plan and then failing to withdraw it during your lifetime. Both of these penalties were widely attacked as "success taxes," punishing people, in essence, for having the fortitude to save large amounts of money.

Now, only two penalties remain: the "too early" penalty (10% for making withdrawals prior to age 59½) and the "too late" penalty (50% for failing to withdraw minimum amounts beginning at age 70½).

My grading for all this is as follows:

The Deductible IRA: B+.

Greatly expanding eligibility for deductible IRAs is excellent, but no A will be awarded until every working American is eligible—which is how the law read prior to The Tax Reform Act of 1986.

The Roth IRA: C-.

Nice idea, but poorly executed and clouded with too many restrictions. It also requires far too much computation to determine its viability and suitability for each taxpayer's situation. We worry that too many people will use the Roth IRA who shouldn't, and others won't who should. Such results can only be blamed on poorly structured legislation. Still, we're pleased to see that no one will have any excuse for contributing to a non-deductible IRA anymore.

The Education IRA: F.

Any new opportunity to save on a tax-advantaged basis is excellent (the pure definition of an "A" grade), but $500 seems an awfully small number considering the massive cost of college these days. And people who don't have children will feel very left out. Where's the car-buying IRA for childfree Americans? Finally, the fine print is horrible.

Elimination of the two Goldilocks Rules: A-.

That's great as far as it goes, but Congress has two more to go to score that A+.

Overall: C+.

The new law offers average improvement, but much more is needed.

Much Fanfare but Little Change for Estate Taxes

Without question, this is the most fraudulent section of the new law. Both Congress and the president are bragging about the improvement they've made in this area, but their claims are a sham.

Under the old law, individuals who die may pass up to $600,000 in assets to their heirs with no estate tax. This figure has not been raised in years, and with tremendous gains in the stock market and real estate values over the past 15 years, many more Americans were falling victim to this ultimate "success tax" than Congress intended. Therefore, the new law increases this exemption to $1 million—or so everyone in Washington wants you to believe.

But it's a scam. Here's why: Under the new law, the exemption does not increase to $1 million on January 1, 1998. It does so on January 1, 2006—*almost 10 years from now!* For 1998, the exemption rises a paltry $25,000, to $625,000. Here's the schedule of increases, according to the new law:

```
1998 = $   625,000
1999 = $   650,000
2000 = $   675,000
2002 = $   700,000
2004 = $   850,000
2005 = $   950,000
2006 = $ 1,000,000
```

By the time you are able to shelter $1 million in assets from the estate tax, guess what? Thanks to inflation (let alone a healthy economy) your net worth will have more than doubled—meaning you'll have the very same tax problem in 10 years as you have today.

Assuming, of course, that Congress makes no changes in the next 10 years. *But that's maybe three presidents from now!* Are you willing to bet no more changes to the law will occur between now and then? Our conclusion: this "increase" in the exemption will have no effect on our estate planning strategies, or indeed, on the need for you to complete a comprehensive estate plan.

Congress and the President also are high-fiving each other over the new protection for family-owned farms and businesses. Many are destroyed when the parents die, because the kids are forced to sell the business to raise the cash to pay the taxes—which not only causes the children to lose the family farm or business, but also throws them out of work.

To solve this problem, the new law lets owners of family farms and businesses exclude their farm or business (up to $1.3 million worth) from the estate tax. Sounds great—until you look at the fine print, which is a doozy:

- The farm or business must represent at least 50% of your net worth, which penalizes those who manage to save money by creating and operating a successful business.

- If you use the $1.3 million exemption, you can't also use the $600,000 exemption—which means, effectively, that by protecting your business, everything else you own will be taxed—at rates ranging from 37% to 55%.

- In order to use the $1.3 million exemption, your heirs must materially participate in the business *for at least five of eight years* within 10 years of your death. How in the world are you going to assure that—and what if your heirs aren't involved in the business *now*?

These conditions are so onerous that the new law offers little relief to anyone (except perhaps for business owners whose primary asset is their business, and who have all their heirs working full-time in the business, and provided that the owner dies within the next few years, before the $600,000 climbs to $1 million).

Despite the truth about the new estate tax law, you are sure to hear our elected officials proclaim how they've helped affluent Americans, farmers, and family businesses. This is politics at its worst. Grade: F.

Others Items Worth Noting

NEW DEDUCTION FOR STUDENT LOAN

Further demonstrating the President's efforts to make college more affordable, beginning in 1998, you can deduct some of the interest you pay for student loans, even if you don't itemize deductions on your tax return. You can now deduct up to this much of student interest each year:

1998	$1,000
1999	$1,500
2000	$2,000
2001 and after	$2,500

- **If you are married,** you lose some or all of this deduction if your adjusted gross income is $60,000 or more.

- **If you are single,** you lose some or all of the deduction if your adjusted gross income is $40,000 or more.

But note: you get no deduction for student loans you incurred prior to 1998.

PENALTIES WAIVED ON ESTIMATED PAYMENTS

With many retroactive changes in the new law, 1997 underpayment penalties have been waived if, as a result of the changes, you underpaid your taxes.

RULES RELAXED REGARDING BUSINESS USE OF THE HOME

Starting in 1999, you will be entitled once again to take a tax deduction if you use a portion of your home exclusively for business, provided that you conduct substantial administrative or management activities there. Congress passed this section in order to overturn a 1993 Supreme Court ruling that severely restricted most home-based business owners from taking the deduction. But beware of a new tax trap: if you *ever* depreciate the home office, you won't *ever* be entitled to the full $500,000 exclusion when you sell your home. (Under the old law, this wasn't a problem provided you didn't take the home office deduction in the year you sold the house. No longer.)

UNDERPAYMENT PENALTY EASED

Individuals who do not fall under one of the special "safe harbor" rules and underpay their estimated income tax (either through withholding or estimated payments) for tax years beginning after 1997 do not have to pay an underpayment penalty if their total underpayment is less than $1,000. Under pre–1997 tax law, the threshold is $500.

CHARITABLE MILEAGE RATE INCREASED

To 14 from 12 cents per mile, effective January 1, 1998.

ESTIMATED TAX PAYMENT RULES HAVE BEEN MODIFIED
BUT ONLY FOR A WHILE

Under current law, if you have a significant increase in income *this year,* you can pay 110% of *last year's tax* (evenly throughout the year) and then ante up the balance next April 15th, interest- and penalty-free.

Under the new law, the 110% figure will be changed to 100% for 1998, 105% for 1999–2001, 112% for 2002, then back to 110% for 2003. Considering we'll end up where we started, it makes you wonder why Congress has gone to such trouble to rewrite the law.

And finally...

FEEL FREE TO PAY BY CREDIT CARD

Starting in 1999, you'll be able to pay your taxes with your credit card. I refuse to comment on this development.

And Just So Congress Could Prove It Has a Sense of Humor

Sec. 908. Modifies the tax treatment of hard cider. No word about soft cider.

Sec. 910. Clarifies authority to use semigeneric designations on wine labels. I don't know about you, but I never drink generic wine.

Sec. 911. Grants authority to postpone tax deadlines by reason of presidentially declared disaster. Gee, sorry to hear that your house was swept away by a flood. But look at the good news: You don't have to file your income taxes by April 15. (Of course, you'll owe interest for every day you delay; Congress merely waived—and for just three months—the *penalty* for failing to file on time, lest it be perceived as being too nice.)

Sec. 935. Places a moratorium on defining what a limited partner is. Good thing, too, because no person who has ever ventured into that hole has ever come back alive.

Sec. 966. Timeshare associations are to be taxed like other homeowners associations. Glad they cleared that up.

Sec. 969. Reporting has been simplified for business meal expenses for individuals involved in federal criminal investigations. I assume they're referring to the federal investigators, not to the crooks being investigated.

Sec. 1021. Reporting of certain payments made to attorneys. I'm afraid to ask what kind of payments Congress is talking about.

Sec. 1033. Restoration of Leaking Underground Storage Tank Trust Fund taxes. I didn't know there *was* a leaking underground storage tank trust fund, or that it once paid taxes. Nevertheless, I'm glad it will pay taxes once again.

Sec. 1034. Application of communications tax to prepaid telephone cards. Glad to see that Congress is keeping up with technology.

Sec.1283. Repeal of authority to disclose whether a prospective juror has been audited. What bothers me is that this requires *repeal*.

Sec. 1418. Foreign embassies may purchase domestically produced beer tax-free. Like this is going to encourage the ambassador from Germany to order a Bud Lite.

Sec. 1419. Beer may be purchased tax-free for destruction. This one is going to require *a lot* of explanation.

Sec. 1435. Skydivers are exempt from the airline ticket tax. They successfully argued that since skydivers don't land with the plane, they should be exempt from having to pay. But what happens if one guy chickens out?

RULE #70 THE TIME TO DO YOUR TAXES IS NOW JUNE 1, NOT APRIL 15.

April is no longer the time to focus on your tax return. Instead, you need to think about taxes in *the preceding June*—while enough time remains in the year for you to make changes that can really help you avoid penalties next tax season.

You have two goals: First, you don't want to owe the IRS any money when you file your taxes in April. Second, and equally important, you don't want to get a big tax refund, either—because if you do, that means you've overpaid your taxes for the year and have given the IRS free use of your money. Getting a refund might be a nice feeling, but it reflects poor money management. So here's how to make sure you're planning for your taxes correctly:

First, do you expect this year's taxable income to be more or less than last year's?

If this year's income will be higher than last year's income

Did you earn[167] **less than** $150,000[168] last year? If so, then during the year, make sure you send the IRS an amount at least equal to what you owed last year. This is known as "the 100% rule."

Did you earn **more than** $150,000 last year? If so, then during the year, make sure you send the IRS an amount at least equal to 110% of what you owed last year. This is known as "the 110% rule."

If this year's income will be lower than last year's income

During the year, you need to send the IRS at least 90% of what you actually will owe this year. This is known as "the 90% rule." In order to determine how much you'll owe, you first have to estimate how much you'll earn—and that's not always easy, because the year isn't over yet! To help you determine this, answer these questions:

---

[167]To be more accurate, I should ask "Is your taxable income . . ." because what you owe isn't necessarily based merely on what you earn. See footnote #158.

[168]Watch out! Numbers like these change all the time, so I wouldn't be surprised if the IRS has modified them between the time I wrote this and the time you're reading it. You should check with a tax advisor to verify that all the dollar figures and percentages you see here are still accurate—assuming (*cough cough*) that they ever were (*wheeze*).

About your income.

How much taxable income do you think you will have received (from all sources) by the end of the year? If your income is not expected to change much during the year, you can simply multiply your monthly income by 12. If you are working and receive a biweekly salary, multiply by 26.[169]

About profits and losses.

By the end of the year, will you have received any profits from selling an asset, such as real estate or stocks? What about losses from such sales? Net gains are added to your taxable income, but net losses (up to $3,000) are subtracted. Factor these into your overall income.

About one-time paychecks.

Will you have received any one-time bonuses or commissions? Add them to your total income.

Until you have an estimate of your income, you cannot even begin to estimate your tax liability. But even if this year's income will be similar to last year's, the tax you owe might differ dramatically from what you owed last year. That's because many other aspects of your life affect what you'll owe in taxes. Two examples:

Your marital status.

Your status as of December 31 is what counts, as far as the IRS is concerned. When you look back on this year, will your marital status be different from what it was on January 1? Married people don't pay income taxes at the same rate as single people, even though their total household incomes might be the same. When your marital status changes, your tax scenario does, too.[170]

---

[169]Biweekly pay is different from getting paid twice a month. But you knew that.

[170]By the way, according to the IRS, you are either married or you're not. *Separated* doesn't count. There's no such thing as *divorced*, either. Both are considered to be single unless or until they remarry. But none of this might matter, anyway, because it might be better for you to file as "head of household," "married filing separately," or as a "qualifying widower." Since there's a "qualifying widower," there must be an "unqualifying widower," too, but I've been afraid to ask.

Children and parents.

Will any children be born to you this year? Will you find
yourself caring for a parent? By the end of this year, will
anyone you were responsible for last year have left the
household or your care, or died? You get a tax deduction
for each dependent you have at year's end. If you can
claim a higher number of dependents than last year, you
may get a bigger deduction; if you have fewer dependents, you get a smaller deduction.[171]

And there's much more. Mortgage interest, business
expenses, medical costs, moving allowances—all the things
that happen in life[172] find their way onto your tax return. I
know you would love to see a paragraph that shows you
how to easily and accurately determine how much your tax
will be, *but you've got to be joking.* Accurately estimating
your income tax requires substantial knowledge not only of
your particular situation, but of current tax exemption
thresholds, itemized deduction phase-out limits, effective
tax rates, and other details of the tax code. Therefore, most
readers should talk with a qualified tax expert who can run
various "what if" scenarios for you.

By talking with your tax advisor in the summer, you'll
have plenty of time to make changes in your payroll deductions or estimated tax payments, which in turn will help you
avoid penalties next April. For more on those estimated
payments, read on.

RULE #71　DETERMINE IF YOU NEED TO MAKE ESTIMATED QUARTERLY TAX PAYMENTS.

You know you have to pay income taxes. But did you know
you have to pay those taxes as you earn the income? If you
don't, you could incur penalties and interest.

---

[171]The more your income, the less your deduction for personal exemptions.
[172]Well, all the expensive things, anyway.

That remark might have scared you. But if most of your income comes from a job, you can relax, because your employer automatically sends a portion of your pay directly to the IRS on your behalf.[173] All you need to do is make sure that your boss is sending the proper amount—not too little, or you'll pay penalties, and not too much, or you'll be wasting money.[174] (You also need to verify that your boss really is sending the money off to the IRS, and not pocketing it or using the cash to pay other bills. To learn the warning signs, and for related horror stories, read Rule #86.)

But if most, or simply *much,* of your income doesn't come from a job, then you might need to make your own estimated tax payments during the year. Do you have to worry about this? Yes, if you get a lot of income from:

- Social Security or a pension, and no taxes are being withheld for you;
- The sale of real estate or other investments;
- Interest or dividends;
- Self-employment activities, or your own business; or
- Alimony.

Even if you currently receive the bulk of your income from your paycheck, the day will come when that's no longer true. At some point you will begin to receive the bulk of your income from the above sources, and unlike your job, they won't send your tax payments to the IRS for you;[175] you'll have to do it yourself.[176]

Say your income is steady, and you think your tax liability will be $10,000. You'd need to make four quarterly payments of $2,500 each. You cannot wait until the fourth quarter to make the entire payment of $10,000 (unless all

---

[173]How nice of them.

[174]As Rule #70 explained.

[175]Even if some of them will, they rarely will send enough to alleviate the need for you to make payments on your own.

[176]As your parents might already be required to do. Have you checked with them to make sure they're doing what they're supposed to be doing? See Rule #54.

the income was earned in the fourth quarter); if you do, you'll be subject to an "underpayment penalty."[177]

This sounds easy enough—except for those whose income fluctuates dramatically throughout the year. Take the owner of a ski shop. He'll do much more business in the winter months than in the summer, and that makes it particularly difficult to make accurate estimated tax payments. Or the retired investor who might sell a lot of stock in September. It's not a regular occurrence, and it changes how he must handle his estimated tax payments.

Fortunately, there is something called "the annualized method," which allows you to calculate your tax payments based on the income you earn each quarter. By observing Rule #70 and reviewing your tax payments in the summer, you still have half a year to make adjustments. Say you determine that you need to withhold an additional $1,200 by the end of the year, in order to meet the 100% rule (as described in Rule #70). If you wait until November, you'll have to withhold an additional $600 in each of the final two months of the year—and with the holidays fast approaching, that could prove to be quite a burden. But by starting in July, you would only need to withhold an additional $200 each month. That would certainly prove to be much easier on your pocketbook!

Lest you thought this story would have a happy ending, read this: Adhering to Rule #70's description of the "90% rule," the "100% rule," or the "110% rule" does not necessarily mean you have paid your taxes in full. It merely means you will avoid underpayment penalties (and the interest charges that accompany them)! Indeed, it's quite possible that you'll owe even more to the IRS, but at least you have until April 15 to cough up the balance.

---

[177]This is particularly important to people who sell stocks or real estate early in the year. They often think the taxes aren't due until the following April, but they're wrong. You must pay the tax in the same quarter that you receive the money, unless you meet the 100% and 110% rules. See Rule #70.

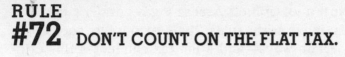

RULE #72 DON'T COUNT ON THE FLAT TAX.

One of the most consistent headlines these days is tax reform. Will we see a major change in our tax code? In a word, no. At least not while President Clinton is in office. The President has made his position very clear: He believes most of the problems in our tax code lie with administrative and procedural problems within the IRS. The solution, the administration says, is not to replace the IRS, but to fix it.

Even if the President changes his position, or if his successor feels differently, there are many reasons why you should not expect to see a flat tax. For one thing, a flat tax could cause municipal bonds to lose their tax-advantaged status, which in turn would reduce their appeal among investors. That would force the states to increase interest rates on their muni bonds, resulting in an increase in state income and property taxes. Once people realize this, support for tax reform could fade.

Also, a flat tax would eliminate deductions for mortgage interest and property taxes (the latter of which would increase as noted above), making homes less affordable. Foreclosures could rise and home values could drop—as much as 25% according to some estimates—followed by a severe recession affecting home builders, real estate agents, mortgage companies, and settlement firms. Ditto for the millions of people who work directly or indirectly in the tax and accounting field, because eliminating the tax code would put all these folks out of work.

But the real reason that Congress will not eliminate our current, convoluted tax system is, quite simply, self-interest. Congress uses the current system to push its social agenda. Want to provide low-income housing? Offer a tax credit to developers. Want to rebuild inner cities? Establish tax-free enterprise zones. Need to preserve historic buildings? Create a Historic Rehabilitation Tax Credit. Need to employ disadvantaged, inner-city youth? Give employers a Targeted Jobs Tax Credit. Want to discourage consumers from buying cars that burn a lot of fuel? Assess a gas guzzler's tax. The tax code is filled with rules that encourage society to behave in certain ways—and a flat tax eliminates this critical tool. Policy-makers know this, and they're not about to give it up.

Yet a lot of people are already acting like the flat tax exists. They are not buying homes out of fear that real estate prices will fall, even though homes are not investments;[178] they are sitting on massive capital gains, unwilling to sell their assets (even though they want to) because they think the flat tax will eliminate the tax liability on those profits; and they are failing to keep up with actual changes in the tax law, thinking that the changes won't matter because the flat tax will soon become law.

Think about it: If the flat tax were about to replace the current tax code, why would Congress have bothered to pass the biggest changes to the law in 11 years?[179]After all, if you were about to throw out a pair of old blue jeans, you wouldn't waste energy stitching them up first.

Even if all this proves wrong, and a flat tax is created, don't get too excited, because the flat tax will not cause your taxes to go down. Indeed, the proposal merely simplifies our tax code; it doesn't reduce the amount of money the government collects. Therefore, don't delay financial and tax planning on the mistaken assumption that the flat tax eliminates this need. You'll need to plan as much as ever. A flat tax might change the strategy, but not the need.

RULE #73   YOU WON'T BE IN A LOWER TAX BRACKET WHEN YOU RETIRE.

"I don't want to earn any more money right now, because if I do, it'll just push me up into a higher tax bracket."

Sound familiar? Well, it's wrong.

---

[178]See Rule #20.
[179]See Rule #69.

That presumption is based on a set of tax rules that haven't existed for more than 11 years, but it's remarkable how many people still act as though the Tax Reform Act of 1986 was never enacted.

Prior to TRA, there were 16 separate income tax rates, starting at 14% for incomes below $3,400, and increasing about every $7,000 until you reached the 70% top bracket for those earning more than $108,300. When this multi-bracket system was created, people tended to stay within their bracket. But with high inflation in the 1970s, employers started awarding 10% pay raises to help workers keep up with the cost of living. Then the 1980s brought huge—and taxable—profits, as the stock, bond, and real estate markets skyrocketed. These increases in income led to a phenomenon called "bracket creep," where making more money (in some cases only a few hundred dollars) pushed you into a higher tax bracket.

As a result of bracket creep, people discovered that a $5,000 pay raise could cost them $3,000 in additional taxes. Why bother earning more money if the government was just going to take it? This led to deferred-compensation programs, tax shelter deals, and other games of the early-to-mid-1980s. Back then the tax code forced you to figure out ways to defer your income, because deferring—which enabled you to avoid paying taxes on your profits—allowed your money to grow more quickly.

Then, just as people began to realize that pay increases weren't so great, they also discovered that when you entered retirement, your lower retirement income placed you in a lower tax bracket than you were in before you retired. Sort of the opposite of bracket creep.[180] Thus, millions of Americans adopted the attitude that if they deferred income from the present to the future, they'd accumulate more money, and if they waited until retirement to spend it, they'd also pay less in taxes.

None of this is true any more.

The Tax Reform Act of 1986 is a great example of **The**

---

[180]Bracket crash?

New Rules of Money. Among other things, TRA replaced the 16 different income tax brackets with just three. Later legislation increased that to the five we have today: 15%, 28%, 31%, 36%, and 39.6%. With only five brackets for all taxpayers, it is highly unlikely that you will move from one bracket to another, even when you retire.

For example, if you are married, you are in the 28% tax bracket if your income is as little as $41,200, or as high as $99,600. Even if your income is as high as $151,750, you'd still only be in the 31% bracket—a three-point difference. Therefore, it is highly unlikely that a person who is currently in the 28% bracket will ever pay only 15%. By contrast, under the pre-TRA tax code, a $41,200 income would have been in the 33% bracket, and a $150,000 income would have been in the 49% bracket—a 16-point difference.

So you can forget about enjoying drastically lower taxes once you enter retirement. That means you can stop acting like earning more money will merely raise your taxes. It won't, so go ahead and put your money where it'll earn that higher profit.[181]

RULE #74 DO NOT MAKE TAX-MOTIVATED INVESTMENT DECISIONS.

Here's a list, in random order, of the things you need to consider when making investments:

- Costs
- Tax implications
- Profit potential
- Liquidity
- Risk

---

[181]Please note that this Rule should not lead you to conclude that tax deferral is no longer of value. See Rule #84, then #76.

Now, go ahead and rank them, most important to least important.

I'll wait.

Done? I hope you put taxes at the bottom of the list. All too often, investors don't. When evaluating investment opportunities, they sometimes get themselves sidetracked, focusing on minor—or even trivial—issues instead of the things that really count.

It reminds me of a lesson my dad once taught me, although I'm not sure he did it on purpose (I think he was just trying to win the game). Anyway, one of the greatest things my dad ever did for me was to teach me how to play chess. Anyone who is willing to play chess with someone so inferior has to be a great guy—because doing so must be, without question, the most boring thing in the world to do.[182] But Dad did it over and over with me, for years. What a guy!

Anyway, back to the story. I was maybe 10, and still nowhere near as good as Dad, when he started goofing around (bored, I guess). He brought his queen out far too early in the game, so I, with nothing better to do—and not knowing any better either—started attacking it. Pretty soon I had his queen cornered; no matter what he did, it was mine on the next move. He started grumbling to himself, and I was feeling mighty pleased, let me tell you.

After a long pause, Dad said, "Oh well," and made a move I hadn't expected (which was not hard to do). I studied the board and realized what Dad had done: If I took his queen, he'd take my rook. Now, it's true that the queen is a much more valuable piece than a rook, but I thought I was going to capture her for free. To discover that my rook now would be traded for her, well, that simply was not acceptable. I looked and looked for a solution. My thinking went from "How can I get his queen without losing my rook?" to "How can I keep my rook while still getting his queen?" to "How can I keep my rook?" Eventually I advanced a pawn, saved my rook—and forgot to take his queen! Without pausing for

---

[182]Okay, maybe playing tennis with someone much worse than you would be as bad.

a moment, Dad fired his queen to safety, along the diagonal that was opened up by my dumb pawn move.

"No way!" I shouted. "Let me have that move back!"

"Sorry," Dad said. "A move is a move."

He was unyielding—but a 10-year-old can be pretty unyielding too. I stomped off to my room, and I wouldn't come out for a month. Well, okay, a half-hour.

Maybe Dad was just glad to keep his queen, but he taught me something I have never forgotten: Keep your eye on the big picture. Stay focused, and don't let problems get you off track of your goals.

(Maybe Dad learned something, too. He never risked his queen like that again.)

Therefore, when searching for the right investment, your evaluation must be done properly. The correct way to evaluate an investment is as follows:

1. Profit potential.

Start here, and if the thing can't make any money, stop looking.

2. Risk.

If the profit potential isn't worth the risk it takes to make that money, stop.

3. Liquidity.

If you unexpectedly need to get your hands on the money sooner than you anticipated, can you? At what cost and under what conditions? Liquidity is not a requirement—you might well choose an investment that has none—but consideration of liquidity is.

4. Costs.

If a comparison of two different investments suggests that they seem equal in all of the above criteria, choose the one that's cheaper to buy, maintain, and sell.[183]

---

[183]Attention all you folks who love to buy no-load funds: By setting "no-load" as your primary sort criterion, you eliminate from consideration two-thirds of the mutual fund universe, including many funds that are so good, their performance more than compensates for their fees. Loads are the fourth consideration, not the first.

5. Tax implications.

As with costs, select investments based on their tax effects only after you've evaluated everything else.

Remember: If all you really want to do is make sure you're not going to have to pay taxes, I can show you a very easy way to accomplish that goal.

RULE #75 STOP INVESTING IN MUNICIPAL BONDS.

Suppose you're in the 28% tax bracket. Which investment will help you create greater wealth, a 7% taxable bond fund, or a 5.5% municipal bond fund? The old school of planning says the muni fund is a better deal, because its interest is tax-free, while the 7% bond fund's after-tax rate is just 4.62%.

The old school of planning is wrong.

If you don't believe me, try this little test: Using a financial calculator,[184] determine the value in 20 years of investing $10,000 at the taxable bond fund's rate of 7% per year, compounded annually. The answer: $38,697.

Now, try it again, this time using the tax-free fund's rate of 5.5% per year. The answer: $29,178.

As you can see, the account containing the taxable bond fund has more money. It's that simple: You should invest in taxable bond funds instead of tax-free bond funds.

But, wait, you say. I'm cheating. Interest from the taxable bond fund is subject to taxes, but I failed to adjust for that in my calculations. Therefore, you say, I've reached an unfair conclusion.

Your objection is overruled.

What you're suggesting is what just about every financial advisor and economist suggests—that tax-free rates of return cannot fairly be compared to taxable returns without first adjusting them for their differences in tax treatment.

---

[184]I didn't say this was going to be an easy test.

Since one fund is tax-free and the other is taxable, I'm making an apples-to-oranges comparison.

To which I say, *So what?*

Look at it from a different perspective. I can argue that the 7% return from the taxable bond fund also is tax-free. Why? Because when the time comes to pay the tax, *you'll find the money elsewhere.* So while it may be true that the fund creates a tax liability, it's not true that this means the account can't compound at the rate of 7%. It can—because you'll leave it untouched.

Think about that. Do you ever touch your mutual fund investments? Of course not. So, when you receive 1099 statements in the mail each January, where do you get the money to pay the taxes that are due? From your checkbook, most likely. Or perhaps the 1099s simply mean you end up with a smaller refund.

However you handle it, my point is this: By not cashing out the bond fund itself, *the interest it earned stays invested,* where it compounds year after year. The result: You have $38,697 in 20 years—36% more than you would have accumulated if you had invested in the muni fund!

Therefore, **The New Rules of Money** are clear: Choose taxable bond funds over tax-free bond funds.

Note: There are two possible exceptions to this Rule. First, if you invest for current income, muni bond funds can make sense, because by withdrawing the interest each year, there is no compounding effect. Second, if you have a highly diversified, well-balanced portfolio, munis might be an appropriate addition, because muni bonds offer shelter from some risks that are present in other investments, and a risk-adjusted return can be more important than return alone. These exceptions aside, it's a bad idea to invest in muni bonds and muni bond funds.

RULE #76

FOR THE MOST POWERFUL ANTI-TAX INVESTMENT AVAILABLE, TURN TO VARIABLE ANNUITIES.

Annoyed that you must pay taxes each year on your mutual fund's profits? You might want to consider a variable annuity, which enables you to continue investing in your favorite mutual funds, but without having to pay taxes until you actually withdraw the money from your account.

Rule #84 explains that you'll accumulate more money when profits are tax-deferred than when profits are taxed annually. So even though variable annuities cost more than mutual funds—up to 1.5% per year more—the benefits of tax-deferral can more than offset this additional expense.

If variable annuities are so much better than mutual funds, why not place all of your money into them? For these three reasons:

1. You're not supposed to touch money in annuities until retirement. Withdrawals prior to age 59½ are subject to income taxes plus a 10% penalty.
2. Profits withdrawn from annuities are taxed as income, not as capital gains. That means the taxes could be much higher than if you had invested in mutual funds. Again, years of tax-deferral can more than compensate for this.
3. Variable annuities offer no "step-up in basis."[185] This means that heirs of annuities will incur a tax that heirs of mutual funds avoid. Most people don't care much about this, feeling (rightly) that they'd rather give the tax problem to their kids than incur it themselves.

Because of the fine print, my colleagues and I at The Edelman Financial Center limit our clients' use of variable annuities. Still, we acknowledge that variable annuities can be an excellent choice for retirement planning purposes, especially for people in their 40s and 50s, and absolutely

---

[185]Explained in Rule #56.

ideal for people already past 60—since the IRS penalty no longer applies.

Under **The New Rules of Money**, variable annuities offer one of the best opportunities for your investments to improve your tax picture.

RULE #77   NEVER ADD MONEY TO A NON-DEDUCTIBLE IRA.

IRA accounts, like company retirement plans,[186] are important retirement planning tools—except the Non-Deductible IRA. Here's why:

1. You get no tax deduction.

2. You must file IRS Form 8606, *Nondeductible IRAs (Contributions, Distributions, and Basis),* which tells the IRS that you have made a non-deductible IRA contribution. Lots of Americans don't know about this form—or the fact that there's a $50 penalty for failing to file it. One of my clients learned about this only when he came to me—six years after he started using a Non-Deductible IRA. His error cost him $300 in penalties—plus interest for every year he had failed to pay the penalty.

3. As annoying as Form 8606 is, *not filing it* is even worse. When you withdraw money from the Non-Deductible IRA, you're supposed to be able to withdraw your original contributions tax-free (since you never took a tax deduction on those funds in the first place). But if you can't show that you had filed Form 8606, you'll have to pay taxes on your original contributions—even though you paid taxes on that money years ago!

4. Even if you do everything right, you'll never be able to withdraw money tax-free from a Non-Deductible IRA. Say

---
[186]See Rule #85.

you've contributed over the years a total of $10,000 to your Non-Deductible IRA. Further, say the account is now worth $30,000. Since your contributions are one-third of the total value, only one-third of any withdrawals you make will be free of tax. Despite what you thought, you can't just withdraw "your" money now, and the "taxable" money later.

You can beat all these hassles by investing in a variable annuity, as the previous Rule described. Indeed, variable annuities are the closest thing to a Non-Deductible IRA, and offer all of the advantages but with none of the headaches.

Not only that, but with variable annuities, you are not limited to a $2,000 annual contribution (you can invest an unlimited amount of money instead), and you can delay withdrawals until age 85. (IRAs require that you begin making withdrawals at age 70½.)

So instead of using a Non-Deductible IRA, invest in a variable annuity. Having and eating cake. Cool.[187]

RULE #78 DO NOT TURN TO TAX PREPARERS FOR FINANCIAL PLANNING ADVICE.

You're trying to decide which mutual fund to choose for your IRA. You have a lot of taxable interest income, and you'd like to lower your taxes. You are now 62 and are trying to decide how much money you should withdraw from your IRA. You want to know how much money you'll need in order to retire comfortably. You want to help a child buy a house.

To whom will you turn for professional advice?

If you said a tax preparer, get ready for bad financial advice. Because by training, tax preparers—which include

---

[187]And if you've already made non-deductible IRA contributions, read Chapter 61 of *The Truth About Money*.

Certified Public Accountants and Enrolled Agents, as well as the part-time seasonal help found in many tax preparation services—are financial *historians*, not *planners*. They are trained, first, to review and document the past (not to project into the future), and second, to help you lower your current tax liability. They generally have little or no training in the fields of investments, insurance, mortgages, or wills and trusts, and therefore they can be quite inappropriate advisors in such matters. Although tax experts would seem to be suited to handle all the above scenarios, they are either not qualified to do so, or their answers could be so narrowly focused as to constitute dangerous advice.

To illustrate, let's examine each of these issues:

1. You're trying to decide which mutual fund to choose for your IRA.

IRA accounts are best known for their tax advantages, so it seems natural to ask your tax preparer for help with investing your IRA. But that's like asking an auto mechanic to drive your race car. Sure, he understands the principle of internal combustion, but that doesn't mean he'll handle the stick in a tight corner. Likewise, the accountant can discuss the tax deductibility limitations of IRAs, but that doesn't mean he or she knows anything about mutual funds—if mutual funds are even the best vehicle for your IRA. Feel free to ask your accountant about the tax implications of an investment, but never about the investment itself.

In fact, tax preparers hate when their clients ask their opinion about an investment. Why? Because if the investment fails after the preparer told you to proceed, he can be liable for the losses. That's why smart tax advisors always tell their clients "No!" when asked if an investment is a good idea.[188] The broker, insurance agent, or financial advisor who sold you the investment, however,

---

[188]If you've never been able to understand why your accountant always seems to hate any idea you mention, now you know why.

is shielded from liability (provided that they met the standards under the Investment Advisor Act of 1940, the Investment Company Act, and other sundry regulations).[189]

2. You have a lot of taxable interest income, and you'd like to lower your taxes.

Prior to the Tax Reform Act of 1986, tax preparers were able to show their clients many wonderful and creative ways to lower their taxes. Those days are gone, and under **The New Rules of Money**, you no longer turn to tax experts mainly for help in *lowering* your taxes; you now turn to them primarily for help in *preparing* your taxes. With the incredible complexity of today's tax code, that's challenging enough.

If you insist on asking for ways to lower your taxable interest income, your preparer will have no choice but to recommend tax-free bonds, because that's about the only option available. The problem is, although municipal bonds might be a good tax solution, they constitute a terrible investment decision (as explained in Rule #75). Besides, if all you want to do is lower your taxes, there's a much simpler and more effective way: Stop earning an income!

3. You are now 62 and trying to decide how much money you should withdraw from your IRA.

Any tax preparer worth his or her fee will tell you, quite simply, not to withdraw anything from your IRA. After all, any distribution would be taxable—and since withdrawals are not required before age 70½, you can avoid paying taxes simply by not taking any withdrawals. So unless you really need the income to support yourself, most preparers will try to discourage you from making a withdrawal from your IRA.

---

[189]In about half the states now, accountants are permitted to sell investments, provided they obtain a federal securities license. Therefore, it's quite possible that your tax preparer also is able to serve as an investment advisor.

The only problem is that this might be bad advice. Depending on the value of your account, delaying your first distribution to age 70½ could cause you not only to pay the income taxes at that time, but also substantial penalties as well. In such cases it's much better to take a distribution from your IRA right now, even though doing so is not mandatory. This is a good example of the tendency among tax preparers to focus solely on this year's tax return, and not on the client's complete, long-term financial situation.

4. You want to know how much money you'll need to retire comfortably.

Turning to your tax preparer for help with this concern is a mistake not unlike that made in example #3 above. You're worried here about income, and income is a word closely and commonly associated with taxes. Unfortunately, this question requires a look into the future, and that's a direction tax preparers are not trained to view. This question is more properly asked of a financial planner.

5. You want to help a child buy a house.

A tax preparer will happily tell you about the tax limitations of making gifts to your child, or of the tax implications for providing your offspring with a loan. This information will trick you into thinking that you've turned to the right person for help. Unfortunately, the preparer often will have nothing to say about the legal and estate planning issues surrounding this idea, nor will he or she warn you of broader family issues that only a holistic, family-based financial planning perspective can provide. Finally, the preparer will not tell you about alternative ways that you can help your child that are more appealing but which you might not have considered, such as a shared equity program.[190]

---

[190]*The Truth About Money,* Chapter 58.

In each case, it is clear that turning to a tax preparer for anything other than pure tax issues can be a big mistake. That's why you must be very careful where you get your advice, and why you should turn to a financial planner, who is trained in these broader financial issues.

The world of financial planning is very complex, and taxes play a critical role in your struggle to achieve financial success. Still, it's a foolish client who relies on a tax preparer for financial planning advice. That's why you need to see a financial advisor in addition to the tax advisor, and that's why my firm's planners and I routinely work with outside tax advisors, lawyers (see Rule #67), and insurance agents (see Rule #83), as well as referring our clients to our own in-house experts.

Whom should you see first? Assuming all parties are competent, it doesn't really matter, because we all know when to refer you to the other. As a financial planner, I'd suggest[191] that it probably makes sense to see the financial advisor first, because no matter what the issue is, it often comes down to the money. Because we're good at identifying the issues, we can point you to the right type of specialist, whether it's a retirement plan specialist, third-party administrator, independent trustee, valuation expert, appraiser, mortgage broker, real estate agent, psychologist (!), attorney, or, yes, a tax preparer.[192]

---

[191](with a certain amount of bias)

[192]Are you experiencing *déjà vu*? If it seems like you read this paragraph before, it's because you did—in Rule #67. And you'll see it again in Rule #83.

the new
insurance rules

RULE #79 NEVER BUY LIFE INSURANCE ON YOUR CHILDREN.

Back in the days when families had many children, all working daily on the farm, the death of a child was not merely the worst tragedy that a parent could experience—it represented a loss of a good farmhand as well. In those days the case for having life insurance on your children might have made sense. After all, the kids worked on the family farm for free, while Dad would have had to pay other folks to tend the fields and livestock.

Things are a little bit different today.

It's highly unlikely that you have 11 children all under the age of 18. It's equally unlikely that you live on a farm, or that your kids work to support the family. Therefore, if there ever was economic justification for maintaining life insurance on a child, those days are long gone. Today, buying life insurance for your children is simply a waste of money.

And yet 19% of all life insurance policies sold in this country cover children under the age of 12. But unless your child earns a wage, you would face no economic loss upon the child's untimely death. The key phrase here is *economic loss*, for economics is the only reason for purchasing a life insurance policy. Since the child earns no wage that must be replaced, there is no need for insurance.[193]

When insurance agents pitch child policies to their clients, they stress that you need to get the coverage while Junior is an infant, because—for the moment anyway—he or she is healthy enough to qualify for the coverage. The implication is that as your child grows, he or she might develop some illness that would prohibit him or her from being able to buy insurance later.

---

[193]If you are concerned about funeral costs, add a $10,000 child rider to your own policy. It'll cost less than $25 a year.

To which I say, *So what?*

If your child were to tragically die as a young adult or earlier, the question again surfaces: Who exactly suffered a financial loss? No one, likely—which means that, again, there was no need for insurance. *You should never buy insurance merely because you're able to.*

"But what if your diabetic son marries?" the insurance agents counter. "He'll then have a need for life insurance—but he won't be able to get it."

Yes, he can—if group coverage is available through work or a membership organization.

"But group coverage might not be available," the insurance agents say. "And that'll leave him without coverage."

Again, *so what?* I say that because there really is no effective solution to this problem.

"Yes, there is," the insurance agents say. "Buy a policy today!"

That sounds reasonable, so I looked at a policy one agent pitched to a client of mine. My client was told to buy a $75,000 policy for his newborn, costing just $26 a month.

Sounds great—except for two problems. First, if the child dies today, his parents don't need the $75,000. And I doubt they would feel like they just won the lottery.[194] And if the child died at age 30, after being married with two kids, by then the $75,000 will be virtually pointless—about as pointless as the $5,000 policy your parents bought for you 40 years ago. Indeed, assuming inflation continues into the future at the same pace of the past, $75,000 in 30 years will have the purchasing power of just $12,450. Is twelve grand supposed to put your child's kids through college in the year 2043?

If you really want to make sure your child will have enough money to protect his family when he's 30, you will need to buy a lot of insurance. But doing so not only would

---

[194] Having worked with many clients who have received large sums due to a loved one's untimely death, or from the settlement of a medical malpractice claim, I can assure you that the money offers no consolation. In a great many cases, the client never touches the money, because it is associated with feelings of loss, anguish, and pain. I assure you, those who deservedly receive large settlements never feel like victors.

be far too expensive, you'd be asking for so much coverage that the insurance company would decline your application. They might even tell you to see a psychiatrist.

This is why the argument collapses under its own weight. By insuring children, you essentially are trying to solve a problem that doesn't yet exist. That's rather pointless.[195]

The second problem is that buying an insurance policy is a very inefficient way to save money. The agent told my client that his proposed child policy would build up a cash value in 21 years of $5,410—essentially creating a savings plan for my client's child. Although that's true, it's also true that investing that same $26 per month for the same 21 years (assuming a 10% annual return) would produce $22,138—four times more than the policy!

So if you own insurance policies for your children, cancel them and invest your money elsewhere. If an insurance agent tells you to buy a child policy, as I said in *The Truth About Money,* ask yourself whether the agent is thinking about the benefits to your child—*or his or hers!*

RULE #80 NEVER BUY LIFE INSURANCE FOR INVESTMENT PURPOSES.

Look, I hate writing about insurance as much as you hate reading about it. So why don't we just cut to the chase, and save everybody a lot of time: Never "invest" in life insurance.

The purpose of insurance, as explained in the previous Rule, is to protect against a financial loss, not to produce a profit. But because many insurance policies create what's known as a "cash value buildup," insurance companies have figured out that if you throw an awful lot of money into those policies, that cash value *really* builds up—and later

---

[195]Insurance companies insure against possible *current* losses; they will not provide coverage against possible *future* losses. If you don't agree, try buying auto insurance if you don't have a car. Go get a car, the insurance industry will tell you, and then we'll insure you.

on, if you haven't died, they'll let you "borrow" it back out to use as you wish. Thus, a lot of insurance agents tout their products as excellent vehicles for long-term savings, because the cash value grows on a tax-deferred basis. As Rule #84 explains, growing money tax-deferred produces much better results than if you are taxed annually.

Sounds nifty, but there's a major problem with this idea. When you put money into a cash-value life insurance policy, not all of your money is actually invested. Some of the money is siphoned off to pay for the underwriting expenses, policy fees, mortality charges, agent commissions, and so on, and *what's left* gets invested and grows. But all these costs place such a drag on the policies that you'll never be able to earn as effective a rate of return as you would have gotten if you had just bought a plain ol' investment, such as a mutual fund.

But isn't the tax deferral worthwhile? Indeed it is, so read Rule #76 to learn how you can get it without all the underlying insurance costs.

Does this mean I think that cash-value life insurance is a rip-off, that you should always "buy term and invest the rest"? Not at all. Cash-value life insurance (which comes in many forms, such as whole life and universal life) are outstanding products. When used correctly, they offer you the opportunity to obtain the insurance you need at a cost that is—and will remain—affordable for the rest of your life. But when used improperly, such as for the purpose of saving for college or retirement, you will simply waste huge amounts of money—while enriching your insurance agent, of course. Because the blunt truth is that insurance agents earn commissions that are *10 to 25 times higher* when selling you a whole life insurance policy instead of a mutual fund or variable annuity.

So if you're about to buy an insurance policy that you think you'll keep for more than 10 years, by all means choose a cash-value policy. But if your agent starts bragging about the investment benefits of that policy, find another agent.

RULE #81
STOP *WORRYING* ABOUT LONG-TERM CARE COSTS—AND START *TAKING ACTION.*

There is perhaps no clearer example of **The New Rules of Money** than the subject of long-term care.

As little as five years ago, you probably had never even heard of long-term care. But by now you are at least somewhat familiar with it. Perhaps a family member is in need of long-term care services, or maybe you've seen a neighbor, friend, or colleague at work deal with the issue on behalf of a family member.

You're starting to hear about long-term care more and more. You've seen the statistics, and they're really starting to worry you:

- Life expectancy for Americans, which in 1900 was just 47, is now 76.
- In 1870, only 2.5% of all Americans reached age 65. By 1990, that percentage had increased fivefold to 12.7%.
- Whereas the leading causes of death in the United States in 1900 were communicable diseases, most deaths today are caused by hereditary illness, lifestyle, and the environment.
- The fastest-growing age group in this country: Those over 85.
- If you and your spouse both reach age 65, one of you can be expected to reach age 90.
- In fact, 90% of all the people in world history who ever reached age 90 are alive today.
- More than half the women and about one-third of the men who reach age 65 will spend some time in a nursing home.
- Seven couples in 10 can expect at least one partner to use a nursing home after age 65.
- Two out of five people 65 and over will need long-term

care. Half will stay in a facility six months or less, while the rest will stay an average of two-and-a-half years.

- The average cost of a nursing home is more than $50,000 per year.
- Medicare does not pay for long-term care, nor does your health insurance.
- Half of all older Americans who live alone will spend themselves into poverty after only 13 weeks in a nursing home, while 56% of couples will spend their income down to the poverty level after one spouse has spent six months in a nursing home.

You've seen these statistics, and they worry you. In fact, according to a 1996 survey by the National Council on the Aging:

- 87% of respondents said long-term care is a very or fairly big problem.
- 60% worry that they or their spouse will require long-term care at some point in their lives.
- Adults 35–44 are more worried about needing long-term care than those either older or younger than themselves. This age group also is the most worried about how to pay for it—for themselves and for their parents.

So, yes, you're worried. But that's probably because *you simply haven't done anything about it yet.* Only 13% of adults own a long-term care insurance policy, which corresponds with the NCA's study where 11% said they've done "a great deal" of planning for long-term care. Another 41% said they've done "some" planning, while the remaining 48%—half of all Americans—say they have done no planning at all.

The irony is that a lot of this worry is for nothing. While 86% agree that buying long-term care insurance would solve the problem, 40% were unable to estimate the cost at all, and most of the remaining 60% wildly overestimated the actual cost of LTC insurance. Maybe that's why 68% of the survey's respondents felt that they couldn't afford the coverage, when in fact they can. Not only that, but the sooner you act, the cheaper it is to solve the problem, as this chart shows:

Age	Years of Coverage	Annual Cost for Basic Policy*	Total Cost to Age 85
50	35	$396	$13,860
55	30	$540	$16,200
60	25	$744	$18,600
65	20	$1,068	$21,360
70	15	$1,656	$24,840
75	10	$3,000	$30,000

*A basic policy—good enough for many families—provides $120/day in benefits for three years, but with no inflation protection. A more comprehensive policy—which you should obtain if you can afford it—would pay benefits for six years and increase the daily benefit to keep pace with inflation.

LTC coverage is inexpensive at young ages because the insurance carrier knows it probably will be years before you file a claim—and it gets to invest your premium dollars in the meantime. So even though a 50-year-old is buying a policy potentially decades before he or she needs the coverage, doing so enables him or her to get the policy for just $45 a month. Virtually any family can afford that cost, while few could afford the thousands of dollars per year that a 75-year-old must pay.

There's another reason to buy the policy when you're younger: You're still healthy enough to qualify for it. Insurance companies are notorious for giving coverage only to those who don't need it, so the last thing you want is to find yourself looking for a policy just *after* the doctor gave you the bad news.

Why am I stressing insurance as the only viable solution to the problem? Because it *is* the only viable solution to the problem! Oh, sure, there are four other solutions, but they are not very practical. Still, for those who insist on trying them, here they are:

1. First, you can simply make yourself poor. If you transfer all your assets to your kids, you'll be broke. That will make you eligible for Medicaid.[196] But as Rule #66 explains, this strategy is not only unethical, it's illegal.

2. Second, if you're married, get a divorce. Under your divorce decree, have the institutionalized spouse leave all the assets to the community spouse, because Medicaid cannot claim assets that have been transferred in such a manner. This has all the same legal and ethical problems as the first idea. Besides, I can't imagine too many people saying to their spouse, "Sorry you're not feeling well, honey, but I'm outta here."

3. Third, have enough assets so you can pay for it. An extra $547,000 (generating an 8% income stream) ought to do it.[197]

4. And the fourth solution is simply NGO—NEVER GET OLD. But until we come up with a way to do that, I don't think you ought to rely on it.

Therefore, I really don't think you're likely to find as cost-effective a solution to your long-term care worries as simply buying a long-term care insurance policy. While you're at it, get one for each of your parents as well as for yourself and your spouse. After all, who do you think will pay for your parents' care after they've run out of money? You'll much prefer to pay a few thousand dollars *per year* for your parents' policies instead of many thousands of dollars *per month* for their actual care.[198]

Under **The New Rules of Money**, worrying is out. Action is in.

---

[196]Medicaid, the joint federal/state welfare plan for the poor, pays for long-term care. Medicare, the federal health plan for retirees, does not.
[197]I can see your grocery list now: *Pick up a loaf of bread, a gallon of milk, and an extra half million dollars.* Yeah, right.
[198]Trust me on this one.

RULE
#82
STOP THINKING THAT GROUP INSURANCE IS THE BEST WAY TO SOLVE YOUR INSURANCE NEEDS.

If you need insurance, think twice about buying a life, disability, or long-term care policy offered by your employer or affinity organization, because group coverage can cost you substantially more than an individual policy.

Group policies are offered by companies for their employees and by associations for their members. Although group insurance once was an excellent benefit, today they can be poor choices, because they often cost more than policies you could buy on your own, and they offer fewer benefits than you can otherwise get.

Case in point: Marylee, 54, and her husband Jerry, 63, are in good health. They are school teachers in the same county, and they've been offered the chance to buy a new nursing home policy the county is making available to its employees. They looked at the plan, and from the limited options it offered, they selected a daily nursing home benefit of $115, with a maximum home health care benefit of 60% of that, or $69. In other words, if one of them goes to a nursing home, the insurance company will pay $115 per day; if they need at-home care, they'll get $69 per day.[199]

Marylee and Jerry also selected a benefit period of five years and the optional compound inflation feature. This means they could receive benefits for five years, and the benefits would increase 5% per year to keep up with inflation, while the cost of the policy would remain the same. The cost for their group policy was almost $3,700 per year.

But Marylee and Jerry were smart. They compared their employer's group plan with other insurance companies that offer individual plans, and the results were astounding. Not only did they find one quote for $600 less than the group

---

[199]To qualify for these benefits, a person must become cognitively impaired, or be unable to perform certain tasks by themselves, such as bathing, eating, dressing, toileting, transferring from bed to chair, or maintaining continence.

plan, the same insurer sponsoring the group plan actually offered Marylee and Jerry an individual policy for $720 less than what they were offering via the school program! With better benefits, too: Both of the individual policies offered a daily benefit of $120—not just $115; 100% of the daily benefit applied to both nursing home *and* home health care (instead of getting just 60% of the benefits for at-home care); and the total benefit period would be six years, not five. And both policies matched the compound inflation feature of the school plan.

Why was the school system's plan so inferior?

The answer, in part, is based on what the insurance company anticipates it will pay in claims. In group plans, all members of the group are automatically accepted, regardless of their health, and everybody pays the same rate at each age level. If the group consists primarily of older or unhealthy people, the insurer is likely to experience a higher number of claims. To compensate, the insurance company must charge everyone more. Thus, healthy folks who buy into the group plan—those who could have qualified for a policy on their own—in essence subsidize the not-so-healthy folks (the ones who *must* choose a group plan because they cannot qualify for a policy on their own).

Other disadvantages of group insurance are:

- The company or association can cancel the coverage at any time;
- The insurance company can cancel the benefit or increase the cost at any time; and
- You may lose the benefits if you leave the company or association that sponsors the group policy.

So if you are in good health, talk with your insurance agent or financial advisor to see if an individual policy for life, disability, or long-term care would be better for you. Chances are, it will be.

RULE #83

STOP TAKING FINANCIAL ADVICE FROM INSURANCE AGENTS.

You want to save for your child's college education. You need estate planning. You want to lower your taxes. You'd like to earn tax-deferred income.

To whom will you turn for professional advice?

If you said an insurance agent, prepare to be parted from your money. Because although many insurance agents might be quick to offer insurance-based solutions to these problems, each is really a financial planning matter, and insurance is not the best answer for any of these issues.

That's why you must be very careful where you get your advice. Insurance agents are excellent at selling insurance, but sometimes they sell it even when it's not best for you. Therefore, turn instead to a financial planner, who is better trained in these broad financial issues.

How can you tell if your "planner" is really a planner— and not just an insurance agent trying to make a sale? After all, many outstanding planners are former insurance agents, and many current insurance agents are highly skilled professionals who know when they're the right resource for their client—and when they're not. Here are some tips to help you determine if your planner is really "just an insurance agent."

1. **His business card carries the name of an insurance company.**

   If so, or if his telephone at work is answered with a carrier's name, then you're talking to an employee or representative of an insurance company. Although there are exceptions, you can expect that everything he recommends will involve the purchase of that company's products.

2. He makes money strictly from the commissions he earns from the policies he sells.

There's nothing wrong with being compensated strictly from commissions, but true financial advisors are not compensated strictly by *insurance* commissions. How objective can he be if he only makes money from selling you an insurance policy? It's easy to find out how he's compensated: Just ask. If he tells you that he makes money selling all sorts of products, including investments, don't worry that he might be lying. If he is, you'll discover it through the next point.

3. All of his recommendations involve the purchase of insurance policies or annuity products.

If he's truly an independent advisor, you can expect to get recommendations involving investments, mortgages, taxes, wills—*and insurance.* If he talks about little other than insurance, odds are high that you're dealing with an insurance agent. That in itself is not a problem, provided you know it.

4. He is not a Registered Investment Advisor.

Under federal law, any person holding himself out to be a financial planner or advisor for compensation is required to register as an investment advisor with the U.S. Securities and Exchange Commission or with your state regulatory agency. Insurance agents are exempt from registration, so if your advisor is not registered, he could well be an insurance agent.[200]

5. He does not hold a federal securities license.

Virtually every true financial advisor holds the National Association of Securities Dealers Series 7 license, which is required in order to handle investments for a client. Some advisors hold the Series 6 instead, which limits the

---

[200]He could be a stockbroker, accountant, or attorney, too—because each of these professionals also are exempt from RIA registration. But it's pretty rare for insurance agents to pose as accountants or attorneys, and as for stockbrokers, well, I'm not sure the agent will be improving his image much by pretending to be *that.*

advisor to recommending mutual funds. If your insurance agent does not hold a securities license, his work is limited by law to the sale of insurance products.[201] To find out if your agent is licensed, ask him. If you don't believe him, contact the NASD at 1–800–289–9999.

6. He's willing to come to your house any evening you want to discuss your case.

I'm including this one merely to annoy all the insurance agents who are reading this.[202] Actually, it's a nice touch and a good demonstration of personal service to make house calls, but I don't know of any physicians, attorneys, accountants, financial planners, or other professional advisors who routinely do this—at least none who have been in practice for any length of time. But I know of lots of salesmen who are happy to visit you at home.

The world of financial planning is very complex, and insurance plays an important role—but it is a limited role. Therefore, it's a foolish client who relies on an insurance salesman for financial planning advice. Sure, you can turn to the agent to buy an insurance policy. But is the agent aware of the legal implications of having you own that policy instead of a trust? Does the agent know what happens, for example, if you name a minor child as a beneficiary?[203] Insurance agents are trained in matters of insurance, not necessarily in issues relating to personal and business finance. Often they are as unaware of the broader financial implications of a decision as you are. That's why you need to see a financial advisor at the same time that you see the agent, and that's why my firm's planners and I routinely work with outside insurance agents, lawyers (see Rule #67),

---

[201]Note that I said that *virtually* all true advisors hold an NASD license. Some do not. There are some advisors scattered around the country who are compensated exclusively by fees, and they do not hold *any* type of license—securities *or* insurance. They are, however, registered with the Securities and Exchange Commission (or the state) as Investment Advisors.

[202]It's so easy to make them mad.

[203]See Rule #57.

and accountants (see Rule #78), as well as referring our clients to our own in-house experts.

Whom should you see first?[204] Assuming all parties are competent, it doesn't really matter, because we all know when to refer you to the other. As a financial planner, I'd suggest[205] that it probably makes sense to see the financial advisor first, because no matter what the issue is, it often comes down to the money. Because we're good at identifying the issues, we can point you to the right type of specialist, whether it's a retirement plan specialist, third-party administrator, independent trustee, valuation expert, appraiser, mortgage broker, real estate agent, psychologist (!), accountant, attorney, or, yes, an insurance agent.

---

[204]See Footnote #192.
[205](with a certain amount of bias)

the new rules of retirement

RULE
#84 TAKE MAXIMUM ADVANTAGE OF
YOUR COMPANY RETIREMENT PLAN.

You know you need to save for the future, so I won't belabor the point. But what you may not know is the most effective way to do it. Without question, if you do only one thing for your financial future, it should be to participate in your company retirement plan, and do so to the maximum extent that you are permitted.

There are several reasons for this, including:

1. All contributions are tax-deductible.

Say you earn $50,000, and you decide to place 10% of your pay into the company retirement plan. By putting that $5,000 into the plan, your taxable income is now just $45,000. So instead of paying $8,892 in federal income taxes, you pay just $7,492—a savings of $1,400. If your state levies a state income tax, you save even more.

Here's the nifty part: Thanks to the tax savings, that $5,000 you invested into the plan cost you, on an after-tax basis, just $3,600. That's a fabulous start to building wealth.

2. Your money will grow tax-deferred.

This is even more important than the tax deduction. Let's face it: A dollar that is not taxed will grow more quickly than a dollar that is.

To illustrate, say you invest a penny for your retirement. Now that doesn't sound like much, but this is a pretty special penny. It's got the ability to grow in value at the rather remarkable rate of 100% per year. Since your retirement is 30 years away, how much money do you suppose that penny will be worth at that time?

Would you believe that it will be enough to satisfy all of your retirement income needs? Probably not.[206]

Lessee now. In one year, your penny will have grown to two pennies. After five years, you'll have a whopping 16 cents. I know, you're overjoyed. And I doubt you'll be much happier in 10 years, because your penny will have grown to just $5.12. Even after 15 years, you've got less than $164. And in 20 years—when you're two-thirds of the way to retirement—you've got just $5,200. Sure, five grand is a big gain over one penny, but it won't "satisfy your retirement income needs," as I said just one paragraph ago.

In fact, by now, you're getting pretty darned annoyed at the whole thing. I mean, you've been saving diligently for *20 years,* and all you have to show for it is a measly five grand. Why, that won't even buy a fraction of what five grand would have bought 20 years ago. And who knows what it will buy in another 10 years, as you're entering retirement! So, you figure, you're not inclined to let the money just sit there. Besides, you're in your early 50s now, and your kids are starting to collect college catalogs. You're going to need a *ton* of money for that, and, well, hey, you've got $5,000 in your retirement plan. So you figure you might as well liquidate that account, and use that cash to help pay for college. Although it's not much, using it does mean that you're five thousand dollars closer to paying for their college tuition. It's no big deal to raid the retirement account anyway, you figure. After all, you need the cash now, and besides, that account hasn't grown to anything huge. Why, at the rate it's been growing—heck, it took 20 years just to collect a lousy five grand—pulling it out now won't make much difference in your retirement prospects. So you withdraw the money, and your special penny stops doubling.

That's too bad. Because if you had allowed the penny

---

[206]Unless you're assuming that this is a trick question, in which case you'll say yes. But saying it and believing it are two different things. Ask yourself, do you *really believe* that a penny doubled every year for 30 years could solve your retirement planning needs?

to continue doubling for the remaining 10 years, *it would have grown to more than five million dollars*. That's right: Although it takes 20 years to go from one penny to five thousand dollars, it takes only 10 years to go from five thousand to almost $5.4 million.[207]

This example demonstrates the incredible power of compounding. Its importance cannot be overemphasized. Neither can my message: In order for you to truly enjoy the benefits of compounding, you must give it time to work. Indeed, compounding is effective only when allowed enough time. This explains why so many people fail to achieve financial success: They're too impatient. Dissatisfied with the performance to date of your penny, and faced with other, more immediate financial concerns, you are tempted to liquidate your account. It doesn't appear doing so will cause much harm, but you couldn't be more wrong.

You see, the penny was two-thirds of the way to reaching $5.4 million in value. But by stopping the clock when you did and spending the money, you effectively started that clock over—*pushing your retirement date back another 30 years*.

This is why you must *never* use the money in your retirement plan for any purpose other than **retirement**.[208] I know you need the cash. I know you have other financial needs and problems. *Tough*. All of them pale beside the money you're going to need later, and your retirement plan is the only thing you've got to help you get there.

But I digress.

Let's return to my original point, which was the fact (in case you forgot) that money which grows without having to pay taxes grows much more effectively than money that is required to pay taxes. There's no better way to illustrate this point than by returning to our penny.

---

[207]I know you don't believe me, so pull out a calculator and see for yourself.
[208]That's why they call it a *retirement* plan, not an *I-wanna-buy–a-house* or *pay–off-some–debt* plan.

You know that the penny, left untouched for 30 years, is now worth $5.4 million. But that's because the penny's profits were allowed to double each year *without taxation*. If the profits had been taxed annually—which is typically what happens when you invest outside of a retirement plan—can you guess how much money you'd have in 30 years, assuming a 28% tax rate?

You probably figured that you'd lose half. I'll explain why you thought that (and why you're wrong) in a moment. But first the correct answer. Please, don't yell. You'll wake the person who's sleeping next to you.

You'll have $48,000.

I'm serious. By taxing the profits each year at 28%, your penny will never grow to $5.4 million. It'll grow to just 48 grand. Here's why: In the original tax-deferred example, one penny became two pennies, representing a one-penny profit, and those two pennies became four pennies in the third year. But by taxing each year's profit, something very different happens. That first year's profit of a penny gets taxed. Cost: $0.0028. Consequently, only $0.0172 is left to double. It does, becoming $0.0344, but this new profit of $0.0172 is taxed, costing $0.004816. Thus, after the third year, you have only 2.95 cents, compared to the tax-deferred version, which had four cents. Keep going for 30 years, and you'll discover that your taxed penny grows to $48,714.41 after taxes, while your tax-deferred penny is worth $5,368,709.12.

But wait a minute, you say. That's not fair. At retirement, the tax-deferred penny *now* will be taxed, because all withdrawals from a retirement plan are subject to taxes. That's true. But if you withdraw all the money at once, in retirement, you'll lose half to taxes,[209] still leaving you with $2.7 million—a whole lot more than the $48,000 you got by paying taxes each year on the pay-as-you-go system.

---

[209]Assuming that your now-huge net worth has pushed you into the 50% estate tax bracket, rather than the 28% income tax bracket used for the taxable penny.

This is why I said you were wrong four paragraphs ago.[210] When you estimated the tax, you merely cut the total by the tax rate.[211] What you failed to do was compound the tax cost, which is what happens, effectively, when you pay taxes each year. So this serves as yet another powerful example of the principle of compounding.[212]

Got the message? Retirement plans allow your money to grow tax-deferred, a tool too important for you to ignore in your efforts to accumulate wealth.[213]

Your employer just might be adding to your wealth.

In addition to putting your own money into the plan, many employers add money to the account on your behalf as well. There are three ways employers do this:

1. *A basic contribution.*
   This is usually a percentage of payroll. If you earn $40,000 a year and your employer contributes 1% of pay to the plan, you get $400.

---

[210]You thought I forgot, didn't you?

[211]And you used lousy math, too, which is how you arrived at $2.7 million instead of $3.9 million—which is the figure you should have arrived at by lopping off the taxes at the 28% rate like my question told you to.

[212]There's another lesson built into our humble penny, and if you haven't awakened your bedmate yet, this is sure to do it. It's clear to you by now that, by taxing you annually on the profits, your ability to accumulate great wealth is destroyed (or at least severely hampered). Yet by doing so, can you guess how much the IRS gets? Some would calculate that by reducing your net from $5.4 million to just $48,000, the IRS must take the difference—several million at least. But it doesn't. By taxing you as you earn the money, the IRS collects over the entire 30-year period a grand total of just $19,000—and it gets almost all of it in the last four years.

   Indeed, by preventing you from achieving wealth, the government deprives itself of taking it, for if it had instead allowed you to accumulate the $5.4 million, it then could have gotten its hands on $2.7 million. Instead, it gets only nineteen grand. Too bad our friends in Congress have never figured this out. Now go apologize for waking that sleepyhead next to you.

[213]There are two other ways to grow money on a tax-deferred basis. The first is to invest in variable annuities (Rule #76). The second is to buy growth stocks (meaning those that pay little or no dividends) because their profits are not taxed until you sell them. If you keep them for 30 years, they become, in essence, tax-deferred investments. This is not very practical, though, because it's unlikely that you'll buy a stock and never sell it in the course of 30 years, and even if you did, it might very well start to pay dividends along the way, thereby ruining the tax-avoidance strategy.

2. *A matching contribution.*

This is a percentage of what you contribute. For every dollar you place into the plan, many companies add 25 cents, 50 cents—or even a whole dollar, up to 3% or 5% of your pay.

3. *A profit-sharing contribution.*

Many companies contribute a portion of their profits to the plan, as much as 3% or more of your pay.

Like your own contribution to the plan, all of the money deposited to the plan by your employer on your behalf is free of income taxes, and it grows tax-deferred.

Your employer's assistance has an awesome effect. If you contribute 10% of your pay to your company plan and work for a company that contributes on your behalf, you easily could double your money *before your money is even invested!*[214]

Without question, your retirement planning needs will be met most effectively by fully participating in your employer's retirement plan.

Keep this point in mind: Most companies don't allow employees to participate in their retirement plans until the employee has been with the company for at least a year, and sometimes longer. So if you're working for a company that contributes to the plan for you, think before you change jobs: Moving to a new employer means you lose that contribution.[215]

In fact, taking a new job where you've been offered a 10% increase in pay actually could *cost* you money. Say you earn $50,000. A 10% increase in pay takes you to $55,000. But that's before taxes. Your take-home pay would be just $35,750 (assuming a 35% combined federal/state income tax bracket). But say you instead kept your current job, where you are able to put 10% of your pay into a retirement plan

---

[214]Talk about pennies!
[215]See Rule #3.

that earns 10%, and where the first 50% of your contributions are matched by your employer. If you stayed, your take-home pay would be $29,250—and you would have another $8,250 in the retirement plan—for a total of $37,500, or $1,750 more than what you'd have from the job that offered you a 10% pay hike!

Conversely, of course, if you are working for an employer that does not add money to your retirement plan, it might behoove you to look for work elsewhere. Indeed, even working for a bit less in pay might be more profitable for you if the new employer's retirement plan benefits are superior to those offered by your current employer.

Think carefully before changing employers, and make sure you participate fully in your company retirement plan.

RULE #85

PLACE 100% OF YOUR COMPANY RETIREMENT PLAN EXCLUSIVELY INTO STOCKS.

Since company retirement plans enable people to save so much money so effectively, and since the majority of workers are indeed participating in their company plans at least to some degree, one would assume that everything will be hunky-dory, right?

Wrong.

The sad truth is that many people are thwarting their own efforts to achieve wealth, because they are investing their company retirement plan contributions incorrectly. As explained in Rule #31, people tend to focus on safety instead of performance. As a result, according to the Institute of Management and Administration, American workers place 33% of all retirement plan contributions into guaranteed investments. On the other extreme, 42% of assets have been placed into the employer's stock—which is equally dangerous, but for very different reasons. Indeed, only 18%

of all the money placed in retirement plans is invested in diversified stock mutual funds—which is the correct choice.

To understand why the fixed account and the employer stock are wrong choices, just compare Colin, Jeff, and Nancy. Colin and Jeff are 40; Nancy is 39. Each earns $40,000, and they work for the same company, each contributing 10% of pay to the company retirement plan. But that's where the similarity ends.

Colin, the most nervous of the three, places all his money into the fixed account, called a GIC (for Guaranteed Investment Contract). It's similar to a CD but is offered by an insurance company, and it pays 5% per year, with the interest rate reset each year for the next 12 months.

Jeff puts his money into the diversified stock fund, and over the course of his career, he earns an average of 12% per year—though there are lots of ups and downs along the way that would make Colin crazy.

Nancy buys company stock with her money, which grows 14% per year, a bit more than Jeff's fund.

Assuming no salary increases, Colin's account at retirement is worth $214,000. But Jeff's is worth $674,000—more than three times as much! As with Rule #84's penny story, the power of compounding is astounding. Because Colin emphasized safety, he finds himself with a fraction of what he could have had.

And Nancy? She retired the year after Jeff and Colin. Having placed 100% of her money into company stock, which earned 14% per year for 30 years, Nancy found herself at retirement with *absolutely nothing*. Why? Because a product her employer has been manufacturing for 50 years has been found to cause cancer, and the class-action lawsuits are flying. Wall Street says there's no hope for the company, and the only way out is for the company to enter Chapter 7 bankruptcy. Its stock is worthless, and Nancy's retirement account, which had been doing even better than Jeff's up to now, is wiped out.

This is why you must never invest in the stock of the company for whom you work, regardless of how successful you expect your company to be. I do not say this because I don't like your company, but because you have only two fundamental assets—time and money—and diversification demands that you invest them separately. Put your money somewhere other than where you put your time. Since you're already investing 10 hours per day in the company, do something different with your money.

If you think what happened to Nancy can't happen to you—because your company is too big, too successful, too *whatever*—then you are being extraordinarily naïve. Don't say I didn't warn you.

RULE #86 YOU MUST NOW WATCH OVER YOUR EMPLOYER'S SHOULDER, TO MAKE SURE YOUR COMPANY RETIREMENT PLAN IS SAFE.

Dear Ric,
I work for a company in northern Virginia. The current and former employees are concerned about our 401(k). Effective December 1997, I stopped contributing. The others are not receiving their statements in a timely manner. As of this date, I have not received my statement for the July to December 1997 period. We asked for a phone number to get information and were told there is no number, that only the human resources manager can call. Former employees are experiencing difficulties in receiving their money from the 401(k). Some have requested lump-sum distributions or rollovers to their current 401(k) plans at their new jobs. The employees have tried calling, and some have written letters to the personnel department requesting their money. For some reason, the former employees' telephone calls are not being returned. It is a known fact that this company is experiencing financial difficulties. There are some questions that need to be answered, such as what are our rights and what should we do. Why

would the company hold the employees' money, and to whom should we complain or report this information?

The above letter, which I received from a viewer of my TV show, is one I hope you never have to write. Think about it: When you voluntarily reduce your paycheck to make a contribution to the company retirement plan, you are acting on faith that your employer is actually investing your money as you've instructed.

But how do you really know your employer is doing so? After all, if the boss is having financial difficulties, it can be mighty tempting for him or her to use your money to pay other bills. The Department of Labor, in fact, has already identified more than 600 companies that have misappropriated employee contributions, and its investigation has only just begun. Because your company retirement plan is funded primarily—if not exclusively—by contributions you make out of your own paycheck, it's critical that you keep a close eye on the money.

I'm not talking about investment performance here; I'm talking about fraud. If you discover a problem, you must deal with it quickly. But what should you look for? Here are the 10 warning signs to help you detect possible misuse of your 401(k) funds.

1. Your statement arrives late or at irregular intervals.

2. The balance appears to be inaccurate.

You know how much money you're putting into the plan. (If you don't remember, just look at your pay stub.) Your statement ought to reflect that amount.

3. Employee contributions have been held for more than 15 days.

Your employer should be putting your money into the plan as soon as it is deducted from your paycheck. Some employers used to play a game called "the float," meaning they'd take the money from your paycheck but not invest it for three to six months—and use the cash in the meantime. To stop that abuse, Congress passed a law requiring employers to deposit their employees' retirement plan contributions within 15 days. Your statements should reflect compliance with this new rule.

4. **A significant drop in your account balance cannot be explained by the normal fluctuations of the stock or bond market.**

If the investment world is doing fine, but you notice a sudden drop in your account's value anyway, perhaps your employer is siphoning money from your account. This is more likely to occur if your employer is experiencing cash flow problems and needs money to pay its bills.

5. **The 401(k) statement shows that contributions from your paychecks were not made.**

You know your employer withheld money from your paycheck, but the 401(k) statement doesn't reflect it.

6. **Investments that are listed in the account balance were not authorized.**

Most employees have the option of choosing where their money is to be invested. Make sure your money is going where you authorized it to go.

7. **Former employees have trouble getting their money on time or in the correct amount.**

8. **The statement reflects unusual transactions, such as a loan to the employer, a corporate officer, or one of the plan trustees.**

It is inappropriate—if not outright illegal—for an employer to withdraw money from your account without your expressed authorization. The money in the plan is yours, not theirs—even if they contributed some of the money to the plan for you.

9. **The employer makes frequent or unexplained changes in the investment managers or consultants.**

Employers often hire outside pension consultants or 401(k) managers to handle the plan's administrative paperwork. If the employer tries to play games with the cash, the administrator will raise questions, and the easiest way for the employer to stop the questions is to fire the administrator and hire somebody new. Beware when your employer frequently changes retirement plan administrators.

10. **The employer has recently experienced severe financial difficulty.**

Although the vast majority of companies are properly handling their employees' retirement plan assets, you should keep your eyes open and be ready to act. If you notice any of these problems, contact the Pension and Welfare Benefits Administration, Division of Technical Assistance and Inquiries, at the U.S. Department of Labor, at 202–219–8776.

RULE #87   FROM NOW ON, WHEN YOU LEAVE A COMPANY, TAKE THE MONEY WITH YOU.

When you leave your company, you will be offered the choice of leaving the money in your retirement plan with your former employer, depositing the money into your new employer's retirement plan, or rolling the cash into an IRA. If you are retiring, you obviously cannot move the money to a new employer, but you can elect to receive a monthly income from your retirement account, based on the amount of money you've accumulated.

Having just read Rule #86, it should be clear that you do not want to leave money with a former employer. Nor do you want to move money to a new employer. Just look at what happened to the staff of Job Shop Services. In what the Department of Labor has called the largest theft of 401(k) assets in the country, 200 of Job Shop's 750 aerospace workers lost $3 million when the firm's owner, Ralph Corace, raided the company retirement plan, using the money to pay company bills in an effort to keep the firm afloat. Among the 200 employees who lost money were several new hires who had transferred their retirement accounts from previous employers into Job Shop's plan.[216]

The irony is that there is absolutely no tax or profit incentive to let an employer—any employer, past or present—manage your assets. If you leave a company, don't leave your money there and don't forward it to your new employer. Instead, transfer the money to an IRA account. There are no tax implications to do so, and you'll be in total control of your money.

And when it comes time to retire, never choose to receive your retirement plan in pieces, such as in the form of a series of monthly checks. If you have the option of receiving one single check, take it, for all these advantages:

- You, not your former employer, will be in control of your money;
- You will have unlimited investment options;
- You can generate a monthly income that is certain to be more than if you allowed your employer to provide that income for you;
- Generating your own income allows you to adjust your income as the cost of living rises. When checks come from most employers, they don't increase with inflation; and

---

[216]In exchange for Corace's guilty plea to embezzlement, prosecutors agreed to recommend a prison sentence of no more than 24 months. And the money? The Department of Labor intended to demand that Corace give to the retirement plan, as partial restitution, the $2 million he received when he sold the company, but the IRS grabbed the cash for back taxes. DOL was trying to convince the IRS to put some or all of the money into the retirement plan, but as of this writing, that hasn't happened. The workers, meanwhile, are suing both Corace and two companies that advised Corace on the plan. So far it's been more than four years since the workers have seen their money.

- When you die, whatever money you have not spent will pass to your heirs. Checks from your employer stop with your death,[217] leaving no inheritance for children.

For all these reasons, you're much better off investing your own money. So, from now on, when your employer offers you that check, take the money and run.

RULE #88   RETIREMENT, THE MOST AWESOME SOCIAL INNOVATION OF THE 20th CENTURY, WILL NOT EXIST IN THE 21st CENTURY. PLAN ACCORDINGLY.

My client Yale just retired as an electrical engineer at NASA. But he never has time to visit, because he's just started a construction company with his son. Another client, Renee, 79 and a former nightclub singer, is so busy running the volunteer department at the local hospital that she's had to hire a maid to clean her house. I know this because I had to increase the money Renee gets from her investments to boost her cash flow. A third client, Jean, is a management executive who retired several years ago and now writes children's books.

Ask a financial advisor about the three-legged stool of retirement, and he or she will tell you about Social Security, pensions, and investment income. For several generations these three legs supported every retiree.

Well, get ready to turn that stool into a chair.

Retirement as you know it is over. Although still practiced by some, it will flat-out not exist by the time you reach, *uh*, retirement age. Instead, you'll install a fourth leg under that stool, and it's called *earned income*.

Notice that I did not call it *work*. You've been doing *that* since you got out of school. You look forward to that day

---

[217]Or the death of you and your spouse, if you choose to receive income based on both your lives. This protects your spouse, but lowers the income you both receive.

when you can leave *work* behind. But having watched lots of my clients enter and live in retirement, I can tell you something: They get bored.

This is a critical development, and a substantial shift from what used to happen to retirees. You see, a generation ago, shortly after a person retired, something very different would happen. They would not get bored. Instead, they would die.

Not any more. Today's 65-year-olds have a life expectancy of 82; today's 85-year-olds can expect to see 91, and there aren't supposed to be any 92-year-olds.[218]

I watch as each of my clients go through the same metamorphosis when they enter retirement: First, as the last day of work approaches, they experience a variety of emotions—excitement and optimism, sure, but also fear and anxiety. After all, leaving work—which you've done for the past 40 years or more—is a major event. It's hard to think of anything that you'd done for as long as that. You haven't been married that long. You haven't had kids that long. If your parents have died, you might not even have been a child for that long.

So the first thing you do is *nothing*. It's a pretty remarkable thing, my newly retired clients tell me, to wake up and not have to go anywhere. This is not a sad thing, mind you, for there's a big difference between *not having to go anywhere* and *not having anywhere to go*. Work, by its nature, dominated everything about your daily routine: When you woke, how you dressed, where you drove, when (and often where) you had lunch, with whom you interacted, and, of course, what you did. Now, in work's absence, you are once again in control of your time. Completely and totally, like you haven't been since, well, it's been too long to remember since when.

If you're not yet retired, don't kid yourself that you can imagine what retirement is like merely because you have occasionally gone on vacation. There's no similarity between the two. Vacations are planned to the smallest

---

[218]Please don't tell my 100-year-old grandmother.

detail. Vacationers deliberately alter their lifestyle, knowing it's only for a short time, and they consciously seek mental diversions to get away from their "real life." Most important, vacationers know that *work* is waiting for them to return.

Retirees, on the other hand, need plan for nothing. They are not deliberately altering their lifestyle, for work—by its sudden absence—has altered it for them. Retirees need no mental diversions, because there's nothing they can do to escape what is now their real life. Most important, retirees know this never needs to change.

At first, retirees revel in their newfound freedom. They do many of the things they've always done, but they do them at odd times. Like not shaving or applying makeup even though it's not Saturday. Or going to the movies in midday. Or driving to see the kids on a weekday. But fairly soon the novelty of retirement wears off, and retirees settle into a new routine.

They return to hobbies they'd left years before, or they pick up new ones. They get back into their golf game. They harass their children more, because they've got more time on their hands.[219]

There are, though, two items at the top of every retiree's (and near-retiree's) agenda. They book appointments to see their doctor and their financial advisor. And they get "bad news" from both, and when you reach retirement age, you'll get the same "bad news": You'll discover you're in good health, and thanks to that three-legged stool, you have plenty of income.

Oh, great. Now what? It's at this point that today's retirees begin to realize that retirement for them is going to be very different from their grandfathers' retirement. Back in the 1940s and 1950s, when Granddad retired at age 62, he got a gold watch, a pension, and a Social Security check. He owned his home outright—the only house he'd ever bought, and aside from a stint in the Army, one of only two houses he ever lived in—and that income, though small, was enough to support him and his wife during retirement.

---

[219]Mom and Dad, I'm certainly not referring to *you* in this paragraph.

Not that it had to support them for long, because they died within a few years.

This short life expectancy made retirement something special—sort of like a long vacation. It was certainly unique, for Granddad's granddad never got to retire at all. Back in the early 1900s and earlier, if you were alive, you worked. You had to, or you'd starve. Indeed, the pinnacle of the new American prosperity was the creation of something called *retirement*—the ability to live comfortably, and even to support others, without having to work or produce an income.

So Granddad looked forward to retirement, to being able to spend his few remaining years enjoying his wife and his family. But Granddad's children have begun to look at retirement a little differently. Why limit that last "vacation" to just a few years—and to a time when your health might be too poor to let you do all the things you've planned to do? Today's workers have watched as Dad or Granddad died or became ill before fully enjoying retirement, and they are determined to avoid that fate.

They have a simple solution, too: Just retire sooner. Don't wait until age 65. Retire at 50. That way, you'll be able to enjoy life for 15 or 20 years instead of just three or four. This is a nice strategy, but it's got three major problems: First, quitting work at 50 deprives you of 15 of your most productive years, and seriously erodes your ability to accumulate the money you'll need to support yourself in retirement.[220] Second, you're not going to die at 67 like Granddad did; you're more likely to die at 87, which means your money must last you a lot longer than Granddad's money had to last him. And third, you have to contend with inflation. Your granddad didn't, partly because inflation barely existed back then, and partly because he wasn't alive long enough for it to affect him to any significant degree.

Add all these factors together, and you discover that you are not going to experience the same kind of retirement your grandfather did. In fact, because of these reasons, retirement as you know it will not even exist.

---

[220]See Rule #84.

This sounds both incredible and horrifying, but actually it's neither. Instead, it is both a natural evolution of society and very reassuring. Because what many retirees discover after a while is that they've become just plain *bored*. Going to work can solve that problem. Work can be mentally challenging and stimulating, and lots of fun—especially when you know you're doing it because you want to, and not because you have to.

That is how work after retirement will differ from your current job. School teachers will not return to the classroom and pilots will not resume flying. You'll do something completely different, as Yale, Renee, and Jean are doing. First, you'll go back to school, beginning with a class here and there, perhaps at an adult education center or the local community college. Maybe you'll enroll in a degree program at a university. (In 1997, 89-year-old Mary Fasano obtained a BA from Harvard University, becoming the oldest person ever to get a Harvard degree.)

If you do return to your career, it'll likely be as a consultant, mentoring younger workers. You'll also probably engage in volunteer work. Pretty soon you'll be as busy as ever—and quite possibly busier. That's good—and not just for your pocketbook. As Robert Kahn, a research scientist emeritus at the University of Michigan, says, "People who are productive score higher on tests of functional ability, both cognitive and physical." He made the comment to *Forbes* magazine, whose June 1997 cover story declared that the key to a successful retirement is "a second career."

If you want to enjoy a successful retirement, you won't dismiss this advice. Trying to retire as your parents and grandparents did simply will not work for you. You'll live too long, the cost of living will increase too much, and your income from Social Security[221] and company retirement plans simply will not be able to keep up.

Face it. If you want to succeed in today's world, you must adapt to **The New Rules of Money**.

---

[221]Ha! Like there *will* be an income from Social Security.

Index